"*Color-Courageous Discipleship* combines biblical insights, cultural commentary, tender personal testimony, and a rich collection of interviews with seasoned leadership voices. This essential resource equips you with sustainable practices to grow in color-courageous discipleship for years to come."

—Jo Saxton, cohost of *Lead Stories Podcast* and author of *Ready to Rise*

"As one who speaks to many groups about issues of racial and social justice, I often hear some variation of 'What does all this have to do with the gospel?' Now, rather than explain, I'm just going to hand them *Color-Courageous Discipleship*. This book will mobilize God's people toward racial righteousness in the service of the gospel."

—Al Tizon, affiliate associate professor of Missional and Global Leadership, North Park Theological Seminary

"Deeply practical, cogent, and beautiful—and accompanied by helpful interviews with antiracist Christian leaders and pastors—this book is a gift to Christians and churches who are seeking to do justice and love mercy and walk humbly with God."

—Tish Harrison Warren, Anglican priest and author of *Liturgy of the Ordinary* and *Prayer in the Night*

"There are many excellent books on racism and fine books on discipleship, but I know of none which combine the two in depth as Michelle Sanchez does. This book can play a vital role in the healing of our divided churches in North America and beyond."

—Leighton Ford, founding president of Leighton Ford Ministries, Charlotte, NC

"*Color-Courageous Discipleship* not only brings together helpful paradigms for dismantling racism, but it also offers essential spiritual practices to form us into Christlikeness as we work toward the beloved community God desires for humanity!"

—Lisa Rodriguez-Watson, national director of Missio Alliance

COLOR-COURAGEOUS
DISCIPLESHIP

COLOR-COURAGEOUS DISCIPLESHIP

FOLLOW JESUS, DISMANTLE RACISM, AND
BUILD BELOVED COMMUNITY

MICHELLE T. SANCHEZ

WATERBROOK

To Mom and Dad,
with so much love and gratitude

Have I not commanded you? Be strong and courageous.
Do not be afraid; do not be discouraged, for the LORD
your God will be with you wherever you go.
—JOSHUA 1:9

by Ed Stetzer

Throughout Scripture, we find a God who confronts, challenges, and upends our prejudice—in particular when it arises from racial or ethnic biases. The Exodus story bears witness to delivering an oppressed Hebrew nation from the bonds of Egyptian slavery. The story of Ruth is one of God providentially placing a young Moabite woman in the lineage of Israel's greatest king and, eventually, the Messiah—who would be not for Israel alone, but for all nations of the world.

The advent of the Holy Spirit at Pentecost led to a miraculous understanding of diverse languages. The dispersion of believers following the martyrdom of Stephen led to the gospel spreading throughout the diverse cultures of the Roman world. And John's vision in Revelation 7 of people from every tongue, tribe, and nation singing as a unified choir before the throne of God is a vision of *after* the final resurrection; meaning, John bore witness to the diversity of all God's people that was still represented by their glorified bodies.

Scripture consistently testifies that God's presence works through our cultural and ethnic diversity rather than collapsing it. The witness and worship of the church is enriched when we model gospel-centered diversity.

The task before us—especially those who are White American evangelicals—is to produce evidence that we are serious about, and driven by, the timeless truth of the Bible and that we are formed by God's love for all people. We cannot do that without listening to our brothers and sisters of color. And we cannot do that without facing the reality of our own struggles on race and ethnic bias and being discipled into a more excellent way.

This is why I am so grateful for this book. Michelle Sanchez paves that more excellent way for followers of Jesus to be discipled out of our racial prejudices, which is precisely what we need. When we come across any issue that is reflected in Scripture, we must look at it from the perspective of discipleship. We cannot separate an issue such as racism into a category that is divorced from our spiritual life. The Bible doesn't compartmentalize things like that.

A discipleship approach that ignores the marginalized—those who have been historically (and presently) discriminated against—is not a fully orbed discipleship. Such a discipleship falls short of being discipleship in the way of Jesus, who consistently concerned himself with those who were victims of the unholy stewardship of power.

What's more, when we consider that an issue like racism has caused such serious divisions within the church, we must admit that it directly affects discipleship in the church. So we must consider Paul's frequent calls for churches to strive for unity—not to pretend that our differences don't exist but rather that, through our shared identity in Christ, those differences would become a feature of beauty where before they were a point of contention.

Michelle writes from a perspective we need to hear. First, she is a discipleship leader. She has worked in the area of discipleship, in her local church and now in her denomination. For Michelle, discipleship is not just a subject to be considered; it is at the very heart of our relationship with Christ.

Second, Michelle is an African American woman. She has experienced the realities of racial inequity firsthand. So when she seeks to cultivate ethnic harmony through discipleship, she writes as one who has been working toward this harmony all her life. As a White male, I was both moved and challenged to continue cultivating a posture of listening and receptivity so that I might continue to learn from my brothers and sisters of color.

She writes honestly (and sometimes painfully) from her own experience of prejudice while being a devoted follower of Christ. Through this she shows us how we cannot separate our growth in discipleship from our view on race. She brings both topics—discipleship and race—together to show how we can grow in Christ even as we learn to love others.

Michelle gives us keen insight into the issues that mark our time. She writes in a balanced and hopeful tone, yet she doesn't deny the historic and current problems in the church regarding race. She gives clear evidence and personal testimony to the challenges that are still too common among us. She calls for the community of faith to lament together, to bear one another's pain, and to come together to seek answers.

Weaving biblical content, awareness of the pertinent topics of our current setting, and compelling stories, Michelle pleads for a racial awakening in our time. She calls for all of us, regardless of political leanings or racial identity, to be transformed by Jesus to bring glory to God—by facing the issue of race and resolving to be disciples who engage head-on the challenges before us that stand in the way of true unity and interdependence. We should listen to Michelle's call for transformation and respond with open and humble hearts.

We are living in a time of reckoning. Passions are high, tempers are short, and division runs deep. But we who love Jesus and serve him as Lord believe change is possible. Fences can be turned into tables. Mistrust can be replaced by mutuality. When we make these changes, we can stand together as disciples in service to our king.

—*Ed Stetzer, professor and dean, Wheaton College*

CONTENTS

PART ONE

INTRODUCTION TO COLOR-COURAGEOUS DISCIPLESHIP

INVITATION TO A RACIAL DISCIPLESHIP JOURNEY

Discipleship has long been my passion. After serving for a number of years as a discipleship pastor in a local church, I could hardly believe it when I was invited to lead discipleship for an entire North American denomination of churches. It was a dream come true. As it happens, I am also an *African American* discipleship leader.

Is that significant? What does race have to do with discipleship, anyway? I'll be honest with you. For most of my life, I did not make many connections between race and discipleship—much less challenge myself to be a "color-courageous" disciple. I have always been *for* Jesus and *against* racism. Most disciples I know would say the same thing. So . . . aren't we good? Racism is such a fraught and depressing topic. I'd much rather talk about Jesus!

But see, that's just it: What I've come to discover is that race and discipleship aren't actually in completely separate categories, like apples and clementines. They are profoundly interrelated. In this book, I will tell the story of my awakening to that fact as both a disciple and a discipleship leader. And here's the crux of it: I now understand that one of the most meaningful ways to get to know Jesus better is to go deeper with him into our racial challenges. Our generation has a unique invitation to strengthen our connection with Jesus through color-courageous discipleship.

One of the most meaningful ways for our generation to get to know Jesus better is to go deeper with him into our racial challenges.

So back to our question: What does race have to do with discipleship? A whole lot, as it turns out. And my eyes are now open to the reality that by missing that connection, I had been missing out on more of Jesus. Looking back, I'm so grateful that I (finally) accepted Jesus's invitation to the adventure of racial discipleship. Although I'll be sharing more of my story, ultimately this book is about *your* story. Consider this your personal invitation to join the adventure of racial discipleship. Or, if you are already on the journey, consider this your invitation to experience rich and colorful new vistas. I don't want you—or any other disciple—to miss out on *all* that Jesus has for you.

DISCIPLESHIP DEFINED

Since this is a journey about discipleship, let's first get clear on what discipleship is. My favorite definition of **discipleship** comes from Jesus's invitation to his first disciples: "Follow Me, and I will make you fishers of people" (Matthew 4:19, NASB). In this brief but brilliant invitation, we discover three elements of discipleship: A disciple (1) follows Jesus, (2) is transformed by Jesus, and (3) is on mission with Jesus.

First, a disciple *follows Jesus.* A disciple's life is completely centered not on religious principles but on the person of Jesus

Christ. A disciple worships Jesus as Lord and Savior of his or her life and of the entire world. A disciple is a friend of Jesus who seeks ever-deepening knowledge of him and intimacy with him. And a disciple looks for opportunities to get to know Jesus better through the Word of God and through every experience.

Second, a disciple *is being transformed by Jesus.* In fact, a disciple submits to a continuous process of being transformed into the likeness of Christ day by day and in every way. There is no area of a disciple's life that is outside of the transforming influence of Christ—character, family, friendship, sexuality, work, politics, you name it. A disciple's holy ambition is to love Christ by obeying him and aligning every aspect of life with his lordship.

Finally, a disciple *is on mission with Jesus.* Disciples are both reconciled reconcilers and disciples who make disciples. They are reconciled reconcilers in that they collaborate with Jesus to see everything broken made whole again. Together with Jesus, disciples bring reconciliation to the world both vertically with God as well as horizontally with one another. They seek to reconcile the world at every level—individuals, families, people groups, systems, and creation. Furthermore, healthy disciples make disciples who make disciples who make disciples. Thus, like Jesus, they have an exponential impact as they multiply disciples who are themselves ambassadors of reconciliation (2 Corinthians 5:11–21).

SO WHAT IS *RACIAL DISCIPLESHIP*?

In the same way, robust racial discipleship encompasses all three discipleship dimensions. Racial discipleship is about following Jesus more closely as we engage racial challenges; being transformed by Jesus as we remove sinful racial tendencies and put on better ones; and embarking on mission with Jesus as we foster shalom and multiply disciples who do the same. As we pursue all three dimensions, we will pursue antiracism not as a societal trend but as an ongoing expression of our discipleship—which is exactly what it should be.

This brings us to what might seem like an unconventional idea: *You have already been racially discipled.* In other words, we each have already been shaped and formed by the racial dynamics of our society. We have all been subtly conditioned by the culture, practices, and perspectives of the family we were reared in, the place we grew up, and even the era that we find ourselves in. The question is not *if* you have been racially discipled; the question is *how.* The problem, of course, is that much of the racial discipleship you have received throughout your life has been unconscious, unintentional, and—in many cases—misaligned with God's heart. But that doesn't make your racial formation to this point any less real.

That is why what many disciples need now is to embark on a different kind of racial discipleship journey. Different, in that this time it will be intentional. Different, in that this time we will orient ourselves as disciples of Jesus Christ to engage effectively with the racial challenges we face, in Jesus's name. When it comes to race, most of us need to be intentionally "rediscipled."[1] That is, we need to be discipled again. What's more, on this journey we will discover that racial discipleship is not just about resisting racism or transforming the world. It is certainly that, but it is far more: Racial discipleship is about being personally transformed so that you can experience more of Jesus. And *that* is what has been the most exciting part of the journey for me.

By the way, yes, this invitation is for you—whatever your race. The journey of racial discipleship is for people of every race and ethnic background. It is not for Whites only, nor is it a journey that is the special preoccupation of pilgrims of color. As fallen creatures in a fallen world, we have all been infected with sinful inclinations and wedded to imperfect perspectives on race, whether we realize it or not. Ironically, this may perhaps be especially true today in more subtle and insidious ways for people of color—like me. Imagine my surprise when I gradually came to understand that I, as an African American woman, was reinforcing racism in different ways myself! We all need awakening, transformation, healing, and fresh vision for a new day.

Although our individual racial discipleship journeys will have different starting points and milestones, in our racialized world, I believe the journey itself is universal. As disciples of Christ, we are all invited to awaken to the broken racial realities of our world and to see how we may have contributed to them. Rather than unintentionally perpetuate existing problems, we are all invited to courageously discover and advance God's solutions.

NOW IS THE RIGHT TIME TO DO *SOMETHING*

While racial unrest in our world is nothing new, many experienced the devastating death of George Floyd in 2020 as an important juncture. A brief review: George Perry Floyd, Jr., was an African American man killed during an arrest in Minneapolis, Minnesota, on May 25, 2020. Despite Floyd's desperate pleas of "I can't breathe," Derek Chauvin (one of four police officers who were at the scene) knelt on Floyd's neck and back for nine minutes and twenty-nine seconds. After Floyd's untimely death, protests quickly spread across the United States and around the world. Polls estimate that in the summer of 2020, between fifteen and twenty-six million people participated in the demonstrations in the United States, making these protests the largest in U.S. history.

In the wake of these events, many have asked new questions and taken steps to learn and grow. People of all backgrounds and faith traditions have been asking questions like "What does this all mean? What am I supposed to do? Given my particular place in the world, what *can* I do?"

As followers of Jesus, we are also prompted to ask additional questions in light of our primary allegiance to Christ. Questions like: "Jesus, what are you inviting me, as your disciple, to do? What are you calling the church, as your discipleship community, to do? And how can we grow closer to you in the process?"

Why this book when so many others have been written? As a discipleship practitioner, I have also been enriched by reams of excellent books on *discipleship*. I have also read many enlightening books on *race*. My intention is for this book to take us on a deeper dive into the many life-transforming connections between the two.

I believe that Jesus is grieved by both personal and systemic racism, and as disciples of Jesus, we can choose to be either more faithful or less faithful to him as we face our racial challenges. I believe that our generation of Jesus followers has been given a unique opportunity to understand that it's no longer enough to identify as "not racist." As disciples, our call is not simply to avoid racism. We will best align with the heart of God as we pursue not *non*racism but *anti*racism. These days, antiracism means a lot of different things to a lot of people—and we'll soon talk more about that. But at its heart, antiracism is simply about making the needful move from *passive* to *proactive* in our resistance of racism. And guess what? That requires courage.

But first things first. I think one reason we get stuck in our conversations about race is that we assign the same words different meanings—and then talk past each other. So let's first get clear on some key words and ideas that we'll return to again and again.

RACE VS. ETHNICITY—WHAT'S THE DIFFERENCE?

We will not be using the words *race* and *ethnicity* interchangeably. From a biblical perspective, there is a difference between race and ethnicity, and it is helpful for disciples to understand that difference.

I once attended a conference where an African American speaker asserted something like this: "God did not create race. In the beginning, there was no race." At the time, I was scandalized. What was he talking about? Of course God created race! He loves race! I even remember singing the song about it by C. Herbert Woolston at church: "Red, yellow, black and white, they are precious in His sight." Right? Well, over time I have come to the surprising realization that the provocative presenter had made a legitimate point. Actually, I was the one who was mixed up. What God created—what God delights in—is not race but *ethnicity*. Let's get clear on the difference by beginning at the beginning.

One day, not so far from today, you will open your eyes in paradise. Imagine: How you arrived—whether by an abrupt accident, a long and excruciating illness, or a soft final sigh—will be a fuzzy memory. In a flash, your former life will be a dream. You are now fully and deliciously awake.

You greedily gulp the air—heavy, fresh, and sweet—as your unfamiliar eyes adjust to the light . . . if this elixir can be called "light." This light is not insubstantial and fleeting like the light you knew on Earth. No, this radiance is pure, pulsing, weighty. *Light* is too small a word. You are bathed in glory.

What's more, the *prism* of this glory defies description. This is no monochromatic world. You are awash in color—and what colors these are! Brilliant, mercurial colors you have never before seen, sparking new emotions that you have never before felt.

This glory also glimmers . . . with personality. It welcomes you, floods your heart, embraces your soul, rejoices over every no-longer-hidden part of you. Love, sheer love, unobstructed love, crazy love! Now you understand. Paradise is not a place. It is a Presence. Paradise is love, the very presence of God. Sweet relief. God is here. God is with you in this place, real and tangible, closer to you than your own self. You will never be afraid again.

You become aware of the gentle trickle of a stream. When you look, you see not a stream but a river of pure crystal. It, too, seems alive. You begin to follow the river and its glory toward their source—a cascading garden city. And you can tell there is a party going on!

You join countless others, transfigured saints of every color, every hue, every variety imaginable. Together you promenade down transparent streets of gold toward the city's center. Without being told, you know this motley crew: These are your friends; this is your family. And only when you're together with them do you see it: love itself, sitting on a throne, ensconced with a rainbow. You erupt with these saints in a symphony of worship, captivated by the *sheer rainbowness* of it all—this gorgeous rainbow God, surrounded by a rainbow throne, worshipped wildly by rainbow people from every tribe, nation, people, language, and culture. And it is in this prismatic moment that you finally behold something that you have been waiting your whole life to see: the forever smile of God.

————

In this depiction of the new creation, the Bible paints us a beautiful picture of shalom. Quite simply, **shalom** is "the way things ought to be."[2] It's what we experience whenever and wherever the kingdom of God is realized. Although sometimes translated as "peace," *shalom* entails far more than a mere ceasefire or state of tranquility. Biblical shalom entails wholeness and flourishing in every dimension of creation, including ethnicity.

The book of Revelation tells the story of how history will climax in a new creation where people from every nation that ever existed will gather to worship God: "After this I looked, and there before me was a great multitude that no one could count, from every nation, tribe, people, and language, standing before the throne and before the Lamb" (Revelation 7:9). This will be the breathtaking fulfillment of the Great Commission that Jesus gave us to "go and make disciples of all nations" (Matthew 28:19).

But wait—let's take a closer look at the word these texts translated as *nation*. When most of us hear the word *nation,* we probably think of a nation-state—a sociopolitical entity like Botswana, Qatar, or Argentina. And that is certainly a legitimate translation. However, the Greek word is *ethnos.*[3] It's where our contemporary word *ethnicity* comes from. So *ethnicity* may actually be a pretty accurate translation of *ethnos*—if not a better one.

Why is this significant? Because the broader translation of *ethnicity* or *ethnic group* would remind us of our call to reach, reconcile, and make disciples of diverse ethnic groups right where we are. It would also keep us focused on the ultimate vision: Around the throne, there will be people not just from every nation. There will also be people from every ethnicity within every nation. History will climax in a multiethnic celebration. God's throne will not only be encircled by citizens of the United States of America, but among those citizens we will also discover members of America's diverse ethnic and cultural groups— Apache, Inuit, Hawaiian, Puerto Rican, and beyond.

Here is the definition that we will use for **ethnicity**:

Ethnicity is a God-ordained cultural identity that God delights in as a means of bringing glory to himself and enrichment to his kingdom.

Let's take a moment with each phrase.

First, *ethnicity is God-ordained*. The grand arc of Scripture displays God's passionate intention for diversity—including ethnic diversity—from beginning to end. That arc is often missed, but it's easy to trace: From the teeming diversity of creation, to the inclusion of foreigners in the Exodus, to the temple built for all nations, to the Savior who came as a light to the nations, to the fiery birth of the church at Pentecost, God both ordained and delights in ethnic diversity.

Second, *ethnic diversity brings greater glory to God*. How? Because although we humans were created in the image of God, no one individual, ethnicity, or culture can reflect the fullness of God. We get to know God better when we praise him not only in unity (God is One) but also in diversity (God is Trinity). We learn more about who God is by understanding that he is simultaneously like a man and like a woman, like living water and a consuming fire, like a lion and a lamb.[4] In the same way, diverse ethnicities and cultures better reflect the unimaginably diverse aspects of God himself.

Finally, *ethnic diversity enriches God's kingdom*. The Scriptures present us with a curious new creation preview: All the ethnic peoples of the world stream into the garden city of God with their unique cultural treasures and contributions (Isaiah 60:11; Revelation 21:26). As a connoisseur of multicultural cuisine, I certainly hope those treasures include food. Who knows what delights we may savor in the new creation? Perhaps not only a feast of Vietnamese pho, Ethiopian flatbread, and French ratatouille, but also New Orleans gumbo, Minnesota wild rice, and Southern fried chicken.

Remember: God delights not only in the diverse riches of the sociopolitical nations, but also, and more broadly, he delights in the riches of ethnic diversity as an essential contribution to the new creation. Ethnic diversity—fully redeemed in all its beauty and brilliance—will be one aspect of the new creation that will make it fascinating and fulfilling beyond anything we have imagined.

You may have noticed that I did not mention the word *race* in the previous biblical discussion. That is because race is not a biblical concept. Other than the concept of the human race, you will find no mention of race in the Bible as we understand *race* today. This may come as surprise for you, as it did for me.

Other than the concept of the human race, you will find no mention of race in the Bible as we understand race *today.*

So what is race?

Race is a man-made system used to stratify humans into artificial categories based on visible characteristics like skin color, typically for purposes related to power, division, and hierarchy.

Ta-Nehisi Coates makes the intriguing observation that "race is the child of racism, not the father."[5] Our contemporary understanding of race is relatively new; previously, ethnicity was a far more common means of identification. The concept of race emerged in past centuries as Europeans sought to justify the colonialization of non-Europeans. European colonialists required a simple, cogent system to rationalize the ongoing subordination of some people to others. So race was created as one of the primary solutions, and it was quite an effective one.[6]

One contributor to the creation of racial divisions was Carl Linnaeus, the Swedish botanist of the eighteenth century commonly known as the "father of taxonomy." We still study him today in science class when we learn about his concepts of species, genus, and family. Like an excitable kid arranging his blocks, Linnaeus clearly got a kick out of organizing things into categories. Unfortunately for us, he did not confine his taxonomic efforts to botany and zoology. Linnaeus was one of the first well-known scientists to systematically categorize people along with beasts.[7]

With regard to race, Linnaeus came to delineate categories based primarily on skin color, which included *Europaeus* (white), *Americanus* (reddish), *Asiaticus* (dark), and *Africanus* (black).[8] Clearly, though, these racial categories emerged from a racist perspective (as we have defined it). This was made clear in that Linnaeus did not stop at creating race categories; he also ordered those races in hierarchies. Of course, Linnaeus always ensured that his own race was at the pinnacle of those hierarchies! In his most famous work, he characterized the entire *H. sapiens europaeus* race as "very smart," "inventive," and "ruled by law."[9] Unsurprisingly, the darkest races occupied the bottom of the hierarchy in both position and character. He described dark-skinned *H. sapiens afer* as "sluggish, lazy . . . crafty, slow, careless . . . Ruled by caprice."[10] Actually, Linnaeus is just one example of a long line of thinkers who "created a hierarchy within the animal kingdom and a hierarchy within the human kingdom, and this human hierarchy was based on race."[11]

So, we can now clearly differentiate between *ethnicity* and *race*: Ethnicity was God's idea; race was our idea. Ethnicity is natural; race is artificial. Ethnicity will endure forever; humanity's racial divisions will cease at the supper of the Lamb.

FROM RACISM TO ANTIRACISM

Now we turn to the definition of *racism*. This is a tricky task. The words *racism* and *racist* are often used in such narrow ways that very few people can relate to them anymore. I think that's why we're having so many challenges in this conversation. Moving forward into a better future begins by gaining clarity about what *racism* actually means. We certainly won't fix the problem if we're not clear about what it is. Even some self-proclaimed White supremacists vigorously deny that they are racist. For example, White supremacist Richard Spencer has said, "*Racist* isn't a descriptive word. It's a pejorative word. It is the equivalent of saying, 'I don't like you.'"[12] Spencer identifies as "not racist."[13] If even White supremacists don't think of themselves as racist, we've got some work to do on developing a common definition.

We will define **racism** as "personal racial prejudice and bias plus systemic practices of institutions that lead to racial inequities in society."

Let's examine the first part of the definition: *personal racial prejudice and bias.* Yes, racism obviously includes personal, consciously chosen prejudice by individuals. However, many are awakening to the reality that racism encompasses much more than this. To be honest, I have known very few people who would self-identify as "racist" by the narrow definition of "conscious prejudice." This is the thing: Racism also includes unconscious racial bias, which we all unwittingly exhibit. In fact, we begin to unconsciously form racial biases when we are two years old.[14] One study found that "three- to five-year-olds in a racially and ethnically diverse day care center used racial categories to identify themselves and others, to include or exclude children from activities, and to negotiate power in their own social/play networks."[15] As we get older, as you might imagine, the problem gets worse, not better.

The second part of our definition of *racism* is *systemic practices of institutions that lead to racial inequities in society.* Here we acknowledge that racism has both personal and systemic dimensions. This shouldn't be a surprise. After all, institutions are run by people—the very same people who have those racial biases we just mentioned. By now there is a vast array of evidence that many, if not most, of our institutions are racist in that their practices consistently result in racial inequity throughout society. We see this clearly in the fields of education, health care, criminal justice, incarceration, housing, and many, many others. For example, despite our apparent gains in civil rights legislation, White families continue to hold 90 percent of the national wealth while Latino families hold 2.3 percent and Black families hold 2.6 percent.[16] With regard to education, a 2016 survey reported that despite serving the same number of students, U.S. minority school districts received $23 billion less in funding than majority-White school districts. Better school funding, of course, leads to better educational outcomes.[17] We will explore more examples of systemic racial inequity in chapter 3. Suffice to say, the problem has reached epidemic proportions.

Unfortunately, oversimplified racial categories are here to stay for the foreseeable future. Race, even though it is a false construct, still matters in that it makes a real difference in people's lives—which is why it no longer works for us to have a "color-blind" approach to race. What we need now is to move from move from color-blind to color-courageous. Color-courageous disciples intentionally counteract racism with antiracism. **Antiracism** is essentially racism's opposite: *becoming aware of and uprooting personal racial prejudice and bias* plus *working to dismantle systemic practices that lead to racial inequities in society.* For Christians, the end goal of antiracism is the restoration of shalom.

Given this definition, you may find the task of antiracism to be overwhelming. After hundreds of years of entrenched racism, can we really hope to make any meaningful progress now? If I have been unconsciously biased my whole life, is there really any hope of reversing that? What's more, can average, ordinary people—schoolteachers, youth pastors, plumbers, stay-at-home moms—really do much to dismantle systemic racism?

The beautiful answer is yes. Because here's the thing: Even if you can't change *the* world, you can certainly change *your* world. If we all did just that, imagine the difference it would make.

———

I want to acknowledge that many of us are tired of talking about racism, antiracism, and everything in between. (I am too. I'd much rather talk about my favorite novels and low-carb recipes.) There's already been so much conversation about race, and it's exhausting. Yet being tired of talking about racism is kind of like asking, "Do we really need to keep bringing up sin? We've already talked about it so much." Or "Wouldn't it be better for us to not see sin at all? No one likes to dwell on sin. It's such a downer. We're all quite sorry for the sins we've committed. So let's move on to different topics!"

> *Even if you can't change the world, you can certainly change your world.*

I get it. What helps me continue the conversation is remembering that, at its heart, "the problem of racism is the problem of sin."[18] When we don't comprehensively understand the nature of sin—its hiddenness, its subtlety, its pervasiveness—we are far more prone to perpetuate it. Sin will be a challenge as long as we live. And as long as we inhabit this broken creation, we will need preachers, teachers, prophets, and friends to point out whatever blind spots we may have so that we might better represent Jesus in the world. This may be especially true when it comes to race.

I also want to acknowledge your fears that any talk of "antiracism" is grounded in the secular philosophical framework of critical race theory (CRT). In popular usage, **critical race theory** refers to a framework for processing and understanding the many complex dimensions of how race impacts systems and society as a whole. While I have certainly come across numerous CRT concepts while writing this book, I am not a critical race theorist and this book is not about critical race theory. I am writing from the perspective of a Christian discipleship leader, and in this book, I seek to explore what the Bible has to say to disciples about our racial challenges. Most importantly, my premise is that the core elements of antiracism ultimately stem not from secular philosophies but from the heart of God. (Space does not permit a full examination of critical race theory here, but you can find more of my reflections on this and many other topics at https://michelletsanchez.com/colorcourageous.)

Finally, some have raised important objections to the term *antiracism* itself. They say, "I don't really want to be 'anti-' anything! It sounds so negative." That does make sense on one level. But think about it: Sometimes it is most constructive to call out exactly what you're up against. Why is that? So that you can be more targeted and effective in your resistance. For example, if I'm sick, a good bowl of chicken soup is a delight to have. But if given the choice, I'd prefer a targeted *antibiotic* to rid me of my suffering for good. In the same way, it's lovely for you to improve your scent with the help of cologne or perfume. In the long run, though, it won't do you much good unless you also avail yourself of *antiperspirant*!

Here's another important point: At its heart, being antiracist is *not* about being anti-people. It is about being against *racism itself.* This is a critical distinction. It is not ultimately people we want to oppose; God loves and wants to transform all people. As the Scriptures say, "our struggle is not against flesh and blood" (Ephesians 6:12). Rather, our work is to oppose racist ideas, practices, and systemic dynamics that continue to perpetuate racial inequity generation after generation. And in this, we never "arrive." No one can ever call themselves perfectly "antiracist." More than a label, it is a journey. At any given time, I might be doing things to promote or dismantle racist ideas, practices, and systemic dynamics. By that measure, all people—including people of color—are called to move from racism to antiracism.

All that being said, my favorite phrase when it comes to a Christian approach to antiracism is now *color-courageous discipleship.* Implied in the term itself is a positive, proactive call for disciples to courageously resist racism in Jesus's name. So color-courageous disciples are against racism, but what are they for? What is our end goal? For me, the culmination of color-courageous discipleship is the creation of beloved community—community that is grounded in Christlike agape love for God and for one another across all boundaries of difference. So now we come to our definition of **color-courageous discipleship:** *the courageous, lifelong journey of following Jesus, dismantling racism, and building beloved community.* In fact, the highlight of this journey for me is when we begin to envision and unpack God's gorgeous and inspiring dream of beloved community together (chapter 6).[19]

INVITATION TO A REDISCIPLESHIP ADVENTURE

I'm sure you know by now that following Jesus is not a one-time invitation. After you initially say yes to Jesus, he will present you with many additional discipleship invitations over the course of your life. And guess what? Each one is an invitation to a new adventure. Consider this book your invitation to a new adventure of *racial* **rediscipleship.**

My favorite definition of an adventure is a journey that is both exciting *and* hazardous.[20] For me, this is an excellent reminder of what discipleship is really like. Discipleship adventures are exciting because of all the opportunities they give us to know Christ better and partner with him to see God's dreams come true. Yet discipleship adventures are also inescapably hazardous because they require us to take risks and possibly experience loss and pain. In other words, *every true discipleship adventure requires courage.*

As disciples of Christ, our call to courage is simultaneously a call to the cross.

As disciples of Christ, our call to courage is simultaneously a call to the cross. That's why so many are unwilling to pursue or to persist on new discipleship adventures, including the racial discipleship adventure. I have no idea what your unique cross may entail on this journey, but God may invite you to

- enter into repentance, confession, and forgiveness
- engage in conversations that produce discomfort, anger, and disagreement
- uncover unconscious biases that have caused harm
- revisit painful moments
- acknowledge the shortcomings of the church or other institutions you love
- experience suspicion or rejection by others
- sacrifice in unfamiliar ways as you courageously love God and others

Yet, let's also remember that discipleship never ends with the cross. It ends with *resurrection.* On the other side of the cross, there is always new life. What that resurrection life will entail for you on this journey is God's surprise, but perhaps you may

- grow in your ability to see the world and its people from God's perspective
- understand the gospel more deeply, both with regard to the depths of your own brokenness as well as the heights of God's grace

- awaken to life-changing insights through the racial and ethnic journeys of others
- enjoy new friendships and richer, more authentic community
- experience more extensive liberation from fear, sin, and shame
- discover God's presence and experience him in new ways
- be healed or help others to heal
- become more effective at bringing shalom and beloved community to your world
- celebrate when witnesses to all these events find new life in Christ as a result!

At times, color-courageous discipleship will feel difficult, dangerous, or both—which is precisely why we need Jesus as our leader and the Bible as our anchor. We need supernatural courage for the journey. Courage is the "mental or moral strength to venture, persevere, and withstand danger, fear, or difficulty."[21] Only in Christ will we find the inexhaustible power, wisdom, and grace we need to flourish as color-courageous disciples.

AN OVERVIEW OF THE JOURNEY

Our racial discipleship journey will have three main parts. This is part 1, your invitation to pursue a racial discipleship journey grounded in Jesus Christ. I hope that you will accept!

Part 2 will explore four color-courageous paradigm shifts, which will empower you not only to grow in antiracism but also to experience Jesus in new ways as you do.

Part 3 will investigate the place of spiritual practices (also known as spiritual disciplines) in the life of color-courageous disciples. In this section we will reframe our daily spiritual practices because racism is, at its core, a spiritual problem—which means that racism requires spiritual solutions. Without spiritual practices, we are left to pursue color-courageous discipleship in our own strength. But *with* spiritual practices, color-courageous discipleship can become an intimate and exciting journey with Jesus Christ. What's more, *spiritual practices provide the means for us to be transformed so that we can transform the world*.

This book will likely serve as both a review and a revelation. It may be a review for some in that certain antiracism concepts covered are familiar to you—I hope they are! Yet I have also sought to provide you with a resource that features *in one place* a full range of antiracism concepts and ideas. At the same, this book can also be a revelation, even if you are familiar with antiracism concepts. My project has been to *freshly connect* antiracism principles to the fundamental principles and dynamics of Christian discipleship. Regardless of where you find yourself on the color-courageous journey, I pray that in this work you will find both education and inspiration.

Our entire project will be grounded in and guided by the Word of God. With that in mind, let me make one important point of clarification about the Bible and race: It would be anachronistic to say that the Bible *directly* addresses race. The Bible does not explicitly condemn racism and it does not explicitly encourage antiracism *because the concept of race wasn't invented yet*. Nevertheless, the Bible does portray plenty of conflict between diverse groups, including diverse ethnic groups. For example, in the Bible we do find **ethnocentrism**—the much more ancient belief that one's ethnic group is normative or superior to others. That being said, I believe we can deduce many important insights about race and racism from the Bible by virtue of how Scripture engages ethnicity, ethnocentrism, and other analogous dynamics.

While our journey will be firmly grounded in Bible, along the way we also learn from a wide variety of writers and thought leaders who, I believe, have important insights for color-courageous disciples. To be clear, this does not mean that I agree with or condone the whole of their thought or approach. For example, from my vantage point, secular antiracist movements do lack components that I believe are vital for those committed to a biblical worldview. At the same time, I believe there are many things we can learn. Like the "fair-minded" Berean disciples who "searched the Scriptures daily to find out whether these things were so," we can separate the wheat from the chaff according to God's Word and to the glory of God (Acts 17:11, NKJV). We, too, can hold on to what is helpful, let go of what is not, and faithfully pursue color-courageous discipleship in Jesus's name.

A FEW NOTES ON TERMINOLOGY

Since color-courageous discipleship involves seeing the world in some new ways, it will help us tremendously to have some new words. New vocabulary can open our eyes to racial realities that may have previously been hidden to us. Once we learn to notice and name the unique dynamics at play in our racial challenges, we can also identify more effective solutions. That's why you'll find an extensive glossary in the back of this book. When I was a kid, I read the dictionary for fun. Yes, I'm aware that makes me weird! With that caveat, I'll still say that the glossary is worth a read in itself as a way to expand your world. Throughout this book, you will find glossary words in bold text (usually at their first mention).

When I refer to people, I will use the following terms interchangeably: **people of color** and **minority** as well as **White** and **majority.** I do fully acknowledge the limitations of these terms. For example, the use of the words *minority* and *majority* is waning because they are becoming outdated: The census predicts that by 2045, if not sooner, the United States is projected to be "minority White."[22]

I will use *people of color* to refer primarily to people of African, Native, Asian, Latino, or Middle Eastern descent. Many people push back on the term *people of color* by rightly pointing out that White people have color, too—which of course they do! White people are not the color of snow just as Black people aren't the color of the night sky. At the same time, *people of color* has resonated with many because it meets "a deeply felt need expressed within all of these groups to *build unity*" among themselves.[23] It's also noteworthy that the term has precedent. For example, Martin Luther King, Jr., used the phrase *citizens of color* in his 1963 "I Have a Dream" speech.[24] So, for now, we'll go with it.

A final grammatical note. As of this writing, there is no general consensus on whether the words Black and White—and similar race-related terms of color—should be capitalized. Many commentators have given compelling reasons for why one, both, or neither word should be capitalized.[25] For simplicity and consistency, this text will capitalize both terms.

Now, let's dive in with a story. Hearing stories from your church community—learning about the experiences of other disciples—is one of the most surefire ways to grow. In fact, that's precisely what the Bible does for us. The Bible is a rich repository of stories about the saints who have walked the path of discipleship before us. Their narratives are meant to encourage, to teach, and to inspire. That is why, throughout this journey, we will also explore stories and interviews with a diverse set of color-courageous disciples. These individuals have been profoundly impacted by the journey of racial discipleship, and they seek to foster racial shalom on a daily basis. By sharing their stories, I hope to make color-courageous discipleship concrete and personal. May their stories impact you as much as they have impacted me.

A COLOR-COURAGEOUS DISCIPLESHIP PORTRAIT: DIETRICH BONHOEFFER

Pop quiz! When I say "Dietrich Bonhoeffer," what comes to mind?[26] Perhaps *costly discipleship, anti-Nazi, German prophet, Confessing Church,* or *Christian community.* Far more rarely would someone reply with *Black church, Black theology, Harlem,* or *anti-racist.* But these responses are just as true.

Bonhoeffer became the hero, prophet, and discipleship leader that we know today precisely because of his time worshipping, serving, and learning with the Black church in Harlem. In fact, when Bonhoeffer reflected on the state of his discipleship prior to his sojourn in New York, he bluntly stated: "I had not yet become a Christian."[27]

Dietrich Bonhoeffer spent a year of his theological training studying at Union Theological Seminary in New York City. Unfortunately, he found his predominantly White seminary and church experiences to be mostly uninspiring—with a notable exception. He became quick friends with Albert Fisher, an African American classmate descended from Black Baptist clergy. Bonhoeffer went with Fisher to visit Abyssinian Baptist Church in Harlem, and he never left. He marveled that he was "increasingly discovering greater religious power and originality among the Negroes" and, furthermore, that he had "only heard a genuine proclamation of the gospel from a Negro."[28]

As Bonhoeffer experienced the fresh spiritual power and vitality of the Black church, he simultaneously made salient observations about the American church as a whole. As a foreigner, Bonhoeffer was much more adept at spotting serious contradictions in America's Christian culture. He warned: "For American Christendom the racial issue has been a real problem from the beginning . . . and [it is] a grave problem for the future."[29] In a country that touted freedom, equality, and opportunity for all,

Bonhoeffer was troubled by America's widespread blindness to its own double standard for people of color.

Later, Bonhoeffer wrote about the two incompatible versions of Jesus in America that he experienced—a "Black Christ" and a "White Christ" who were pitted against each other in a "destructive rift."[30] Of the two, it was clear that Bonhoeffer related far more profoundly to the Black Christ. Bonhoeffer did not recraft Jesus into a man of African descent, but he understood Jesus to identify as a co-sufferer with the poor, the marginalized, and the oppressed.

In the Black church, Bonhoeffer learned that discipleship necessitated costly suffering in solidarity with disenfranchised people. And it was in the Black church that one of Bonhoeffer's friends concluded that he was witnessing in Bonhoeffer "a beginning of his identification with the oppressed which played a role in the decision that led to his death."[31]

As many of us know, in 1945 Dietrich Bonhoeffer was executed by the Nazi regime: Bonhoeffer courageously sacrificed his own life for the sake of the Jewish people. Unlike so many of his German colleagues, Bonhoeffer applied what he learned about American racism back in Germany in a surprising way: He resisted the Nazi regime and became a courageous advocate for Jewish lives.

In the racial upheaval and racial awakening of our generation, we must consider, *Why should we as believers expand our understanding of racial realities and injustices?* Like Bonhoeffer, we do so as a matter of discipleship. We do so to experience more of Jesus Christ, who so profoundly identifies with those who suffer. And we do so to open our eyes to all kinds of injustices everywhere, injustices that we might otherwise miss.

We also seek to expand our understanding of racial realities so that we might experience greater joy! Remember that while racism is a scourge on God's creation, ethnicity is a God-ordained cultural identity that God delights in to bring glory to himself and enrichment to everyone in his kingdom—including you. Those who take steps to dismantle racism will undoubtedly discover new opportunities to enjoy more of the surprising riches of God's colorful kingdom.

As you go deeper now into this journey of color-courageous discipleship, may you—like Bonhoeffer—be surprised by how God works both to bring greater shalom to your corner of the world and to draw you closer to Jesus Christ.

FURTHER READING

Bonhoeffer's Black Jesus: Harlem Renaissance Theology and an Ethic of Resistance by Reggie L. Williams

The Deeply Formed Life: Five Transformative Values to Root Us in the Way of Jesus by Rich Villodas

Faithful Antiracism: Moving Past Talk to Systemic Change by Christina Barland Edmondson and Chad Brennan

The Heart of Racial Justice: How Soul Change Leads to Social Change by Brenda Salter McNeil and Rick Richardson

Stamped from the Beginning: The Definitive History of Racist Ideas in America by Ibram X. Kendi

A CHRIST-CENTERED APPROACH TO ANTIRACISM

God was pleased to have all his fullness dwell in [Christ],
and through him to reconcile to himself all things... by
making peace through his blood, shed on the cross.
—COLOSSIANS 1:19–20

As I make my way through the corridors of my office, I'm
keenly aware of my palpitating heart. It's time for my first
performance review with my boss, and I'm thinking, *I've given
this my all, and I've done okay—but what have I missed?*

Quick rewind. Earlier in the year, I'd jumped from leading
discipleship at a thriving local church to leading discipleship for
an entire denomination of churches across North America. And
to be honest, it was a steep jump. I started as both the youngest
executive and the first person of color to lead discipleship for our
movement. So, you better believe that I was giving the job my
all. My main motivation, of course, was to glorify God. But if
I'm honest, I was also striving to prove that those who took the
chance to hire me—young, Black, female me—had made the
right choice.

Here I am. Inhale. I knock and my boss ushers me in with his characteristically warm welcome. We take our seats—the senior White male on one side, the junior Black female on the other. I'm eager as usual to make myself acceptable. We engage in small talk. "How is your family?" he inquires. "Have you found a church you like?" It's not an obligatory exercise. This man was on the search team that chose me, and he was among the first to enthusiastically congratulate me. It's clear to me that he cares—about me, my family, and my flourishing.

The review begins. I remain calm and on top of my game. He showers me with affirmations. Yet my heart is clenched. *Okay—but what have I missed? What else is coming?* I finally sense him shifting gears to constructive feedback mode, and I brace myself. *Have I not been relational enough as a manager? Have I done enough on the ministry field? Have I made enough progress on such-and-such initiative?*

Finally, he ventures, "Michelle, I've noticed a pattern. It seems that most White people within our movement appreciate you, yet there are some Black folks who aren't fans. Why do you think that is?"

What happens next is a blur. My confident facade shatters and, to my horror, I erupt in tears. Now hear me: I don't cry at work. Nevertheless, that day my tears flow, and flow, and continue to flow as we press through the conversation. I struggle to remain in the present, yet I am undeniably pulled to the past. My scars are aflame. I watch my childhood bullies parade by in quick succession. Punching a hole through the wall of years, they taunt me again in this moment with the refrain that I am an Oreo cookie— Black on the outside, White on the inside, and (I fear) ultimately unacceptable to all sides. Once again, I am that little girl, frightened and ashamed. *Will it never stop? Never enough, never enough. I have no home. I am haunted by race. I'm not White, so I'll certainly never be "White enough" for Whites. And apparently I can't be "Black enough" for Blacks. So . . . who am I? And what am I supposed to do?*

I realize that not everyone will have a dramatic incident like this one that prompts them to ask deeper questions about race. That said, I would argue that our generation has experienced some pretty dramatic events as a society, events that galvanized the most widespread protests in U.S. history. As disciples, we are invited to be like the people of Issachar "who understood the times and knew what Israel should do" (1 Chronicles 12:32). And if you do accept that invitation, you might find yourself considering questions like the ones God prompted in me: Who is God calling me to be in this moment? What am I supposed to do? And where do I begin? For disciples of Jesus, the answer to "Where do I begin?" is as simple as it is profound: *As disciples of Jesus, we start with Jesus.*

For my part, I took my racial challenges to Jesus . . . eventually. Previously, I had—quite frankly—not been taught *to engage race as a disciple.* My Christian discipleship had been characterized by a color-blind approach rather than a color-courageous one. So I would be taking this journey without a map.

I left for the day shortly after my review, and on the long drive home, I wailed inside my sedan and soaked my steering wheel with tears. It took me a long time to move past my pain and discomfort and enter into the racial challenges before me with a clear head and a learning posture.

Yet God was patient with me. He whispered, "Hey, there, discipleship leader! Remember that at the end of the day, race is a matter of discipleship too." God was reminding me that the journey of color-courageous discipleship—like any other—starts and ends with Jesus.

If you identify as a disciple of Jesus Christ, I invite you to begin again now with him too. I invite you to ask your king, "What am I missing? How can I grow?" Only Jesus can answer these questions in their fullness. He loves you, and he will show you. Maybe you've already started the color-courageous discipleship journey. Good. Very good. But don't stop now. Ask again. Keep on asking. And I guarantee that Jesus will keep on discipling you in new and surprising ways.

As we recommit to Jesus amid our human factions and controversies, I'm reminded of Joshua's encounter with the "commander of the army of the LORD" prior to the fall of Jericho:

> Now when Joshua was near Jericho, he looked up and saw a man standing in front of him with a drawn sword in his hand. Joshua went up to him and asked, "Are you for us or for our enemies?"
>
> "Neither," he replied, "but as commander of the army of the LORD I have now come." Then Joshua fell facedown to the ground in reverence, and asked him, *What message does my Lord have for his servant?"* (Joshua 5:13–14)

When it comes to race (and everything else for that matter), the ultimate question for a disciple is not "Is Jesus on my side?" The ultimate questions are ones like: "Am I on Jesus's side? Am I centering my racial discipleship on Jesus Christ? And, in all this, *what message does Jesus have for me?"*

To be clear, I do not claim to have all the definitive answers to these questions as it concerns your personal discipleship journey. I am still on the journey too. What I do know, though, is that these are the right questions for disciples to ask. So let's dive in together—starting again with Jesus as Lord and Savior.

CHRIST-CENTERED ANTIRACISM:
JESUS AS LORD AND SAVIOR

I spent two years working with Cru in New York City. During my final summer in 2005, I volunteered at Billy Graham's 417th and final crusade. More than 240,000 New Yorkers descended upon Flushing Meadows Corona Park to hear the legendary preacher at his culminating event.

Like many others, I had been trained by Cru and the Billy Graham Association to share the **gospel** using the well-known phrase *Would you like to accept Jesus as Lord and Savior?* This is a succinct summary of the gospel. The word *gospel* means "good news," and our good news is that Jesus Christ is Lord and Savior. Of course, the phrase *Lord and Savior* did not originate with Billy Graham! It comes to us directly from the Scriptures (for example, 2 Peter 3:18). The good news that Jesus is Lord and Savior never gets old or irrelevant. Of course, there is a pivotal point at which many disciples say yes to Jesus as Lord and Savior for the first time. But the reality is, our journey with him will continue to bring life to the extent that we continue to say yes every day and in every way. Disciples are called both to start and to sustain every new discipleship adventure—including the adventure of color-courageous discipleship—with the good news that Jesus is Lord and Savior.

INVITATION #1: HOW DO COLOR-COURAGEOUS DISCIPLES HONOR JESUS AS LORD?

Is it possible to produce a list of the most influential people of all time? That's debatable, but many have risen to the challenge, including Steve Skiena, a professor of computer science at Stony Brook University.[1] In the same way that Google identifies and ranks webpages, Skiena has meticulously designed algorithms to rank more than one thousand of history's most historically significant people.

You may not be surprised to see that Jesus came out on top. And yet that is precisely the problem. We have become so accustomed to Jesus that we are no longer baffled by him. How in the world did this poor man born into utter obscurity come to dominate world history?

Six of the ten figures on this list commanded armies. Jesus was born in a stable, preached peace, and was executed as a criminal—at which point most of his followers promptly deserted him. The remaining three figures revolutionized the world primarily through the power of their pens. Jesus wrote nothing.

HISTORY'S TOP 10 MOST SIGNIFICANT PEOPLE

1. Jesus
2. Napoleon
3. Muhammad
4. William Shakespeare
5. Abraham Lincoln
6. George Washington
7. Adolf Hitler
8. Aristotle
9. Alexander the Great
10. Thomas Jefferson[2]

More than two billion people, or roughly one-third of the world's population, identify as Jesus's followers. The Bible, the book that tells his story, is by far the bestselling book of all time. Time itself has been split with reference to the birth of Christ.

You might imagine that Napoleon, notorious for his gargantuan ego, would be miffed about ranking second. On the contrary, Napoleon himself marveled at how the lowly Jesus outshone him. At the end of his life, Napoleon seemed preoccupied with the question of how the carpenter from Nazareth continued to dazzle after death. He confessed with wonder,

"Alexander, Caesar, Charlemagne, and myself have founded empires. But upon what did we rest . . . our genius? Upon *force*. Jesus Christ founded His empire upon *love;* and at this hour millions of men would die for him . . . which proves to me quite convincingly the divinity of Christ!"[3]

The only reasonable explanation for Jesus's powerful and persistent impact is that he truly is the Son of God and Lord of all.

The book of Colossians presents an even more astonishing view of Jesus. The apostle Paul was concerned that the Colossians' understanding of the supremacy of Jesus Christ had been compromised. So he wrote a letter to persuade the Colossian disciples to recommit to Christ alone as Lord.

It seems that the faith of the Colossians had become infected with a kind of religious syncretism. **Syncretism** is the amalgamation of different and often contradictory religious beliefs and practices. The Colossians clearly identified as disciples of Jesus. However, they combined their loyalty to Jesus with competing loyalties.

The truth is, we are not so different from the Colossians. In the twenty-first century, most disciples are probably not in danger of renouncing Jesus to worship other gods. We know that's **idolatry.** Our danger is that, like the Colossians, we will worship Jesus *plus* other gods. Even in the Old Testament, when the people of Israel practiced idolatry, they usually did not stop worshipping Yahweh altogether. They just added Asherah or Molek to the mix (see 2 Kings 23).

Today disciples are still prone to combine commitment to Jesus with competing loyalties. One way we do this is through conflicting ideologies, philosophies, or worldviews. An **ideology** is simply a system of ideas. You can often recognize an ideology by its *-ism* ending—like social*ism* and capital*ism,* liberal*ism,* and conservat*ism.* Most ideologies are not harmful in themselves. But problems can arise if we lose perspective on what comes first. By the way, yes, that warning applies to antira*cism!* Even the well-intentioned pursuit of antiracism can compete with our commitment to Christ.

Back to the Colossians. Apparently, their faith had been compromised in just this syncretistic way. So Paul wrote a letter to remind them of the incontestable lordship of Christ. Of course, bullying doesn't really motivate anybody ("Worship Jesus or else!"), so Paul didn't take that approach. He understood that the human soul is deeply motivated by beauty. We will exalt Jesus as Lord in an all-encompassing way to the extent that we become enraptured by his all-encompassing beauty. The appeal of beauty explains why, to convince the Colossians of the supremacy of Christ, Paul used not a polemic but a poem, not a speech but a song. In fact, many scholars believe that Paul's Colossians 1 poem is actually an excerpt from an ancient hymn that savored the supremacy of Christ. It says this:

> [He] is the image of the invisible God, the firstborn over all creation. For in him all things were created: things in heaven and on earth, visible and invisible, whether thrones or powers or authorities; all things have been created through him and for him. He is before all things, and in him all things hold together. . . . He is the beginning and the firstborn from among the dead, *so that in everything he might have the supremacy.* (Colossians 1:15–18)

This Colossian Christ-hymn woos our hearts with a fresh revelation of Jesus as Lord. It celebrates Jesus as God with us, the exquisite image of the invisible God. Humans suffer an insatiable longing of the heart, an existential craving for something that nothing in this world can satisfy. The Germans have called it *Sehnsucht,* a kind of nostalgia for something not yet experienced.[4] Earthly beauty—birds exchanging love songs in the soft brightness of dawn, endless ocean waves reaching beyond the horizon, fireflies suspended across boundless fields—can provide a temporary reprieve from those longings, of course. Yet our nagging nostalgia lingers still. The truth is that our yearning for beauty will only be completely satisfied in glory when we see the face of God—the Source and the Creator of all beauty, the beauty to which all other beauties point.[5] But marvel of marvels, we can enjoy a glimpse of our gorgeous God now in the face of Jesus Christ.

We will exalt Jesus as Lord in an all-encompassing way to the extent that we become enraptured by his all-encompassing beauty.

As disciples we frequently say yes to Jesus in some arenas of our lives while holding back in others. Put another way, we are afraid to trust Jesus with the *whole* of our lives. But just as Jesus urged the Twelve, so he continues to urge us now: "Take courage! It is I. Don't be afraid" (Matthew 14:27). Our hymn reveals that Jesus Christ is Lord not only because he is the image of the invisible God but also because he is, wondrously, the creator of the cosmos. In him, all things hold together and find their meaning—including race and ethnicity. Because Jesus is Lord of all, we have every reason to take courage. We have every reason to honor Christ as the leader of every part of our lives, including race.

Doing this requires a kind of dual intentionality. On the one hand, we clearly need to rid ourselves of all forms of racism and any sense of **racial supremacy,** submitting instead to the supremacy of Christ.[6] Yet on the other hand, we who are committed to antiracism must also guard against making antiracism itself supreme. As a friend of mine says, while antiracism may be a great cause, it makes for a terrible god. In the words of John M. Perkins: "God is all about reconciliation, but we run the risk of missing Him when we allow racial reconciliation, or any kind of reconciliation, to rise as the dominating force—if we allow it rather than God Himself to become the ultimate goal."[7]

We who are committed to antiracism must guard against making antiracism itself supreme.

When it comes to matters of race, Jesus invites us again to courageously say yes to him alone as Lord. Jesus is—truly—the only one who deserves the place of supremacy in our hearts and lives.

INVITATION #2: WHAT DOES IT MEAN FOR COLOR-COURAGEOUS DISCIPLES TO HONOR JESUS AS SAVIOR?

After celebrating Jesus as Lord, the Colossian hymn exalts him as Savior—the one who rescues us from sin and death by his shed blood and reconciles us to God and to one another.

> God was pleased to have all his fullness dwell in [the Son], and through him to reconcile to himself all things, whether things on earth or things in heaven, by making peace through his blood, shed on the cross. (Colossians 1:19–20)

The name *Jesus* means "the Lord saves." An angel instructed Mary to name her son Jesus because "he will save his people from their sins," a feat that Jesus achieved for us through his death on the cross (Matthew 1:21). If we're honest, though, it's actually hard to admit that we need a savior. This, too, requires courage—the courage of humility. Needing a savior implies that we are needy. It implies that we are sinful. It implies that we are truly helpless without God. Nevertheless, to make meaningful progress on the racial discipleship journey, we as disciples must humbly comprehend the pervasive brokenness in our own lives and in every dimension of creation.

Speaking of which, sin is not just an individual problem. Creation is broken on every level and needs to be reconciled on every level. I resonate with how George Yancey puts it in his book *Beyond Racial Gridlock:* "The problem of racism is the problem of sin."[8] Everything has been broken by **sin,** and only God can put everything back together again. That is what **reconciliation** is all about: making broken things whole again. That's why the Colossian Christ-hymn culminates with a celebration of how God is making all broken things whole again through Jesus Christ.

Four Levels of Creation

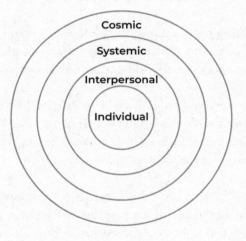

Let's draw this out. We can envision the levels of creation as four concentric circles—individual, interpersonal, systemic, and cosmic—with each having profound implications for how racism works and how to uproot it.[9] Too often, we have sought to deal with racism on only one or two of these levels when we really need to engage every level. All four dimensions of creation are broken, and all four can only be ultimately reconciled through the blood of Jesus Christ.

We can trace this breakdown of creation on every level in the Bible as we progress sequentially through the earliest chapters of Genesis.

Individual Level (Genesis 3:1–10). I first became a follower of Jesus as a little girl. I knelt before a high window and lifted my head to the sky in prayer. As a shaft of light cascaded down on me, I asked Jesus to forgive my sins. Of course, what I had in mind as a child was personal sin. Yet I suspect that most Christians, regardless of their age, continue to consider sin primarily on a personal level. And that makes sense because that's also where Scripture begins with sin: on the individual level.

Our story—the story of everything—began with beauty, abundance, and delight (Genesis 1–2). Tragically, though, the trouble began as early as Genesis 3 when the first humans rejected God in the hopes of becoming "like God" themselves (3:5). Our ancestors' decision to distrust and disobey God put them squarely at odds with the Creator, and we continue to live with the consequences. On an individual level, Adam and Eve sensed an immediate change and clamored to cover their sin with fig leaves—a sad and pitiful picture of the never-ending human attempt to hide the guilt and shame that alienate us from God and from one another. As individuals, we continue to be broken in multiple ways. We suffer emotional distress, mental illness, physical ailments, and beyond. God's intention was for us to enjoy endless life. Instead, we awaken every morning trapped on a high-speed train barreling toward the final destination: a grave.

What does individual brokenness have to do with our racial discipleship journey? The answer is that we cannot make meaningful progress when it comes to race unless we courageously comprehend the depths of our individual brokenness. This is true for disciples of all races. As we will soon see, racial oppressors and racial victims alike possess a sin nature and are called to repentance and grace (Romans 3:23). Just as we are all equally dignified in reflecting the image of God, we are also equally in need of forgiveness and healing at the foot of the cross.

Racial oppressors and racial victims alike possess a sin nature and are called to repentance and grace (Romans 3:23).

When it comes to race, one important dimension of individual brokenness is what theologians call the **noetic effect of sin.** The word *noetic* derives from the Greek words for perception and intellect. The noetic effect of sin reminds us that sin has even impacted our ability to think clearly and to perceive the world accurately. That is one explanation for our human inclination toward **unconscious bias** even from a very early age.

Interpersonal Level (Genesis 3:11–4:16). As I grew up, I came to comprehend sin in more relational ways. When I experienced racial bullying for the first time, for example, I came to understand just how badly hurt people can hurt people. But even more important, God gradually opened my eyes to the ways in which my own sins were spoiling many of the relationships that mattered most to me.

In a similar way, the Genesis story traces the cancerous spread of sin from the *individual* to the *interpersonal level.* Conflict erupted between Adam and Eve, and soon we observe how sin spread to their children and their children's children. We watch with dismay as sin spoils interpersonal relationships through jealousy, abuse, and violence. Now, marriage ends in divorce. Friendships become mired in misunderstanding. Family feuds fester in unforgiveness.

With race, interpersonal sin tends to be easy to see and condemn because it has often taken the form of outright racial **prejudice** and **discrimination.** Thankfully, most Christians no longer approve of racial jokes and slurs, join White supremacist groups, or cling to the conscious conviction that racial minorities are inferior. Yet it helps to understand that interpersonal racial brokenness can take more subtle forms as well.

Systemic Level (Genesis 4:17–26). This book is largely the story of how God has opened my eyes to the reality of the world's systemic brokenness. In some ways, of course, I have always recognized the reality of systemic brokenness. It started with little things. When I was a child, I remember asking my mother why all my (mostly White) friends hosted birthday parties at their homes, but we never did. She told me that she feared my friends wouldn't want to visit our part of town. So many questions followed: *What was wrong with our part of town? And, by extension, what was wrong with us? Why did we all live in different parts of town anyway?* I didn't have the words at the time, but clearly, I was beginning to witness the effects of larger "systemic" dynamics at work. Of course, we all understand systemic brokenness at some level. Whenever we watch the news, we are reminded that it's not only humans but also systems created by humans that are defective. At the same time, it is only recently that God has helped me understand the extent of the systemic brokenness of our world as well as how I have unwittingly perpetuated that brokenness.

Systemic brokenness is an ancient affliction. We see it develop as we watch sin's infection spread to Cain's descendants and, through them, to the city they founded. After Cain killed Abel, he wandered east, farther away from his parents and "from the LORD's presence" (4:16). He established a family in the land of Nod and built a city there. I have lived and worked in cities around the world, from New York City to Minneapolis to Quito to Hong Kong, and I can testify: Every human city is simultaneously glorious and galling. Cain's prosperous first city was no different. As the constructive creativity of the city grew, so did its destructive creativity. As the city grew and multiplied, so did oppression and violence (4:19–24).

The racial awakening of our generation is mostly about our awakening to systemic racism.

I, along with many others of our generation, have been slowly awakening to the ways in which sin has subtly yet profoundly impacted our communities, institutions, and nations. **Systemic racism** is, simply, what racial brokenness looks like at a corporate level. But one of the most cunning characteristics of systemic racism is that it stubbornly persists as a menace to minorities while remaining virtually invisible to the majority. And then as systemic racism becomes widespread, we see a racialized society emerge. A **racialized society** is a society in which "race matters profoundly for differences in life experiences, life opportunities, and social relationships."[10] As I see it, the racial awakening of our generation is mostly about our awakening to systemic racism. That's why we'll be diving deep into systemic racism in our next chapter.

Cosmic Level (Genesis 5–7). Ultimately sin has a cosmic impact: It infects everyone, spreads everywhere, and taints everything. Nature itself has become a constant source of frustration and pain (3:18; 5:29). Many generations after the Fall, Lamech named his son Noah, meaning "comfort," in the hope that somehow Noah would "comfort us in the labor and painful toil of our hands caused by the ground the LORD has cursed" (5:28–29). Later, in a strange and mysterious passage, Genesis 6 reveals how at this time the "sons of God" married the "daughters of humans," resulting in the "Nephilim," often translated "giants" (6:1–4). While the meaning of this passage is unclear, it certainly hints at an unnatural disturbance at the cosmic level that called for divine intervention. Finally, as humankind increased in number across the earth, they also increased in depravity. In response, the Lord was "grieved" that he had created humanity (6:6, NKJV). In fact, "it broke his heart" (6:6, NLT). Grief, more than anger, compelled our Creator to cleanse the earth with a flood. This biblical story illustrates that sin has cosmic dimensions: Everything that lives must suffer and die, and the whole world must be cleansed and reconciled. This was true of Noah's time, and it is still true of ours.

We will be more effective as color-courageous disciples to the extent that we understand that racial brokenness has cosmic dimensions. The Scriptures reveal that there are larger **powers and principalities** at war against God and that as disciples we are called to combat these adversaries in God's power (Ephesians 6:12, NKJV). There is a real cosmic battle raging behind human events, and real, intentional evil is at work in the world. These are the powers and principalities, and they include deceptive and destructive ideologies like racism.[11]

GENESIS
Tracing the Fall on Four Levels

3:1–10
Individual Brokenness *(Adam, Eve)*

3:11–4:16
Interpersonal Brokenness *(Marriage, Children)*

4:17–26
Systemic Brokenness *(Communities, Cities)*

5–7
Cosmic Brokenness *(Creation, Principalities)*

Committing to color-courageous discipleship means working to identify and dismantle racial fallacies and distortions wherever we encounter them. Too often we find ourselves raging against one another when, in reality, "our struggle is not against flesh and blood" (Ephesians 6:12). Thankfully, we have cause to rejoice because Christ is supreme over all powers (Colossians 1:15–18). In the end, Jesus wins. But in the meantime, color-courageous disciples are invited to partner with Christ right now in his ongoing work of cosmic reconciliation.

———

We have been talking about what it means to acknowledge Jesus as Savior in matters of race. Color-courageous disciples, for instance, acknowledge that our world is racially broken on every level, starting with ourselves. As we do, it helps to keep in mind that liberal-leaning and conservative-leaning disciples tend to differ in their ability to recognize what racial brokenness looks like on each level. Depending on our vantage point, we can often easily see racial brokenness on some levels while missing it on others.

Liberal-leaning and conservative-leaning disciples differ in their ability to recognize what racial brokenness looks like on each level.

Here is a pattern I've observed. Liberal-leaning disciples recognize racial brokenness at the systemic level and, to a lesser extent, the cosmic level. In other words, they can often identify when racial brokenness rears its ugly head in institutions and ideologies. They respond by advocating for systemic reforms in areas such as law enforcement and education. But they can miss that reconciliation in these outer circles alone is not enough. Individual transformation in Christ is also vital.

On the other hand, conservative-leaning disciples more easily recognize racial brokenness at the interpersonal level and, to a lesser extent, at the individual level. Most contemporary conservatives now strongly condemn obvious expressions of interpersonal racism. They understand that true transformation requires transformation of individual hearts. However, they miss the extent to which sin pervasively impacts the systems, ideologies, and principalities of our world—and therefore necessitates an intentional response.

START WITH THE *REAL* JESUS

As we start with Jesus, let's remember the importance of starting with the *real* Jesus. Our view of the real Jesus has probably been obscured over many years. After all, the people in every generation and every culture tend to reimagine Jesus in their own image. Let's take a moment to recall just a few key facts about who Jesus actually was:

- a Middle Eastern Jew and a person of color, not a person of European descent
- a member of a marginalized and oppressed minority under the Roman Empire
- a refugee whose parents desperately fled to Egypt to save his life
- a blue-collar worker trained as a carpenter, not an elite religious scholar
- a convicted criminal, tried and sentenced to death according to the law

We have gotten so used to our contemporary conceptions of Jesus that sometimes the real Jesus eludes us. Jesus is a surprising figure in every way, so of course our racial discipleship journey will also yield some surprises!

In the end, I believe that all of us disciples must realize and confess that our world is broken on every level and that we need Jesus to save and reconcile us on every level—starting with ourselves. Honestly, it takes real courage to admit that we cannot save the world. To become effective agents of racial shalom, we learn to humbly say yes again and again to Jesus as Savior.

COLOR-COURAGEOUS DISCIPLES: RECONCILED RECONCILERS

We've been exploring why it is vital to start our racial discipleship journey with Jesus as Lord and Savior. In short, we do so because "Christ is all, and is in all" (Colossians 3:11). Jesus invites us to say yes again to him as *Lord,* making sure to honor him as supreme in every area of our lives, including the areas of race and ethnicity. He also invites us to say yes again to him as *Savior,* which means humbly admitting our racial brokenness and neediness on every level. And, in all things, Jesus Christ remains central and supreme for disciples—even over doing good antiracist ministry in Jesus's name.

Disciples are called not only to serve Jesus but also to allow Jesus to serve through us.

According to the ancient understanding, being a disciple meant following a *particular person.* That's why I believe that only as we recommit to the person of Jesus can our pursuit of antiracism become a *discipleship* journey. I want to encourage us: As we pursue antiracism for Jesus, let's work not for some*thing* (antiracism) but for some*one.* For us, antiracism can become color-courageous discipleship. Antiracism can be about serving Jesus himself, our cherished Lord and Savior.

What's more, disciples are called not only to serve Jesus but also to allow Jesus to serve through us. God has invited us to become "Christ's ambassadors" in his all-encompassing "ministry of reconciliation":

> All this is from God, who reconciled us to himself through Christ and gave us the ministry of reconciliation: that God was reconciling the world to himself in Christ, not counting people's sins against them. And he has committed to us the message of reconciliation. We are therefore Christ's ambassadors, as though God were making his appeal through us. We implore you on Christ's behalf: Be reconciled to God. (2 Corinthians 5:18–20)

God has given his disciples the breathtaking privilege of being **ambassadors of reconciliation.** He has promised to work in us and through us to bring Christ's reconciliation to the world. This means that, by the power of the Holy Spirit, we are now *reconciled reconcilers.* Not just on one level, but on every level of creation. God invites us to reconnect *individuals* to himself through his provision of forgiveness and healing. He invites us to restore our *interpersonal* relationships by being grace-givers and peacemakers. He invites us to dismantle *systemic* racism in communities and organizations. And he invites us to combat *cosmic* evil forces as we identify false ideologies and join with all the saints in prayer against the powers and principalities of our world. As disciples, we have been reconciled to reconcile. Yes, this is a daunting call—but thankfully, we each have unlimited access to the unparalleled power of Christ that is at work in and through us.

Although I didn't realize it at first, that fateful afternoon in my boss's office turned out to be an important step on my own journey of racial discipleship. After I emerged from the fog of my initial pain and discomfort, I saw the truth: *I had room to grow.* Yes, I am a Black woman, and I had experienced some racism. Yet I had also been reared in predominantly White, well-resourced communities, which meant that there were many important aspects of systemic injustice that I had not experienced. That day, I truly began to understand that *I can do more to help.*

That day, I clearly recognized the voice of Christ calling me to grow as a color-courageous disciple for the sake of the church and the world. And—I have to be honest—it was both a mystifying and terrifying invitation. I wasn't even sure what it would entail. What I did know, though, was that it would be a precious opportunity to face my fears and grow. So despite my questions and qualms, I said yes to a new discipleship journey with Jesus, holding tightly to him as Savior and Lord. He invited me then, and he continues to invite us now:

> I am the Alpha and the Omega,
> the First and the Last,
> the Beginning and the End.
> Yes! That is why you can take courage.
> It is I. Do not be afraid.
> Instead of wasting time with fear, be sure of this:
> I am with you always, even to the end of the age.[12]

FURTHER READING

Beyond Racial Gridlock: Embracing Mutual Responsibility by George Yancey

Dream with Me: Race, Love, and the Struggle We Must Win by John M. Perkins

Rejoicing in Christ by Michael Reeves

Why Sin Matters: The Surprising Relationship Between Our Sin and God's Grace by Mark R. McMinn

COLOR-COURAGEOUS PARADIGM SHIFTS

Over the years, I have been captivated by the concept of missional discipleship, of faithfully responding to the rallying cry to make disciples *who make* disciples. In sermon after sermon, I have cast a vision for discipleship that doesn't shrink or stagnate—but multiplies.

Yet on one of these occasions, someone asked me questions that gave me pause. The person said, "Okay, yes, but what kind of disciples are we making? What if we're making disciples who are jerks? I mean, if we're making disciples but those disciples aren't actually much like Christ, what's the point?"

These questions serve as both a revelation and a reminder. Yes, healthy things grow and multiply. But so do unhealthy things—like cancer. We need growth, but more specifically, what we need is *healthy* growth: Christlike disciples who make Christlike disciples. Color-courageous disciples who make color-courageous disciples.

Did you know that one of the earliest slave ships was named *Jesus*?

Two of the first English ships to carry West Africans to the New World had ominous names: *Jesus* and *Minion*. . . . Both ships served the same purpose. . . . Forced aboard *Jesus,* African men and women probably had no idea that the ship bore the name of a man who had been crucified fifteen centuries earlier. They probably had no idea that the vessel outfitted with guns, chains, and dungeons was named for the "prince of peace" who had come to "set the captives free."[1]

Needless to say, a label does not a reality make! A ship with the label *Jesus* does not necessarily reflect who Jesus is; a person with the label *Jesus follower* does not necessarily do what Jesus does. To reflect Christ more deeply, deeper discipleship is needed.

What do I mean by "deeper" discipleship? Let's reimagine discipleship as a diamond. In some ways, all diamonds are the same. For example, they are crystallized forms of carbon. Nevertheless, some diamonds are far more brilliant than others. In fact, jewelers and gemologists use the word *brilliance* as a technical term that indicates the measure of a diamond's shine. Yes, all diamonds sparkle. But generally speaking, the more facets a diamond has, the more brilliant it will shine. Of all the diamond cuts, the "round brilliant" cut is the most brilliant of all: Its fifty-eight facets beautifully refract white light in multiple directions, thus achieving a singularly dazzling effect.

In the same way, healthy discipleship is composed of multiple discipleship facets, which we may also refer to as discipleship dimensions or paradigms. Everyone who follows Jesus is being conformed to his image to some degree. But some will more brilliantly reflect his image than others. It's not because they are somehow inherently "better." The way I see it, these disciples are simply like diamonds of a round brilliant cut, beautifully reflecting more facets of who Jesus calls us to be.

In part 2 of this book, we will consider four different discipleship dimensions that Jesus calls us to embrace so that we can reflect him more brilliantly. To be clear, these are not *new* discipleship paradigms, but they have been *underemphasized*. That is why racial inequity has persisted even in the church, and it's also why our discipleship has been less than color-courageous. In other words, brothers and sisters, we must do some major recovery work when it comes to a fully orbed discipleship experience. Same discipleship but new emphases. Same diamond but new facets.

Color-courageous disciples are simply like diamonds of a round brilliant cut, beautifully reflecting more facets of who Jesus calls us to be.

The church does not need only disciples who make disciples. The church also needs Christlike disciples who make Christlike disciples; ambassadors of reconciliation who make ambassadors of reconciliation; color-courageous disciples who make color-courageous disciples.

This is how God's kingdom comes.

DISCIPLESHIP AS AWAKENING

Open Your Eyes to the Myth of Equality

One of the great liabilities of history is that all too many
people fail to remain awake.

—MARTIN LUTHER KING, JR., *WHERE DO WE GO FROM HERE?*

In the midnight darkness of the Garden of Gethsemane, on the
eve of his crucifixion, the disciples failed to do the one thing
Jesus needed most. Three times Jesus implored his disciples to
stay awake. He urged them to remain attentive, to watch and
pray. And each time the disciples drifted away into the comfortable oblivion of sleep. As a result, they were utterly unprepared
for the trials that came their way. The disciples snoozed right
through one of their finest opportunities to partner with Jesus.
That night, they learned firsthand the essence of what it means
to faithfully follow Jesus: *to stay awake.*

Time and again, the Scriptures call for awakening. And here's
the thing: Overwhelmingly it is believers—*not* unbelievers—
who are called to wake up. Apparently you can be a fully committed follower of Jesus and still remain fast asleep in important
ways.

You were once darkness, but now you are light in the Lord. Live as children of light . . . and find out what pleases the Lord. Have nothing to do with the fruitless deeds of darkness, but rather expose them. . . .

This is why it is said:
"Wake up, sleeper,
   rise from the dead,
   and Christ will shine on you."
(Ephesians 5:8, 10–11, 14)

It goes without saying, of course, that sleep is *not* a bad thing in itself. God designed us to sleep, and God grants sleep to those he loves (Psalm 127:2). Nevertheless, we all know that there are times when falling asleep will get you into trouble . . . like when you're driving down a dark and curvy highway at two o'clock in the morning, for example!

By definition, when we are asleep, we cannot remain attentive to what is unfolding around us in the real world. We are immersed in a comfortable darkness. We inhabit a dream world that seems true but is not. Being unconscious is fine . . . unless there is something dangerous happening around you. And according to the Scriptures, there *is* something dangerous—something spiritually evil—unfolding in the darkness around us. This is why disciples are encouraged to stay awake, expose the "deeds of darkness," and courageously live as children of light (Ephesians 5).

The distinction between slumber and wakefulness can help us by drawing our attention to the true nature of evil. Evil often seems benign. Normal. Acceptable. Evil can sometimes take the form of an enchanting lullaby, comforting and tranquilizing. Just as we aren't aware of being asleep when we are asleep, we aren't always aware of when we're succumbing to the evil of the world, the flesh, and the devil. To wake up, we must become fully conscious to the evil around us and listen for how Jesus wants us to respond. Although you won't find this topic in most discipleship textbooks, *staying awake is a vital dimension of what it means to follow Jesus.* Discipleship is, at heart, a journey of awakening.

AWAKENING TO THE MYTH OF EQUALITY

Not many people can say that their high school graduation was front-page news. But when I graduated as the first African American valedictorian of my predominantly White high school, it was a spectacle that earned me a spot on the front page of the local newspaper.

I had been set up for success by a well-resourced Long Island education, but a good education had not been a given for me. My parents grew up across the street from one another in the South Bronx. They were both descendants of slavery by way of the South (my father) and the Caribbean (my mother). After they were married, my parents purchased a home on the eastern reaches of Long Island through a homeownership program for lower-income families. The greatest reward from that move was a shot for my brothers and me to access a well-resourced school district, something we would not have had in the South Bronx.

Still, my childhood had its challenges. We lived in a working-class Black enclave surrounded by affluent White neighborhoods. I grew up with a myriad of White friends, but I inwardly resented many for their fancier homes, clothes, and vacations. For years I felt homeless: I didn't fit in racially with Whites or culturally with Blacks. (I've already mentioned how, when I excelled at school, Black tormentors accused me of being an Oreo.) Day after day, I would wake up in the darkness of the early morning and think that even death would be better than going back to school. It was agonizing. For so long, people who looked like me had struggled for opportunities to succeed. Why, then, were some Blacks traumatizing those of us who did succeed?

While some people might have responded to such harassment by ditching their studies in an attempt to fit in, I buried myself in books. "By reading and studying hard," my mentors promised, "you will leave the haters behind and achieve the life that you have always dreamed of." So study hard I did.

When I was a kid, my idol was Clair Huxtable, the Black mom from *The Cosby Show*. She had a law career, five kids, great hair, *and* a snazzy townhouse in Brooklyn. If I studied hard enough, I could be her. Over time and as I excelled, the bullying thankfully subsided. In the end, I finished first in my class and scored reams of scholarships. After graduating from NYU, I went to work at Goldman Sachs—the mecca of Wall Street at the time. The formula—study hard, receive rewards, and live like Clair Huxtable—had worked for me. I was well on my way!

It was only after college that a more robust racial awakening began for me. While working at Goldman, I volunteered to teach economics for a day at an inner-city school. As I rode the subway uptown, I was excited for the opportunity to inspire students I imagined were miniature versions of me.

The school was mostly Black and Brown, and I was shocked by the conditions I witnessed there. I honestly never imagined that a school like this one existed in the United States of America: dilapidated facilities, dark corridors, overcrowded classrooms with desks spilling out into the hallways, rowdy and troubled kids who made it impossible for others to concentrate or even to hear. It was as if I had crossed over an invisible border into a developing nation. This school certainly did not feel like it was located in the most prosperous country the world has ever known. I stumbled through my lesson, but it was no use.

Up to that point my understanding of the world had been defined by my version of the American dream formula: study hard, receive rewards, and live like Clair Huxtable. It only took one day of teaching at this school to explode that formula. Questions swirled: *What if the conditions of my school didn't make me want to learn but to escape? What if my education had been—inherently—unequal to others'?*

This experience happened years ago, but I have never recovered. Nor should I. A recent story in *The New York Times* once again left me speechless. It is titled "25-Year-Old Textbooks and Holes in the Ceiling: Inside America's Public Schools."[1] With renewed horror, I realized that the tattered biology textbook featured was the same textbook I had used in my own biology class roughly twenty-five years ago.

My journey toward color-courageous discipleship began with my awakening to the "myth of equality."[2] In a land like America that prides itself on equality, what do we do when faced with the reality of just how unequal American experiences and opportunities really are?

SEVEN SYMPTOMS OF SYSTEMIC RACISM

Education is just one area of our society where racial inequity is the stubborn norm. Racism has been highly adaptive over time, morphing like a monstrous chameleon as the context has changed. Today, racism works itself out in a subtler way through systemic racism and the racialization of society. If a society's systems persistently result in different outcomes for different races, we call that a **racialized society**. There are now many high-quality resources that demonstrate the reality of systemic racism; the copious evidence is only a Google search away. At times, though, the sheer quantity of the research can seem overwhelming. That's why I've sought to provide a compact summary here to catalyze color-courageous discipleship both for you and your community.

One additional caveat: By listing these "seven symptoms of systemic racism," am I claiming that all of the following disparities are 100 percent racially motivated? No, I am not. The reality is that every social problem proceeds from a tangled web of factors. When it comes to our stubborn racial disparities, though, it seems to me that systemic racism is one of those factors. What we have here is a list of symptoms, all in a racialized pattern, that make plain our society's ongoing struggle to live up to our stated aspirations for racial equality. Furthermore, regardless of the causes, I hope that with me, you will find these disparities to be heartbreaking. They represent real people, real families, and real communities that are suffering *now*. As disciples of Christ, I would encourage us to consider: What can we do to make a difference in these tragic patterns in Jesus's name?

If a society's systems persistently result in different outcomes for different races, we call that a racialized society.

So, without further ado, let's take a brief look now at seven ways we can know that systemic racism is present and active in society.[3]

1. Wealth

Median Wealth per U.S. Family (2019)

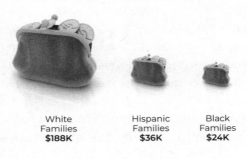

| White Families $188K | Hispanic Families $36K | Black Families $24K |

According to the U.S. Federal Reserve, White families enjoy a median net worth ($188K) that is almost eight times higher than Black families ($24K) and five times the wealth of Hispanic families ($36K).[4] White earners with no bachelor's degree still boast a higher net worth than Black and Hispanic earners that do hold a bachelor's degree.[5] *Overall, White families hold 90 percent of the national wealth while Hispanic families hold 2.3 percent and Black families hold 2.6 percent.*[6]

2. Homeownership

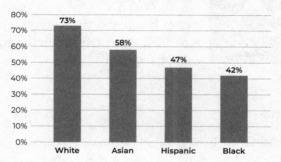

Data Source: Joint Center for Housing Studies (Harvard), 2019

Homeownership is the primary means of building wealth over time and achieving the American dream. In fact, *homeownership is the single largest predictor of racial wealth disparity.*[7] As of 2019, 73 percent of White families owned a home in comparison to 58 percent of Asians, 47 percent of Hispanics, and only 42 percent of Blacks.[8] What's more, Black homeownership continues to hit all-time lows.[9] Among those fortunate enough to own homes, White families have accumulated greater home equity over time: in 2015, the median home equity for Whites was $100K compared to $56K for Blacks.[10] Due to **redlining** and other discriminatory practices, 98 percent of home loans went to White families between 1934 and 1968.[11] To this day, Blacks are less likely to be approved for mortgages.[12]

3. Employment

Black workers are consistently twice as likely to be unemployed as White workers. This has been true for at least sixty years regardless of whether the U.S. economy was booming or busting.[13] Even Black college graduates remain twice as likely to be unemployed as other grads.[14] There has also been a massive income gap between Black and White families that has remained essentially unchanged since the 1960s.[15]

Blacks are **2x** more likely to be unemployed

4. Education

More than half of U.S. children are educated in racially concentrated school districts. As one study revealed, *minority school districts in the United States received $23 billion less in funding than majority-White ones.*[16] White students are more likely than Blacks to be identified as gifted despite similar academic performance, while Black students are three times more likely to be suspended despite similar misbehavior.[17] Once Black children are in the criminal justice system, they are eighteen times more likely than White children to be sentenced as adults, a pattern often referred to as the **school-to-prison pipeline.**[18]

Minority school districts receive **$23 billion less**

5. Criminal Justice

America prides itself on being a land of equality and fairness. Yet justice in America is not blind: When a Black person and a White person commit similar crimes, the Black person is more likely to be arrested.[19] Black people are convicted more often and are more likely to receive a harsher sentence. In fact, the darker the Black defendant's skin looks, the more likely they are to receive the death penalty.[20] People of color suffer more wrongful convictions than Whites do: Roughly 70 percent of convicts who have later been proved innocent through DNA testing are people of color.[21] These realities all shed light on why Black people are incarcerated at five times the rate of Whites. Perhaps, then, it is no wonder that Black people comprise 40 percent of the prison population but make up only 13 percent of the U.S. population.[22] **Mass incarceration** is another peculiar American phenomenon. *Although the United States makes up 5 percent of the global population, it is home to nearly 25 percent of the world's prison population.*[23]

Black U.S. Population

13%

Black Prison Population

40%

Data Source: NAACP

6. Health

The Covid-19 crisis put the existing racial disparities of our healthcare system into sharp relief: Covid-19 had a far more devastating impact on communities of color.[24] Even with recent innovations such as the Affordable Care Act, people of color are less likely to have access to health insurance.[25] Of the thirty million people who remain uninsured, about half are people of color.[26] *Even when people of color do have access to health insurance, they experience lower-quality care.*[27] The

The uninsured are

50%

people of color

most highly trained professionals serve predominantly White communities.[28] Doctors are less likely to order blood tests, CT scans, or X-rays for Black, Latino, and Asian children.[29] African American men are less likely to receive treatment for cardiovascular disease.[30] Another study revealed that, over a twelve-year period, Black patients were 10 percent less likely to be admitted to a hospital than White patients. When they were admitted, they were almost 1.3 times more likely to die there.[31] As a survey of the research reveals, "Put simply, people of color receive less care—and often worse care—than white Americans."[32]

7. Leadership

Society's leaders are the ones who have the power to make a difference in all the categories we have been exploring. *Yet leaders of color have been severely underrepresented in our halls of power at all points of American history.* In 2020 corporate America, nearly 90 percent of Fortune 500 CEOs were White, and as of 2019, only

five Fortune 500 and S&P 500 companies were led by Black CEOs.[33] The pattern in government has been the same. In 2018, for instance, the 116th Congress was the most diverse ever, but only 57 of the 535 voting members of Congress were Black.[34] As of 2020, only two Black governors have ever been elected in the United States, and only six Black senators have been elected since the Reconstruction.[35] A survey from the same year found that 80 percent of the most powerful people in America were White, even as the United States has become more diverse.[36]

Although we're stopping at seven, we could go on. Our society is racialized in countless ways. Research demonstrates persistent inequities in life experiences as wide-ranging as employment outcomes, auto loan rates, mortgage rates, cost of products, respect levels, performance expectations, self-esteem, environmental pollution, child poverty, and more. In the words of one commentator, "Let's wake up, for we are no longer the country we think we are."[37]

AWAKENING TO OUR MOMENT

Over time, the concept of awakening has been commonly understood as a kind of prerequisite for racial justice work. In 2017, the term **woke** emerged and won a place in the Merriam-Webster dictionary to mean "aware of and actively attentive to important facts and issues (especially issues of racial and social justice)."[38] Originally, *stay woke* became a watch phrase "in parts of the black community for those who were self-aware, questioning the dominant paradigm and striving for something better."[39] As I'm sure you've heard, the term *woke* has more recently

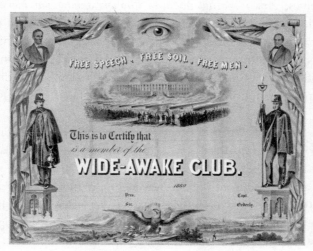

Wide-Awake Club, 1860

acquired negative connotations, often brandished as a pejorative term for extreme political correctness. This, however, is a deviation from the original concept.

Despite recent trends, the concept of awakening to racism is not new. The idea has also been employed historically to signal a growing consciousness of racial inequity. Nineteenth-century abolitionists campaigned for President Lincoln under the banner of the "Wide-Awake Club."

In the twentieth century Martin Luther King, Jr., famously urged awakening:

> One of the great liabilities of history is that all too many people fail to remain awake through great periods of social change. Every society has its protectors of the status quo and its fraternities of the indifferent who are notorious for sleeping through revolutions. But today our very survival depends on our ability to stay awake.[40]

In every generation, followers of Jesus would do well to ask themselves, *Am I snoring my way through a kingdom movement?* Many insist that if they were alive during previous civil rights movements, they would have been on the right side of history. Now is our chance to prove it. We are living through another wave of the Civil Rights Movement, which some have called the "third reconstruction." Hear the words of Jemar Tisby:

> The first reconstruction occurred immediately after the Civil War when newly freed slaves joined in a flowering of black political, economic, and social participation. The second reconstruction happened during the civil rights movement of the 1950s and 1960s when activists assailed the stronghold of Jim Crow segregation. The third reconstruction is happening right now. Careful observers agree that the nation is in the midst of another wave of the civil rights movement.[41]

I believe that our most urgent task is for people of all racial backgrounds to educate ourselves about the reality of ongoing racial inequity. Dr. King candidly stated, "Whites, it must frankly be said, are not putting in a similar mass effort to reeducate themselves out of their racial ignorance. It is an aspect of their sense of superiority that the white people of America believe they have so little to learn."[42]

But people of color need awakening too. This is exactly what I discovered. Today many people of color do escape some of the worst consequences of systemic racism, as I did. *But the reality is, although some people of color might be exceptions to the rule, the rule still firmly persists.*

In the early twentieth century, the activist Marcus Garvey exhorted fellow Blacks to wake up and invest in the uplift of the entire Black community. In the 1972 play *Garvey Lives!* one of the characters says, "I been sleeping all my life. And now that Mr. Garvey done woke me up, I'm gon' stay woke. And I'm gon' help him wake up other Black folk."[43]

What I have personally discovered is that no one is exempt from the need for awakening.

AWAKENING TO THE SPIRITUAL BATTLE

Although this chapter has been full of facts and statistics, make no mistake: Systemic racism is fundamentally a spiritual sickness. The fact is this: "Our struggle is not against flesh and blood, but against the rulers, against the authorities, against the powers of this dark world and against the spiritual forces of evil in the heavenly realms" (Ephesians 6:12). Other Bible translations use the term *principalities* in this verse. Our task is to open our eyes and see that one way that principalities manifest is through fallen institutions and ideologies.

If we remain blind to the spiritual reality behind systemic

racism, we will also remain blind to the spiritual resources available to us. Color-courageous disciples can emulate how Jesus resisted the principalities and powers. He "disarmed [*apekdyomai*] the spiritual rulers and authorities. He shamed them publicly [*deigmatizō*] by his victory over them on the cross" (Colossians 2:15, NLT). The word translated *disarmed* is *apekdyomai*, which literally means to "take off" or to strip. And *shamed them*—from *deigmatizō*—means "to expose to public disgrace . . . to make a spectacle of."[44]

If we remain blind to the spiritual reality behind
systemic racism, we will also remain blind to the
spiritual resources available to us.

From this we discover that *one of the most effective ways to resist the principalities of systemic racism is simply to name them.* That's what this chapter has been about: unmasking systemic inequity while simultaneously calling people to dismantle it in Jesus's name. The mere act of exposing systemic racial inequity is key to stripping it of its power.

Before moving on, let's briefly address an important question about Jesus and justice. Some rightly point out that neither Jesus, nor Paul, for that matter, called out the systemic injustices of the Roman empire. This is largely true; the ministry of Jesus and the apostles majored on making disciples, not reforming society's institutions. What does that mean for us? First, I agree that the primary task of color-courageous disciples, like all disciples, is to *make disciples* (Matthew 28:19–21). Over the long haul, transformed people are the best way to bring about transformation in the world. But second, *context matters:* In Jesus's time, the Jewish people were a tiny, persecuted minority. Their ability to effect systemic change was in any case sorely limited. Today, disciples of Christ have abundant and unprecedented opportunities to bring about systemic change. I think, for example, of disciples like William Wilberforce (1759–1833). While he did support traditional disciplemaking work, Wilberforce also had the monumental opportunity to fight slavery as longtime member of the British Parliament. And fight it he did, laying the groundwork for the abolition of slavery throughout the British empire.

The mere act of exposing systemic racial inequity is key to stripping it of its power.

Jesus Christ made disciples *and* ultimately disarmed larger, unseen powers and principalities by means of the cross (Colossians 2:15). Once awakened, we, too, can engage in holistic reconciliation—doing evangelism, growing disciples, and stripping systemic injustices like racism of their power—as we abide in Christ and bear our cross together with him.

CHRIST WILL SHINE ON YOU

My all-too-brief experience as a volunteer at an under-resourced school awakened me to reality. It also awakened me to my own need for color-courageous discipleship. I finally saw that although I'd had access to an excellent public school education because I grew up in a predominantly White community, the reality is that too many Black and Brown youth still do not enjoy that same access.

American disciples cherish the "self-evident" ideal of equality, the bedrock conviction that God created us equal. But let's not stop at cherishing an *equal creation* that happened at some point in the distant past; let's also strive for *equal opportunity now.* This distinction begins to get at the difference between equality and equity. **Equality** is about sameness: We all possess the same image of God. **Equity** is about fairness: We don't all have fair access to similar opportunities. But it's precisely because all people are created *equal* that all people deserve *equity*.

To be clear, **biblical equity** is not ultimately about socialism, communism, or any other socioeconomic system. It's about greater fairness in every socioeconomic system. What's more, biblical equity is not about *forcing* equal outcomes. It's about doing what we can to ensure that everyone has a fair shot at life, liberty, and the pursuit of happiness. As we've seen, we still have a long way to go.

Let's not stop at cherishing an equal creation *that* happened at some point in the distant past; let's also strive for equal opportunity now.

I love the Ignatian concept of **magis,** which in Latin means "more." The Ignatians (Society of Jesus) have used the concept of *magis* as a reminder that Jesus continually invites disciples to *more*—to see Christ *more clearly* and abide in Christ *more deeply* so that we might bear Christ's fruit *more abundantly.*[45] Jesus says to the church: "Wake up then, and strengthen what remains that was about to die, because I have not found your deeds complete in the sight of my God" (Revelation 3:2, NET).

I have been awakening to the ways in which my own deeds have been *good* but *incomplete.* As long as we have breath, Jesus invites disciples to awaken to more of what he can accomplish in us and through us.

As we awaken, a beautiful reward awaits: "Wake up, sleeper, rise from the dead, and Christ will shine on you" (Ephesians 5:14). Some believe that early disciples sang this as a hymn of repentance to move from being passive partners of darkness to active agents of light. So it is delightfully good news to discover that, in the end, the disciple's reward for waking up is more of Jesus Christ.

In the end, the disciple's reward for waking up is more of Jesus Christ.

Just as he did with his disciples in the Garden of Gethsemane, Jesus is now nudging you to awaken from your slumber. And as you wake up, you will find that you'll experience *more:* more opportunities to courageously transform the world and more of the glory of God.

DANIEL HILL

PASTOR AND AUTHOR OF *WHITE AWAKE*

Daniel Hill is the founding and senior pastor of River City Community Church, a vibrant, multiethnic church in the Humboldt Park neighborhood of Chicago. He is also the author of *White Awake, White Lies,* and *10:10: Life to the Fullest.*

How has God uniquely prepared you for color-courageous ministry?

Years ago, I attended a wedding of a South Asian/Indian friend. It was so festive and colorful, and I wistfully commented to him that I wish I had culture too. He replied, "Daniel, you may be white, but don't let that lull you into thinking you have no culture. White culture is very real. In fact, when white culture comes in contact with other cultures, it almost always wins. So it would be a really good idea for you to learn about your culture."[46] I was *really* unsettled by that—what did he mean? But with that brief encounter God began a process of awakening in me, and it opened up a whole new world.

Why do disciples need to be awakened, and what do we need to be awakened to?

The Scriptures say to "seek first the kingdom of God," but what's that about? I have spent a lot of time pondering Jesus's conversation with Nicodemus where he says, "No one can see the kingdom of God unless they are born again" (John 3:3). Many have focused on being "born again," but what about "seeing" the kingdom of God? That, to me, is the essence of discipleship: awakening to and seeing the kingdom of God more clearly.

What do we see when our eyes are opened to the kingdom of God?

Jesus taught us to pray, "Your kingdom come, your will be done, on earth as it is in heaven." I think that should be a daily meditation for us. God's "kingdom come" is certainly characterized by shalom, equality, and justice. Ultimately, though, the kingdom of God is about love—love of God and love of neighbor. It manifests a beautiful richness in these relationships. And as our eyes are opened to the kingdom of God, we catch glimpses of how God is working toward these rich relationships even now, reconciling all things to himself in Christ.

Your first book on race was titled *White Awake*. But your second book, *White Lies,* counsels disciples to "stop being woke." Tell us more about this seeming contradiction.

Discipleship is about awakening. Yet in my experience, many who begin the journey of racial awakening have an almost manic desire to get to the cool "woke" stage ASAP—in part because there is so much disorientation, shame, and fear on the journey. But as soon as you think you've arrived, it undermines everything. The only trustworthy posture for color-courageous discipleship is an ongoing willingness to learn.

What spiritual practices have you found life-giving on your color-courageous discipleship journey?

Community is essential. When it comes to awakening, I need community to point out my blind spots and keep me accountable. I am also anchored in a deep awareness of God's voice. Jesus's baptism is central to me. I love how he launched his ministry with a reminder that he is the beloved, that God delights in him, that he's a son of God. He also hears those same words at the Transfiguration, and so concludes his ministry in exactly the same way it began. So that is my daily prayer too. I start and end my days listening to the voice of God, and he faithfully reminds me of my identity in Christ: a beloved child of God. With that reminder, I have all I need to continue the work.

FURTHER READING

Disintegration: The Splintering of Black America by Eugene Robinson

Divided by Faith: Evangelical Religion and the Problem of Race in America by Michael O. Emerson and Christian Smith

The Myth of Equality: Uncovering the Roots of Injustice and Privilege by Ken Wytsma

White Awake: An Honest Look at What It Means to Be White by Daniel Hill

White Lies: Nine Ways to Expose and Resist the Racial Systems That Divide Us by Daniel Hill

DISCIPLESHIP AS WARDROBE CHANGE

Take Off the Bias That Holds You Back

> The ancient world, just like the modern, was an elaborate
> network of prejudice...so ingrained as to be thought
> normal and natural.
>
> —N. T. WRIGHT, *COLOSSIANS AND PHILEMON*

Like the ancient Greeks, we tend to envision ourselves as a *tabula rasa*—a "blank slate." We like to think that we embark on new learning experiences with a neutral mindset: objective, clear-eyed, and level-headed. Unfortunately, this blank slate concept is more pagan than Christian.

Our human nature—tainted by sin—inclines us toward error from the get-go. What's more, over time, our minds are further shaped by the sinful patterns of a broken world. That's why the Scriptures insist: "Do not conform to the pattern of this world, but be transformed by the renewing of your mind" (Romans 12:2).

When it comes to race, what does it mean to *renew our minds*? I am convinced that *one important way to renew our minds when it comes to race is to uproot unconscious bias*. A greater deterrent to biblical equity today than *conscious* bias may be *unconscious* bias. A gargantuan gap persists between our *intentions* and the actual *impact* that we are having on the world. This is what I call the **intention vs. impact dilemma.** Somehow, people who have the best of intentions when it comes to race are still fostering racial inequity. How can this be?

Unpacking unconscious bias (also known as **implicit bias**) can help us come to terms with our confounding racial contradictions. Yet unpacking unconscious bias also requires courage. Why? Because it's never fun to look into a mirror and not like what you see looking back! What helps me is to remember that we are all susceptible to unconscious biases, regardless of race. In fact, it's quite common for people of color to experience unconscious bias even toward their own racial group—which I discovered, to my chagrin, was true of me.

People who have the best of intentions when it comes to race are still fostering racial inequity. How can this be?

I serve as a leader for the Evangelical Covenant Church, a denomination known for its multiethnic commitment. One of my most treasured Covenant experiences is the Journey to Mosaic (J2M), a bus tour that travels to sites of civil rights significance for multiple racial groups.

On my own Journey to Mosaic, our first stop was the Nisei Veterans Memorial Hall in Seattle where we listened to one woman's experience in a World War II Japanese internment camp. At the Chinese Reconciliation Park in Tacoma, I heard for the first time about the **Chinese Exclusion Act.** And I will never forget my first visit to a Native American reservation, the Yakama Nation of Toppenish. There, we stood at an unmarked burial ground and commemorated the Indigenous people who perished as they resisted European encroachment.

But my most pivotal growth moment occurred during our final debrief session. Someone broached the topic of racial inequity in Black communities, and cringeworthy thoughts like these automatically welled up in me: *Well, I wish it weren't true, but Black communities are plagued with Black-on-Black crime. Mass incarceration is the sad but obvious result. It's our own fault.* I kept most of these thoughts to myself, but in the group conversation that followed, some of these very ideas were addressed head-on—and unmasked as unhelpful and misleading.

The Chinese Must Go! poster, 1885

That night, I began to realize for the first time the depths of my unconscious bias—*toward my own community.* The Lord placed a mirror before me and I discovered the truth. Although I thought I was looking good, I was actually clothed with the dirty rags of unconscious bias. In fact, my bias had a name: **attribution error.** I was attributing blame in lopsided ways; I was predisposed to blame a person for their plight rather than also reasonably take that person's situation into account.[1] It is because of attribution error that our human tendency is to blame the victim and overlook the victimizer; to blame the oppressed and overlook the oppressive circumstances; to blame a community's culture and overlook the community's history.

When looking at a predominantly Black community riddled with poverty and crime, some might quietly harbor thoughts like these: *Black people must not be as smart or hardworking as others. The fact that more Black people are criminal than others is sad but true. I wonder what it is about Black culture that keeps them in the gutter. Of course, there are exceptions, but in general, these people need to get their act together.* These assessments are all characterized by attribution error, and they do very little to get at the root causes of our society's challenges so that we can find effective solutions together.

Color-courageous disciples seek to ask more constructive questions: *What is leading to such high levels of crime and despair? How might the system itself be failing this community, even unintentionally? What resources are needed for empowerment, growth, and healing? When it comes to crime, what would it look like to take a more restorative—rather than punitive—approach? For that matter, are these citizens being fairly convicted and sentenced to begin with? Why don't more people care about questions like these? And how can I be part of the solution?*

Now, an important caveat: I am certainly not arguing that individuals or communities should never take responsibility for their actions. What I am calling for—and, more important, what the Scriptures seem to call for—is both truth *and* amazing grace. Unconscious bias inclines us to attribute blame in fallacious, legalistic, and coldly detached ways—not an ideal approach for a disciple of Jesus Christ.

The Bible addresses unconscious bias, too, albeit in different terms. In the story of the man born blind, the disciples asked, "Who sinned, this man or his parents, that he was born blind?" Jesus bluntly rebuked them, "Neither this man nor his parents sinned . . . but this happened so that the works of God might be displayed in him. As long as it is day, we must do the works of him who sent me" (John 9:1–5).

Jesus did two intriguing things with this response. First, he pushed back on the disciples' attribution error, rebuking their tendency to blame the victim. Second, he challenged them to get to work. Here is my paraphrase: *When you see a person or a community suffering, it's not time to play the blame game. It is time for you to wake up, collaborate with God, and get to work.*

Even in a story where the individual *had* clearly sinned—like the woman caught in adultery—Jesus's response was beautifully balanced (John 8:1–11). Did this woman deserve death according to Jewish law? Yes, she did (Deuteronomy 22:22). Nevertheless, Jesus did a curious and unexpected thing: He drew attention not to the woman's *overt sin* but rather to her accusers' *covert sin*—their judgmentalism, hypocrisy, and pride. While acknowledging the woman's sin, Jesus declined to condemn her. Instead, he gently and graciously encouraged her toward repentance and life.

When it comes to race, we are not called to conform to the pattern of this world, but to be transformed by the renewing of our minds (Romans 12:2).

CALLED TO A WARDROBE CHANGE

Jesus launched his preaching ministry with a dual call: "'The time has come,' he said. 'The kingdom of God has come near. Repent and believe the good news!'" (Mark 1:15). Here, Jesus named two distinct actions that he requires of disciples: The first is to *turn away* from former ways (repent). Only then can we *turn toward* Jesus (believe). These two simple actions—repent and believe—are the basis for all ongoing discipleship and transformation in Christ.

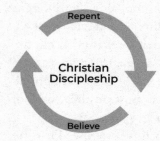

I mentioned earlier that when it comes to spiritual growth, the Bible does not utilize "blank slate" metaphors. Instead, we see metaphors like wardrobe change. Before the Lord, even our best deeds are filthy garments (Isaiah 64:6). Growing as a disciple, then, involves a dual process of wardrobe change: taking off our filthy garments— including our distorted mindsets—and putting on the way of Christ. The Scriptures reveal that wardrobe change is particularly relevant when it comes to ethnicity:

You have taken off your old self with its practices and have put on the new self. . . . Here there is no Gentile or Jew, circumcised or uncircumcised, barbarian, Scythian, slave or free, but Christ is all, and is in all. Therefore, as God's chosen people, holy and dearly loved, clothe yourselves with compassion, kindness, humility, gentleness and patience. . . . And over all these virtues put on love. (Colossians 3:9–12, 14)

Permit me this paraphrase: *Left to your own devices, dear disciples, your default will be to mistreat the ethnic "other" whether you realize it or not. Seek to identify the world's biased mindsets in yourself so that you can take off those rags and clothe yourself instead with the mindset of Christ.*

When it comes to race, we have all been unconsciously discipled by the world's powerful racial narratives. That is why, in the words of my friend and colleague David Swanson, we need to be "rediscipled," especially with regard to our minds.[2] Theologians refer to the impact of sin on the mind as the **noetic effect of sin,** which asserts that even our ability to process information accurately has been compromised by sin.[3]

Researchers estimate that 98 percent of what our brain does, it does without our conscious awareness.[4] This fact sheds some light on our nation's bewildering racial contradictions.

SEVEN CATEGORIES OF UNCONSCIOUS BIAS

Unconscious bias is another term for **cognitive bias;** both refer to a habitual misperception of the mind. Human cognitive biases fall into well-worn patterns. Just as we looked at seven symptoms of systemic racism in the previous chapter, now we will investigate seven categories of unconscious bias—as well as practical ideas for "taking off" each one.

1. Pro-White Preference

The **Implicit Association Test (IAT)** measures the strength of associations between concepts (Black people, White people) and evaluations (good, bad) or stereotypes (athletic, smart, dangerous).[5] IAT results reveal that a significant majority of Whites, Asians, and Latinos manifest anti–Black bias. Tragically, the results also reveal that almost half of Blacks harbor anti–Black bias too.[6] In one study of how pro–White bias works itself out in everyday life, thousands of college professors were sent an email from a fictitious student asking for an appointment to discuss the school's doctoral programs. The emails were identical except for the names of the students, which varied by perceived ethnicity.[7] It turns out that professors *of all races* were far more likely to respond positively to requests to meet with students whom they perceived to be White. This was true in nearly every academic discipline.[8]

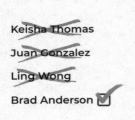

Take It Off: *Before making evaluations or giving out favors, pause and consider how pro-White or anti-Black bias may be impacting your judgment. You can also take a free IAT online.*[9]

2. Blame

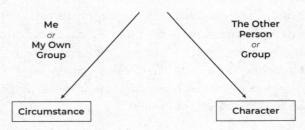

Where Should We Place Blame?

Me
or
My Own
Group

The Other
Person
or
Group

Circumstance

Character

When we encounter a problematic situation, we understandably want to figure out who is to blame. Unfortunately, as I mentioned when I described my own experience with attribution error, we tend to answer the blame question in a biased way. For example, when a person is cut off while driving, she might assume that the offender did so because they are a horrible person (*What a jerk!*)— not because they are in the middle of some horrible circumstance (*This driver must be responding to an emergency*). Color-courageous disciples strive to take a more balanced approach, keeping in mind a person's *circumstances* as well as any concerns about a person's *character*. Disciples are commanded not to judge for the obvious reason that our human interpretation of a person's actions can never be as comprehensive as God's (Matthew 7:1–5). Actually, God calls us to be biased . . . not toward blame but toward grace.

Take It Off: *When you encounter racial inequity, do not automatically assume that something is wrong with a person's character or community. While either of these or both might indeed benefit from positive change, take a step back to consider how circumstances, history, policies, and racial inequity may provide a more comprehensive picture of the situation.*

3. Dehumanization

We tend to assume that people who are not just like us share our humanity to a lesser degree.[10] Once that happens, it's easier for us to mistreat them; sociologists call this **moral disengagement.** We see **dehumanization** happen especially when people feel threatened. In her book *Biased,* Jennifer Eberhardt writes,

> Marginalized groups in countries all over the world are often discredited through animal imagery. Disfavored immigrant groups—Mexicans in the United States, Jews in Germany, the Roma in Italy, Muslims across the European continent—are frequently likened to insects, rodents, and other vermin . . . [it's] been a universal fixture of human history.[11]

In the United States, the dehumanization of African Americans has long been a particular problem. In 2016, police officers in San Francisco referred to Black people in their text messages as "wild animals, cockroaches, savages, barbarians, and monkeys."[12] Further, the association of "Blacks with apes is closely correlated with police officers' use of excessive force against young Black males."[13] To the extent that society believes—even subtly—a racial group to be less than human, it is prone to feel less compassion for those people and to tolerate greater violence against that group.

"I Am a Man," diorama of Memphis Sanitation
Workers Strike, National Civil Rights Museum,
Downtown Memphis, Tennessee*
PHOTO BY ADAM JONES, PhD

Because all people are created in God's image, we must resist even the subtlest forms of dehumanization. I believe this was the heart of Jesus's warning in the Sermon on the Mount:

* https://commons.wikimedia.org/w/index.php?title=File:I_Am_a_Man
_-_Diorama_of_Memphis_Sanitation_Workers_Strike_-_National_Civil_Rights
Museum-_Downtown_Memphis_-_Tennessee_-_USA.jpg&oldid=491566088

"Anyone who says to a brother or sister, 'Raca,' is answerable to the court. And anyone who says, 'You fool!' will be in danger of the fire of hell" (Matthew 5:22). These terms—*raca* and *fool*—are code for the dehumanization that happens by default in the human heart.

Take It Off: *Resist the temptation to dehumanize—even privately— whole racial groups with diminishing tropes and one-dimensional labels. Strive to exercise compassion on the basis of common ground.*

4. Criminalization

Black boys are suspended 3X more than White boys

Black children are perceived to be less innocent than what would be considered normal and natural for their age.[14] Black children are disciplined at much higher levels in schools, reinforcing the school-to-prison pipeline.[15] **Racial profiling** happens when people utilize race as a grounds for suspected wrongdoing. This may be why in one study Black drivers were 31 percent more likely to be pulled over than White ones.[16] Media portrayals are also lopsided; for example, Black individuals are overrepresented as perpetrators of violent crimes in news coverage when compared to actual arrest rates.[17] What's more, the overrepresentation of negative stereotypes in the media is exacerbated by the corresponding underrepresentation of Black individuals in positive portrayals of all kinds.[18]

Take It Off: *If you are in a position where you have the ability to elevate positive role models, ensure that people of color are represented among them. Remain attentive to how people of color are portrayed in the media you consume and expose others to. Think twice before disciplining a young person of color and be sure to take a restorative approach.*

5. Stereotype Threat

Stereotype threat is a phenomenon in which a person's anxiety about confirming a negative stereotype leads to their underperformance. Studies reveal that when students are asked to indicate their race before an exam, Black students tend to underperform. In one study, Black students performed more poorly on standardized tests when their race was emphasized. When race was not emphasized, however, Black students performed equivalently with White students. What we learn is that "performance in academic contexts can be harmed by the awareness that one's behavior might be viewed through the lens of racial stereotypes."[19] This is why it doesn't really help for teachers to take a color-blind approach and behave as if racial stereotypes did not exist. A far better approach is to take proactive steps to reduce stereotype threat.

Take It Off: *Strategies to reduce stereotype threat include removing cues that could trigger worry about stereotypes; clearly conveying that diversity is valued; increasing the visibility and representation of role models from minority groups; and expressing both high standards as well as confidence in a person's ability to meet those standards.*[20]

6. Status Quo Bias

Humans have a natural tendency to resist changes to the status quo even when those changes are shown to be beneficial. Ironi-

Back to Egypt, please!

cally, both the powerful and the less powerful members of a society are prone to defend the status quo. While dominant groups have an obvious interest in preserving the status quo, "subordinates (or disadvantaged groups) are invested in *minimizing further losses*."[21] (*Status quo bias* is also called *system justification bias*.) Re-

gardless of where we might find ourselves on the social scale, we humans prefer stability to change and loss. Consider the Israelites: Despite their miraculous deliverance from Egypt, they pined after their former life when faced with new challenges, and they conspired to find a way back (Exodus 16:3; Numbers 14:4).

Take It Off: *When you, your organization, or your community face change, remember that your natural response will be resistance. Seek to understand—both for yourself and for others—the pros and cons of any potential change.*

7. Truth Distortion

The human mind finds countless ways to distort truth. *Confirmation bias* inclines us to see what we want to see. The *ostrich*

Confirmation Bias

Facts — Existing Beliefs

What you pay attention to

effect predisposes us to avoid unpleasant information.[22] And, most ironically, our *bias blind spot* means even when we understand that bias exists, we are *still* prone to see ourselves as less biased than other people!

Take It Off: *Despite everything, you are still prone to assume that you're less biased than other people. The only solution is Christlike humility. Always resist the temptation to believe that you have "arrived." Proactively seek out feedback, especially from those who are different from you. Always remain open to acknowledging blind spots as others point them out.*

These seven categories of unconscious bias are just the beginning. In considering these, I find myself drawn back to Paul's words in Romans: "I decide to do good, but I don't *really* do it; I decide not to do bad, but then I do it anyway. . . . Something has gone wrong deep within me and gets the better of me every time" (Romans 7:17–20, MSG).

Remember: Wardrobe change is a lifelong discipleship process. Although we may never root out our unconscious biases completely, we *can* continue to learn more about human biases so that we might not be ruled by them.

> **Our bias is unconscious. However, that does not mean it's altogether undetectable or unchangeable.**

This survey of our unconscious biases should reinforce just how badly we need Christlike humility. Color-courageous disciples must be the type of people who exemplify humility. It takes courage to admit that we are imperfect and always will be. With racism—like with so many other challenges—the change must start with us.

There is a level, of course, at which uprooting our unconscious bias is impossible. The whole idea is that our bias is unconscious. *However, that does not mean it's altogether undetectable or unchangeable.* In Christ, we have reason to hope for the transformation of even our most stubborn biases when we both commit to practices that have been proven to counteract racial bias and surrender to the transformational power of the Holy Spirit within us (Romans 8:1–2).

FROM COLOR-BLIND TO COLOR-BRAVE

There's one more racial mindset that we need to address: **color blindness.** Many have wondered, *What's wrong with just being color-blind?* Color-blind people say, "I don't see color." They counsel others, "Try not to notice the color of people's skin. That way, you can steer clear of bias." They quote Martin Luther King, Jr.'s "I Have a Dream" speech: "I have a dream that my four little children will one day live in a nation where they will not be judged by the color of their skin but by the content of their character." We'll return to Dr. King's words shortly, but first, a few reflections.

Most people who embrace color blindness do so with the best of intentions. They acknowledge that racism is a problem, and color blindness is their solution. I think we can all agree that we'd rather not be judged based on the color of our skin. However, color blindness yields a number of unintended consequences.

First, color blindness minimizes both race *and* ethnicity. It is true that *race* has been a harmful human construct, but *ethnicity* is a God-given gift. Those who say that they don't see color are prone to miss out on the valuable contributions of ethnic diversity.

Second, it's impossible to be color-blind. As much as we might like to say that race doesn't matter, our brains behave otherwise. That is why blindness, denial, and nonaction are all ineffective responses to racism.

Color blindness ironically leads to racial inequity—
precisely the opposite outcome of what was intended.

Finally, and most important, color blindness ironically leads to racial inequity—precisely the opposite outcome of what was intended.[23] That is because *those people who do not see race also cannot see racism.* Those who resist racial reality are liable to remain naïvely unaware of their own unconscious racial bias. Those who prefer not to countenance racial categories are often responsible for suppressing the critical conversations that we need to have about race in order to make real progress.

In *The Psychology of Racial Colorblindness,* Philip J. Mazzocco comprehensively summarizes the copious research on color blindness. His conclusion: "Although the preference for colorblindness may be well-intentioned for some, the consequences of colorblindness . . . appear to be almost entirely negative both with respect to racial minorities, and society at large."[24]

We need to move from color-blind to **color-brave.**[25] Those who are color-brave choose to courageously see color for the sake of cultivating biblical equity. When we choose to be color-brave, we can more easily see the racial disparities before us. We can become attentive to our own biases. We can listen to one another's racial stories. And we can seek courageous solutions together.

Those who are color-brave choose to courageously see
color for the sake of cultivating biblical equity.

Returning to Dr. King's famous quote: To deduce that he was color-blind on the basis of one sentence from one speech is to take his words out of context. When we review the scope of his life and work, we will discover that Martin Luther King, Jr., was color-brave.

I would argue that Jesus himself was not color-blind but color-brave. He charged us, after all, with a strikingly colorful commission to make disciples of all cultures and ethnicities—which, of course, color-blind disciplemakers could never fulfill (Matthew 28:19–21).

PUTTING ON THE MIND OF CHRIST

I find it intriguing that clothing has long been metaphorically associated with life. In Greek mythology, for example, the goddess Clotho was one of the three fates who determined the course of a life. Every individual life was a thread. Clotho spun the thread, Lachesis drew it out, and Atropos cut the thread upon one's death.

We have seen that in the Scriptures, too, clothing is used as a metaphor for life. That's why if you want to change your life, you've got to change your clothes. In the Old Testament, we see this illustrated in the life of the high priest Joshua: His spiritual transformation was depicted through a wardrobe change as the angels exchanged his filthy garments of sin for robes of righteousness (Zechariah 3:4).

In the New Testament, wardrobe change is applied to the disciples' need to transform the way they engage the ethnic "other"—Jew or Gentile, circumcised or uncircumcised, barbarian, and even Scythian, a people understood at the time to be the worst of the worst, the savages, the so-called dregs of society (Colossians 3:9–14).

Is taking off our bias even possible? Thankfully, studies have shown that it is, and we've touched upon some of those interventions.[26] But beyond worldly remedies, disciples have something more. In the New Testament, the righteous robe that God clothes us with is Jesus himself (Romans 13:14; Galatians 3:27).

On my own journey with unconscious bias, I have come to understand at a profound level that putting on Christ looks like putting on a courageous mindset of Christlike humility (Colossians 3:12). The Greek word for *repent*—*metanoeō*—derives from *meta-* ("to change") and *-noeō* ("the mind"). Humility may be the very best way to describe the mindset of Christ.

> In your relationships with one another, *have the same mindset as Christ Jesus:*
>
> Who, being in very nature God,
>   did not consider equality with God something to be used to
>   his own advantage;
> rather, he made himself nothing
>   by taking the very nature of a servant,
>   being made in human likeness.
> And being found in appearance as a man,
>   *he humbled himself*
>   by becoming obedient to death—
>   even death on a cross! (Philippians 2:5–8)

The only way to overcome unconscious bias is through Christlike humility. We must humbly comprehend that overcoming bias is—and always will be—a challenge for us. After all, putting on humility means coming to terms with our imperfect inclinations. It means accepting that our intentions do not always line up with our impact. It means forever resisting the temptation to say that we have arrived. Most of all, putting on Christlike humility means we recognize the need to repent and believe, moment by moment, for a lifetime. Ultimately, our daily courageous choice to repent and believe exemplifies what discipleship is all about.

DAVID W. SWANSON

PASTOR AND AUTHOR OF *REDISCIPLING THE WHITE CHURCH*

David is the founding pastor of New Community Covenant Church (Bronzeville), a multiracial congregation on the South Side of Chicago. He also serves as the CEO of New Community Outreach, a nonprofit organization working to increase opportunities for biblical equity in Chicago. He previously served as director of church planting for the Central Conference of the Evangelical Covenant Church. David is the author of *Rediscipling the White Church: From Cheap Diversity to True Solidarity*.

Tell us a little about yourself. How has God uniquely prepared you for color-courageous ministry?

I grew up as a missionary kid in Venezuela, which may explain why I tend to have a unique perspective. Since I was not as strongly formed by U.S. culture, I may be able to identify both the racial dynamics of U.S. culture more clearly as well as how those dynamics form disciples of Christ.

Why do Christians need racial rediscipleship, and where in the Bible do we find encouragement to pursue that?

Rediscipleship implies that we've been discipled already. It assumes that discipleship transcends the church, meaning that we are constantly being discipled all the time by all kinds of different things. If that is true, then followers of Jesus absolutely need to be rediscipled. As disciples, we will still get things wrong sometimes because we are broken and we inhabit a broken and sinful world. As much as I want to believe that the initial call to follow Jesus opens up my eyes to everything I must leave behind, the fact of the matter is, there will be things I must continually wake up to through the Holy Spirit over the course of my discipleship. The biblical term for this is *repentance*. The call to rediscipleship is really just a reminder that repentance is the basic posture of Christian discipleship. Repentance is the lifelong process of taking off what is not of Jesus and putting on what is.

What else do we need to understand as we pursue racial rediscipleship?

Racial rediscipleship is both an individual and a corporate call. For example, the apostle Paul told the Corinthian Christians to examine their hearts before taking Communion. Western people have tended to interpret that individually: "What sin have I committed? Let me confess that." But in Corinthians, Paul was actually calling them to acknowledge their *corporate* participation in a socioeconomic stratification that has left the poor hungry while the wealthy have too much. God invites us to examine ourselves corporately and ask, "In what ways have we conformed to the patterns of this world together, and how are we going to live differently together?"

What spiritual practices have you found particularly life-giving on your color-courageous discipleship journey?

Fellowship with the body of Christ has been the biggest gift. It's not enough to attend a multiracial church; we must also become deeply embedded in a racially reconciled community. It's not just about right information: "I have read the right books, I listen to the right podcasts, I use the right language." The question is, how does all that information translate to real life? Is it impacting who you eat with, who you are accountable to, who's forming your imagination about how to care for children? Without a doubt, I have experienced the deepest transformation in the context of community.

FURTHER READING

Beyond Colorblind: Redeeming Our Ethnic Journey by Sarah Shin

Biased: Uncovering the Hidden Prejudice That Shapes What We See, Think, and Do by Jennifer L. Eberhardt

The Blindspots Between Us: How to Overcome Unconscious Cognitive Bias and Build Better Relationships by Gleb Tsipursky

Whistling Vivaldi: How Stereotypes Affect Us and What We Can Do by Claude Steele

DISCIPLESHIP AS INNER HEALING

Be Healed Before You Heal the World

Only through an inner spiritual transformation do we
gain the strength to fight vigorously the evils of the world
in a humble and loving spirit.

—MARTIN LUTHER KING, JR., *STRENGTH TO LOVE*

The town of Capernaum was a frenzy of enthusiasm! Jesus was home! By then it was common knowledge that he was no run-of-the-mill rabbi. This Jesus could *perform miracles*. Word was spreading like rushing lava that "the Lord's healing power was strongly with Jesus" (Luke 5:17, NLT).

That day we had a front-row seat for the rabbi's miracle. The "house . . . was so packed with visitors that there was no more room, even outside the door" (Mark 2:2, NLT). Along with the crowd, we were enrapt by the rabbi's teaching.

Suddenly, shouts and commotion came from overhead—and the roof was caving in! We took cover, but then craned our necks to observe that the roof wasn't falling but opening up. A rectangle of sunshine burst through, and a shaft of light streamed down. With a shower of straw and debris, a paralyzed man was lowered like a heap of cargo, landing directly in front of Jesus. Unprecedented. All eyes were on the rabbi. How would he respond?

Jesus reacted—as he usually did—in a surprising way. Jesus wasn't bothered by the sudden appearance of the man; Jesus was beaming. He opened his mouth and spoke words of healing— but certainly not the words we were expecting. "Be encouraged, my child!" Jesus declared with elation. "Your sins are forgiven." (Matthew 9:2, NLT).

Wait—what? Instead of showing us a miraculous healing, Jesus perplexed us with talk of forgiveness. Shortly thereafter, in a flurry of further excitement and confusion, Jesus *did* heal the man's paralysis too. Yet he did it almost as an afterthought. We gazed upon the strange rabbi in wonder. He had opened the eyes of our hearts to the peculiar idea that perhaps physical healing wasn't really his primary concern.

For Jesus, tangible miracles were signs and pointers to subtler yet more significant miracles. Today, we are too often just like the paralyzed man and his friends. We respectfully demand that Jesus stop whatever he's doing so he can get to the more urgent business of healing our obvious, tangible wounds. But Jesus yearns for us to experience a far deeper kind of healing.

Jesus seeks to bring about the kind of inner transformation we need to transform our world in God's way.

Together we have taken a hard look at the vast racial brokenness of our world. Seeing this, color-courageous disciples are rightly eager to go about the business of dismantling racism and making a difference. That agenda is good, but Jesus's agenda is fuller and better. Jesus wants to see racism dismantled, but he also wants to liberate us from sin, guilt, and shame. Jesus seeks to bring about the kind of inner transformation we need to transform our world in God's way.

NAMING OUR TRAUMA

When my husband and I went to seminary, we went with bright ambitions to change the world for God. But God's ambition was to change us. . . .

It was the end of the seminary semester, and the Boston chill was beginning to bite the air. I should have been ecstatic—I'd just handed in a final paper! Instead, I was lying on my couch in a fetal position, rocking back and forth in the dark.

During seminary I began to experience severe bouts of panic, depression, and anxiety. I became enraged whenever I felt disappointed in my relationships. I was plagued by anxiety whenever I feared I wasn't making the best vocational decisions. And I was tortured by panic when I felt that I hadn't done something *just right*. On this particular night, I was paralyzed by the terrifying thought that I just submitted a paper . . . that wasn't perfect.

One day I came across a book titled *Perfecting Ourselves to Death: The Pursuit of Excellence and the Perils of Perfectionism* by Richard Winter. I recognized myself on nearly every page. As I began to look at the dysfunctional perfectionism in my life, God helped me to see how racial trauma had played a major role. As a Black girl, I grew up believing the lie that I was a member of the lowest echelon of society. I came to believe that I couldn't merely perform as well as others but that I had to do twice as well as others if I hoped to earn even the exact same rewards. In time, I fully embraced the false narrative that because I was a Black girl, imperfection must not—could not—ever be tolerated. I didn't fully realize it, but this was evidence of trauma. I began to experience healing as I was able to name my wounds and seek healing. In the same way, color-courageous disciples can increasingly defang racism as we grow in our capacity to name the specific trauma that racism has caused, both in ourselves and in others.

> *In a traumatized world, healing, discipleship, and mission are all intimately intertwined.*

My original vision for this book did not include a chapter on healing. But in the process of writing it, and especially while conducting interviews with color-courageous disciples, I came to realize that in a traumatized world, healing, discipleship, and mission are all intimately intertwined. What's more, color-courageous disciples will become far more effective in God's mission to make the world whole to the extent that we are whole ourselves—spiritually, emotionally, relationally, and in every other way.

In addition to grappling with the racial trauma of people of color, though, color-courageous disciples would do well to unpack the surprising truth that *racism traumatizes both victims and victimizers.*[1] As it turns out, White people have been traumatized by racism too, albeit in different ways. So let's consider what racial trauma looks like for both communities, starting with people of color.

RACIAL TRAUMA IN PEOPLE OF COLOR

In her book *Healing Racial Trauma,* Sheila Wise Rowe describes the dizzying array of traumas that racism can inflict upon people of color. From the Greek for "wound," *trauma* describes the spiritual, emotional, and relational wounds that linger and continue to cause pain after a distressing event. It is helpful to understand that racism has not impacted all people of color in the same way. There are some forms of racial trauma that I can relate to, and others I can't. Yet color-courageous disciples know the value of understanding the racial trauma that others have experienced not only in order to dismantle racism but also to comprehensively restore healthy communities in which people of color have had diverse experiences. We'll take a look at racial trauma in three categories: *individual, corporate,* and *divine.*

Individual Racial Trauma

It comes as a surprise to many that *physical hate crimes* toward individuals still happen. In fact, incidents of **hate crimes** rose in 2019 to levels not seen in a decade.[2] In schools, more than one-third of adolescents who report bullying are experiencing *bias-based* bullying. As it happens, bias-based bullying is more strongly associated with diminished health than general bullying.[3]

Emotional wounds inflict real but often hidden damage on individuals. For example, students who experience bullying are at increased "risk for depression, anxiety, sleep difficulties, lower academic achievement, and dropping out of school."[4]

It is particularly helpful to understand that simply witnessing someone else's distress can result in personal trauma too. This is called **vicarious trauma.** For example, after traumatic and racially charged incidents with the police, individuals throughout the Black community experience a heightened stress response for some time.[5]

Corporate Racial Trauma

There has been a widespread awakening to systemic racism, but to make real progress in combating it, we also need to awaken to the systemic trauma that systemic racism causes. Maria Yellow

Horse Brave Heart, a Lakota social worker, devoted herself to unearthing the reasons why entire communities of Indigenous peoples have languished over generations.[6] She unearthed the diagnosis of historical racial trauma, the "collective emotional and psychological injury both over the life span and across generations."[7] The documented effects of historical racial trauma include mental illness, family dysfunction, alcohol abuse, and even premature mortality. Similar historical racial trauma can also be observed among Black communities (dubbed "post-traumatic slave syndrome"), Japanese Americans after the internment camps of World War II, and Jewish communities after the Holocaust.[8]

There has been a widespread awakening to systemic racism, but to make real progress in combating it, we also need to awaken to the systemic trauma that systemic racism causes.

Recent studies on the impact of the Jewish Holocaust across generations have yielded the further discovery of transgenerational racial trauma—trauma that is, astonishingly, passed down genetically.[9] Here's what we know:

Trauma can alter the DNA expression of a child or grandchild's brain, causing a wide range of health and mental health issues, including memory loss, chronic anxiety, muscle weakness, and depression. Some of these effects seem particularly prevalent among African Americans, Jews, and American Indians, three groups who have experienced an enormous amount of historical trauma.[10]

A 2015 study of Jewish Holocaust survivors "demonstrated that damaged genes in the bodies of Jewish Holocaust survivors . . . were passed on to their children."[11] In fact, a new field of scientific inquiry called **epigenetics** has emerged to study "inheritable changes in gene expression."[12]

A third type of trauma is environmental racial trauma caused by **environmental racism,** which happens when communities of color are disproportionately exposed to pollutants. Did you know that hazardous waste facilities are more often located in communities of color?[13] Another example is the water crisis of Flint, Michigan. The city's hundred thousand residents were exposed to toxic levels of lead when municipal leaders switched the city's water source. Tragically, "nearly 9,000 children were supplied with lead-contaminated water for eighteen months."[14]

Divine Racial Trauma

All trauma is harmful, but perhaps the most destructive kind is **divine racial trauma,** trauma that harms our relationship with God. Obviously, our God does not traumatize us, but it sure can seem that way. Why, for instance, does God allow racism and oppression to thrive, bullies to taunt, inequity to be perpetuated? Why has God allowed slavery and other racial atrocities to flourish for so long, especially in a "Christian" country? Questions like these weaken the faith of some and cause others to reject Christianity outright.

The life of Malcolm X is a case in point. He was raised in a Christian family by a father who served as an itinerant preacher. In addition to preaching the gospel, his father also taught people to embrace pride in their Black identity. Unfortunately, as Malcolm recounted, the "good Christian white people" in the area weren't happy about that.[15] When his mother was pregnant with Malcolm, the Ku Klux Klan arrived at their home brandishing torches and rifles and shouting threats. Later, Malcolm said that his earliest memory was his house burning to the ground while the White police and firemen stood by and watched.[16]

Soon after, Malcolm's father was murdered. His body was

found laid across train tracks, his head smashed in and his body severed nearly in half. Although the family had purchased life insurance, local authorities denied the family claim. Over time, the family became destitute, and Malcolm's mother was committed to an asylum. Malcolm rejected his father's faith once and for all. When Malcolm X did eventually return to faith, it was to the Nation of Islam—a religious movement that addressed the evils of racism forcefully and directly in a way that his experience of Christianity never had.

When I think of Malcolm X's rejection of the God of Jesus Christ, my heart aches. His story is exhibit A for divine racial trauma, and there are many others like him. Some have held on to the Christian faith, but their relationship with God has suffered due to the divine racial trauma they have experienced.

APPLES, BANANAS, AND COCONUTS: THE ABCS OF INTERNALIZED RACISM

Let's look at one more example of racial trauma experienced by people of color: **internalized racism.** This is what happens when marginalized racial groups internalize society's negative narratives about themselves.

One of the clearest demonstrations of internalized racism was the famed doll test. In this social psychology test of 1947, Black children were presented with two dolls—one Black and one White. They were asked which doll they wanted to play with and to identify which doll was the "nice" one and which was the "bad" one. A majority of the Black children preferred the White dolls and shunned the Black dolls. The results were so stark that they influenced the deliberations of the 1954 *Brown v. Board of Education* case, which led to the desegregation of American schools.[17] A more recent 2005 documentary recorded similar experiments with similar results.[18]

Internalized racism has destructive consequences for both individuals and communities. For individuals, internalized racism correlates with anxiety, depression, shame, low self-esteem, and other poor health outcomes.[19] For communities, internalized racism actually has the power to pit people of color against one another. One example is the **crabs-in-a-bucket effect.** If you put a bunch of crabs in a bucket, they will do their best to escape. One crab in a bucket can escape without a problem. But a group of crabs in a bucket will drag down individual ones that try to escape, irrationally ensuring the demise of the whole group. I believe this may be why my most vicious bully growing up was not White but Black. And the Oreo label is not unique. A number of other racial slurs derive from food products. You can check them out at the online Racial Slur Database (don't you love the internet?).[20] Similarly painful epithets for people being "ethnic" on the outside but White on the inside are apples (Indigenous peoples), bananas (Asians), and coconuts (Latinos and South Asians), to name a few.

Colorism is another form of internalized racism that assigns higher value to lighter skin tones with grievous consequences.[21] It is already true that "dark-skinned blacks have lower levels of education, income, and job status; they are less likely to own homes or to marry; and dark-skinned blacks' prison sentences are longer."[22] Internalized racism prompts even people of color to discriminate against their own darker-skinned counterparts.[23]

Sadly, internalized racism causes many people of color to betray their own in different forms. Some pursue **assimilation,** downplaying their ethnic distinctiveness in order to better fit in with the dominant group. Others go further, choosing **defensive othering** by distancing themselves from their own racial group. Hate or shame for one's own community is, in many ways, the final frontier of racism. Tragically, racism causes many to say, "If you can't beat 'em, join 'em."

YES, TRAUMA ALSO COMES IN WHITE

When it comes to trauma, we rightly think about victims first, yet trauma harms victimizers too. The truth is that God created humanity to thrive as a community of equals. When God's design for equality is distorted, the victimizer must also pay an existential price.

When God's design for equality is distorted, the victimizer must also pay an existential price.

Consider the example we find in Exodus. For hundreds of years, the Israelites had been enslaved in Egypt, suffering deep trauma as an ethnoreligious minority group. When God sent Moses to deliver them, the story narrowed in on Moses's negotiations with Pharaoh. Of course, the text highlights the trauma that the victim, Israel, suffered. Yet the text also clearly depicts how the act of oppressing others traumatized Pharaoh too. We can see it in the progressive hardening of Pharaoh's heart. We see it in Pharaoh's unrelenting pride, denial, and delusion. We see it as Pharaoh desperately continued to embrace a false narrative of superiority, one that he simply could not bear to give up. Pharaoh may have been in power, but he was also in trouble. He was lost, and ultimately he was unable to cope with reality. In the end, the trauma that Pharaoh inflicted on the people of Israel boomeranged right back to him and led to the downfall of the nation. What's more, Pharaoh missed the beautiful opportunity to play a redemptive role in God's story.

Today psychologists call this **perpetrator trauma** or **Perpetration-Induced Traumatic Stress (PITS),** a form of PTSD that emerges after a person traumatizes someone else. If we understand White Americans to be another traumatized group, we might more sympathetically recognize in them certain symptoms of trauma. We might gain insight into certain reactions that Whites often have when confronted about racial inequity: shock, denial, avoidance, delusion, guilt, shame, and more. These are trauma responses. The truth is, the trauma of racism "has resulted in large numbers of Americans who are white, racist, and proud to be both; an even larger number who are white, racist, and in reflexive denial about it; and another large number who are white, progressive, and ashamed of their whiteness. All of these are forms of immaturity; all can be trauma responses; and all harm African Americans *and* white Americans."[24]

Color-courageous disciples recognize that we *all*—whether we realize it or not—need healing from the trauma that racism has caused. We are all equal at the foot of the cross, and we all need God's healing touch.

SHEDDING LIGHT ON SHAME

One of the most destructive consequences of trauma is shame. Brené Brown's well-known definition of **shame** has resonated with millions of people: "the intensely painful feeling or experience of believing that we are flawed and therefore unworthy of love and belonging—something we've experienced, done, or failed to do makes us unworthy of connection."[25] Ever since Eden, we humans have been seeking to avoid shame at all costs.

If God's heart is for shalom, then the Enemy's plan is to unravel shalom. Shame is one of his most effective strategies. While much work has been done on racism and much work has been done on shame, there has not been as much on the intersection of the two.[26] Just as racism has caused trauma for both people of color and Whites, so, too, has our trauma produced shame in us all. To experience shalom, color-courageous disciples must acknowledge not only racial trauma but also the racial shame that trauma causes.

To experience shalom, color-courageous disciples must acknowledge not only racial trauma but also the racial shame that trauma causes.

What does shame look like for people of color? As a woman of color, I have been tempted throughout my life to believe the powerful false narrative that I am worth less; that I am, in a word, *worthless.* My trauma provoked the painful thought *Perhaps there really is something wrong with me.* My own pursuit of perfection was my fig leaf of choice to cover the shame of being who I was.

But shame also impacts the privileged. Racial shame plays out in White communities in different ways. One way is shame about the past. As White individuals begin to recognize how they or their predecessors have consciously and unconsciously perpetuated racial inequity, shame rears its ugly head. It is *healthy* to feel grief over past mistakes; it is *unhealthy* to feel shame (2 Corinthians 7:10).

Another form of shame that impacts White disciples who seek to be color-courageous is the fear of making mistakes. In fact, I suspect that this shameful fear of making mistakes is what thwarts many racial reconciliation efforts. In *White Fragility,* Robin DiAngelo talks about the dynamic of the good/bad binary that so often stymies antiracism efforts—the idea that if someone points out racism in me, then I must be "bad" rather than "good." Not only is this ridiculously simplistic, but it also misses the reality that growth over time involves a bumpy process of making mistakes, falling, and getting back up again. Andrew Horning, the author of *Grappling: White Men's Journey from Fragile to Agile,* unpacks this:

> We have to realize "I can be a good person *and* have racist pat-
> terns.". . . Patterns we learned are not us; it's learned behavior
> that can be unlearned. . . . The feeling of discomfort or possibly
> shame is only a temporary state, and if we can sustain ourselves
> through it, we can come out the other side confident and free.[27]

Speaking to fellow White men in particular, Horning explains the many benefits that come with embracing the discomfort of racial reconciliation and pressing through shame, benefits
that include stronger emotional capacity, richer relational connections, deeper life meaning, and surprising joy.[28] Color-
courageous disciples of all backgrounds will be more effective to
the extent that we identify and heal our shame, exchanging it for
something better.

HEALING OUR STORIES, HEALING OUR SOULS

To deal with trauma and shame, we must experience rediscple-
ship through the exchange of false narratives for true ones. A
counselor I had once described good therapy as a "process of
demythologization." I love that. Healing happens as we courageously ferret out false narratives and fully embrace the true.

---

*Healing happens as we courageously ferret out false
narratives and fully embrace the true.*

As we have discussed previously, *racism is not just a false idea; it
is an entire false story.* Bryan Stevenson wisely describes racism as
"the narrative of racial difference."[29] That is why we can't only
address our practices. We must also address the story itself, the
story that is making us sick. Our color-courageous discipleship
must become an exercise of reimagination.

Over the centuries, the narrative of racial difference has led to varied experiences of racial trauma for us all. To find healing, we must—together with God—take ownership of our own stories lest we remain "trapped as characters in stories someone else is telling."[30] In the process, we can also "own our stories of falling down, screwing up, and facing hurt so we can integrate those stories into our lives and write daring new endings."[31]

Why is it so hard to own our own stories of falling down, screwing up, and facing hurt? Because doing so requires courage. I love how our word *courage* derives from *cor,* the Latin word for "heart." In fact, "In one of its earliest forms, the word *courage* meant 'To speak one's mind by telling all one's heart.'"[32] What this means is that color-courageous discipleship is not only about performing valiant deeds. It is also about *being vulnerable.* It is about choosing to acknowledge, own, and share the stories of our own hearts, stories that we might otherwise be ashamed of. We do this both for the sake of our own healing and so that we might extend that healing to the world.

Let's now consider two of the core stories that we must recover if we are to find healing.

Story #1: We are created in the image of God. All my life I've heard that I am made in the image of God. But . . . so what? It's kind of like hearing someone say, "You have the same nose as your dad!" It's cute to recognize, but it doesn't make any real difference in my life. But now I'm beginning to get it. Being created in the image of God means that we reflect the royalty of God, that we are called to live as royal characters in God's story.

The narrative of racial difference denies that we are all equally created in the image of God and instead points to race as an important way to measure our value. But the truth is that our value is not a matter of pedigree, race, or achievement. Our royal identity is grounded in the image of God in us, an incontrovertible inheritance from our creator. Knowing at my core that I'm royalty? That you are royalty? That people of every ethnicity, culture, and background were created to reflect God's royal image in unique ways? Yes, *that* makes a difference.

We must address the story itself, the story that is making us sick.

Story #2: We are deeply loved by God. God's love is the narrative that lies at the center of the cosmos, the narrative of all narratives. God's love surrounds us like an ocean as he works out his good purposes in us and through us using all that happens in our lives (Romans 8:28).

As Henri Nouwen understood, "Becoming the Beloved is the great spiritual journey we have to make."[33] God is still speaking over us the same words that he spoke over Christ in Matthew 3: *You are my beloved; in you I am well pleased.* We must attune our hearts to that voice.

> It is certainly not easy to hear that voice in a world filled with voices that shout: "You are no good, you are ugly, you are worthless, you are despicable, you are nobody—unless you can demonstrate the opposite." . . . Self-rejection is the greatest enemy of the spiritual life because it contradicts the sacred voice that calls us the "Beloved." Being the Beloved expresses the core truth of our existence.[34]

When we embrace our identity as God's beloved, we can more easily embrace **post-traumatic growth,** that positive transformation we can experience as a result of our struggle with a traumatic event.[35] From one vantage point, the entire Bible is a story of post-traumatic growth; it's the story of how God continues to grow his good purposes in the world even after the great tragedy of the Fall. And of course, we now follow the One whose death—the most traumatic event in history—has made possible the salvation of the entire world.

We cannot force growth to happen, but we can intentionally foster growth as we reframe our story in light of God's love.

We cannot *force* growth to happen, but we can intentionally *foster* growth as we reframe our story in light of God's love. The result can be the rediscovery of beauty from among the ashes. We don't pretend everything is okay, but as we tell our stories, "we are transformed from victims of uncontrollable events into well-informed authors, and our life stories become meaningful works of art."[36]

In light of God's love, I know for certain that no part of my story will prove meaningless. Instead, my story—every single part of my story—is becoming a meaningful work of art in God's hands. No chapter of my story has ever been lived outside the reach of God's love. Not only this: but God is able to transform the pain I have endured into a means by which I can extend his love to others.

Trauma is never good, but trauma can be repurposed into a redemptive force.

Trauma is never good, but trauma can be repurposed into a redemptive force. This truth echoes the famous words of Joseph, who was traumatized by his own brothers: "You intended to harm me, but God intended it for good to accomplish what is now being done, the saving of many lives" (Genesis 50:20). Even through our trauma, our foundational truth is that we are caught up in the story of God's love.

THE FREEDOM OF FORGIVENESS

Desmond Tutu, South African Anglican bishop and civil rights leader, is renowned for his ministry as an anti-apartheid activist. Apartheid was the legal system of racial segregation and discrimination that existed in South Africa through the 1990s. When apartheid finally fell, many predicted that the country would descend into chaos. After all, South Africans of color finally had their opportunity for revenge. But to everyone's surprise, chaos didn't happen—thanks largely to Desmond Tutu. Through his leadership of the Truth and Reconciliation Commission, Tutu inspired victimizers to confess, apologize, and make restitution, and he inspired victims to experience the freedom and joy of forgiveness. Tutu understood that there was no other way for the nation to move forward *together.* There simply can be no future without forgiveness.[37]

The cross bears witness to the truth that forgiveness is what ultimately brings lasting healing and freedom. Let's return to our story of Jesus and the paralytic. What the paralytic wanted was to walk again. Instead, Jesus proclaimed, "Your sins are forgiven!" Jesus understands that true healing entails forgiveness. "Forgive us our sins, for we also forgive everyone who sins against us" (Luke 11:4)—these are perhaps the most liberating words we can pray.

"Forgive us our sins." When we are forgiven by God, we are liberated from sin, which is our true disease. Jesus died for the sin of the world not only *out there,* but also the sin *in here,* the sin that is present and active in every human heart and leads only to death (Romans 6:23). Undeserved forgiveness is the beating heart of our faith (Romans 5:8).

An important note: As color-courageous disciples, we must remain alert to the subtler sins that are likely to infect our own hearts. We may no longer engage in blatant racial apathy or discrimination. However, we can too easily fall into the subtler but equally poisonous sins of self-righteousness and pride. "Forgive us our sins" applies to all of us at every point of the racial discipleship journey.

As color-courageous disciples, we must remain alert to the subtler sins that are likely to infect our own hearts.

We are also to "forgive everyone who sins against us." Forgiveness places us firmly on the path to the ultimate goal of restored relationships in a beloved community. But we can only enjoy restored relationships if we acknowledge that we are all equal at the foot of the cross. As Miroslav Volf writes in *Exclusion and Embrace,* "Forgiveness flounders because I exclude the enemy from the community of humans even as I exclude myself from the community of sinners."[38]

Beloved community is the end goal, and our courageous choice to forgive is what makes it possible. In the words of Dr. King: "We can never say, 'I will forgive you, but I won't have anything further to do with you.' Forgiveness means reconciliation, a coming together again."[39]

FLOURISHING AS WOUNDED HEALERS

George Orwell's classic *Animal Farm* is a brilliant cautionary fable. A barnful of animals become fed up with the oppressive regime of the farmers. Led by the pigs, the animals successfully carry out a coup against the farmers. In time, however, the pigs adopt the values and practices of their former oppressors until they themselves form a new ruling and oppressive class indistinguishable from the old one. The pigs even wear the farmers' clothes and sleep in the farmers' beds! *In fighting evil, they became evil themselves.*

This vicious cycle has repeated throughout human history.

Volf puts it this way: "People often find themselves sucked into a long history of wrongdoing in which yesterday's victims are today's perpetrators and today's perpetrators tomorrow's victims."[40] This is precisely the pattern that color-courageous disciples must resist, as Martin Luther King, Jr., taught his followers in *Strength to Love:* "Forced to live with these shameful conditions, we are tempted to become bitter and to retaliate with a corresponding hate. But if this happens, the new order we seek will be little more than a duplicate of the old order. We must in strength and humility meet hate with love."[41]

While seeking to defeat evil, we must not in the process become ensnared by evil. It is the very nature of evil to do this. As Volf observes, "Evil generates new evil as evildoers fashion victims in their own ugly image."[42] This is why inner healing is so vital for color-courageous discipleship: We pursue healing so that we might "not be overcome by evil, but overcome evil with good" (Romans 12:21). To heal the world, we begin with humility, restoration, repentance, and forgiveness. In other words, we begin with the pursuit of healing for ourselves.

While seeking to defeat evil, we must not in the process become ensnared by evil.

Perhaps one reason Jesus continued to visibly bear the scars of the trauma he suffered—even after the Resurrection—is to demonstrate to us that we, too, can become wounded healers. In the words of Nouwen, "Thus like Jesus, he who proclaims liberation is called not only to care for his own wounds and the wounds of others, but also to make his wounds into a major source of his healing power."[43] Then, as we go deeper into God's love and courageously extend that same love to others, we can become co-builders of that which God has envisioned for us: a rich and colorful beloved community.

SHEILA WISE ROWE

THERAPIST AND AUTHOR OF *HEALING RACIAL TRAUMA: THE ROAD TO RESILIENCE*

Sheila Wise Rowe has counseled abuse and trauma survivors for more than twenty-five years in the United States and South Africa. Executive director of the Rehoboth House, an international healing and reconciliation ministry, she is passionate about matters of faith and emotional healing.

How has God uniquely prepared you for color-courageous ministry?

My family has always placed a high premium on education and growth despite racial challenges. On my mother's side, we have a proud legacy of establishing "freedom schools" for Black children—we established one of the first on family property in the 1930s to '40s in Virginia. Later, my parents migrated, and I was born and raised in Boston—part of a generation that was bused out of my own neighborhood to a mostly White school. Of course, I had to deal with the inevitable resistance. Another example: Growing up, it was clear that predatory lenders were targeting communities of color, including mine. My parents fell victim too; at one point, we lost our home. So, in my background you will find racial trauma—but you will also find deep resilience.

What does inner healing have to do with discipleship?

For me, discipleship is a process of being transformed by the renewing of our mind. Our thoughts deeply influence our ability to love; so, to love well, we need to pursue the deep healing and transformation of our thoughts. I also believe that discipleship involves living fully into the image of God, becoming all that God created us to be. But we must first acknowledge our broken-ness. Most of us just want to skip right over the brokenness, but that's not how it works! Healing doesn't just magically happen; it requires surrender and an intentional willingness to become more like Christ over time.

Why is it valuable for disciples to understand the process of healing from racial trauma?

My whole book is about that, but here's an example. For our re-lationship with God to flourish, we need to deal with moral in-jury. A moral injury happens whenever our relationship with God and others suffers because of some perceived harm that was not prevented. As people of color experience racial trauma, we can become angry and distance ourselves from God for al-lowing the harm to happen. Honestly, we are seeing this every-where. Due to racial trauma and disillusionment, many Black and Brown folks are just "done" with the church and with God. People of all ethnic backgrounds must learn to recognize and engage racial moral injury if we hope to foster a thriving multi-ethnic church.

How have you drawn closer to Jesus as you have pursued antiracism?

One way has been through the process of healing from my own moral injury. I had to process the racial trauma I have suffered, and I had to process how my perceptions of God suffered too. Did God really love me? Was he really going to provide for me? Would he protect me and my children? Why had God allowed others to cause me harm? I had to grapple with these questions and really work through them. Ultimately, God led me to a place of healing, forgiveness, and freedom.

What advice would you like to give to growing color-courageous disciples?

Color-courageous discipleship is hard. There will be opposition. You will be challenged. But it is worth it. Also, don't worry about having the answers or being the expert; just keep learning and growing. Most of all, don't forget that antiracism isn't just about helping others. You, too, have a lot to receive. There are gifts that God wants to give *you,* but you must choose to remain open to receive them.

FURTHER READING

Emotionally Healthy Discipleship: Moving from Shallow Christianity to Deep Transformation by Peter Scazzero

Healing Racial Trauma: The Road to Resilience by Sheila Wise Rowe

Life of the Beloved: Spiritual Living in a Secular World by Henri J. M. Nouwen

My Grandmother's Hands: Racialized Trauma and the Pathway to Mending Our Hearts and Bodies by Resmaa Menakem

The Unapologetic Guide to Black Mental Health: Navigate an Unequal System, Learn Tools for Emotional Wellness, and Get the Help You Deserve by Rheeda Walker

DISCIPLESHIP AS BELOVED COMMUNITY

Experience Christ-Shaped Solidarity

> The end is reconciliation; the end is redemption; the end
> is the creation of the beloved community.
> —MARTIN LUTHER KING, JR., "FACING THE CHALLENGE OF A NEW AGE"

Any discipleship journey must ultimately find its destination in love. For Jesus, love was the point. He taught that the culmination of the law was love (Matthew 22:36–40). Everything else is a footnote. And as we have learned, a Christian approach to antiracism entails both dismantling and building. So we seek to dismantle racism and to build . . . what? As Martin Luther King, Jr., increasingly emphasized toward the end of his life, our aim as color-courageous disciples of Christ must be beloved community:

> I do not think of political power as an end. Neither do I think of economic power as an end. They are ingredients in the objective that we seek in life. And I think the end of that objective is a truly brotherly society, the creation of the beloved community.[1]

On my own journey, I have pondered, *What distinguishes a Christian approach to antiracism from a secular one?* Although there are many distinctives to Christian antiracism, first among them is our destination: Color-courageous disciples seek to create communities characterized by Christlike love.

Unfortunately, the word *love* has become hackneyed and dull for most of us. So, on this leg of the journey, our task is to remember how God defines *love* and to reimagine our purpose in light of that definition. The concept of beloved community, popularized by Martin Luther King, Jr., is a beautiful starting point.

One distinctive of Christian antiracism is our destination: a community characterized by Christlike love.

This may be an appropriate moment to pause and say a word about Dr. King's contributions. I am well aware that he was not faultless in his life or in his work. At the same time, as I have reviewed the prodigious scope of King's speeches, writings, and legacy, I believe that we have so much more to learn from his pioneering thought leadership with regard to a Christian approach to antiracism. For me, King's conception of the beloved community is one of his most important contributions, a gorgeous idea that he tragically never had the opportunity to develop. The concept of beloved community continues to be echoed by contemporary color-courageous leaders like John M. Perkins, who reminds disciples that "love is the final fight."[2] I fully agree.

So back to our task: remembering God's love and reframing our purpose as color-courageous disciples in light of that love. For me, the most compelling way to talk about love is as the Scriptures do: in both prose *and* poetry. So let's venture to reimagine God's love now in three poetic acts.

Act I: Created by Love

Before the beginning, there was Love—glorious, rejoicing, beautiful Love.
A tripersonal community, an everlasting embrace, a Beloved Community.
Listen closely, and you can hear its cadence . . .
the gentle beating heart at the center of the universe.
Unity-in-diversity. Unity, not uniformity.
Three partners
delighting in difference, savoring the dance.
Love lacked nothing, required nothing.
Love was satisfied.
Yet this love could not be contained!
So Love overflowed in a burst of fire and light.
Love took a three-dimensional canvas and painted:
day and night, sky and sea, flora and fauna, and then the crown—
Man and Woman
delighting in difference, savoring the dance.
And Love flared into song
over its children:
"Welcome to Beloved Community!
In you I am well pleased!
You are blessed
to love and to multiply Beloved Community
throughout the earth!"
And Love rejoiced in the goodness and wonder of
its manifold masterpiece.

Our God is triune love—Father, Son, and Holy Spirit, a Beloved Community existing in an eternal trinitarian embrace (1 John 4:13–16). What an astonishing truth, that *we were created by and for beloved community.* Of course, the kingdom of God will only be fully realized when Jesus returns. Yet we live in the era of the "already but not yet," which is to say that although the kingdom is present in the world, it is not yet pervasive. Still, color-courageous disciples are called to bear witness to God's reign even now.

A point of clarification. Is the *kingdom of God* the same thing as *beloved community*? For me, the two do overlap, but they are slightly different. Beloved community is a dimension of the larger kingdom of God, and **kingdom of God** is the overarching term for the rule of Jesus Christ that includes every dimension of creation. **Beloved community,** on the other hand, narrows our focus to how a diverse community of people interact with one another in God's kingdom.

There are, unfortunately, many impediments to beloved community. Our focus has been on how racism impedes beloved community. But to truly pull up racism from the roots, we must understand the shape of the sin that lies at those roots. Is that sin hatred? Disgust? Envy? Apathy? Ibram X. Kendi, author of *How to Be an Antiracist,* has wrestled for years to identify the roots of racism, how it developed, and why it persists. Although he doesn't write from a Christian perspective, his conclusion on this question resonates with a biblical worldview: "My research kept pointing me to the same answer: The source of racist ideas [is] not ignorance and hate, but self-interest."[3] Compare this, for example, with James 3:16: "Where jealousy and self-interest exist, there will be disorder and every evil thing" (BLB).

This is a profound insight. *Self-interest is the antithesis of beloved community.* By *self-interest,* we are not referring to normal and natural self-care. The word translated "self-interest" in James 3:16 is *eritheia,* the pursuit of one's own interests with little regard for the interests of others. In other words, sin turns us inward. Our sin nature inclines us to look out for ourselves even when it disadvantages others. In beloved community, however, we lovingly look out for others even when it disadvantages us. Beloved community turns outward in a posture of generosity and embrace.

But this bears further reflection—*why* are we inclined inward? *Because we are afraid.* We live in a fallen world. We are vulnerable to scarcity, suffering, sickness, and death—so it is perfectly logical that we would be afraid. Yet the greatest tragedy of fear is that it frustrates love: "The one who fears is not made perfect in love" (1 John 4:18). Fear destroys the very possibility of beloved community. How can I share with you, honor you, pay attention to you, sacrifice for you if I fear that these same things won't be done for me?

I believe that George Yancey correctly identifies the "fear factor" as the final frontier of racial reconciliation.[4] For example, in conversations about race, White individuals may fear being misunderstood, labeled a racist, or shunned for committing a racial faux pas. They may also fear the consequences of making waves with their White colleagues and friends. A person of color may fear being dismissed, discounted, or labeled a troublemaker. And, of course, they may fear that their efforts will not yield results. And here's the thing: *These are all real possibilities.* Not only do we live in a broken world, but the sin nature that resides deep within every human heart means that we will inevitably hurt each other on the journey toward beloved community. Our persistent pattern, in Yancey's words, is to perpetuate a vicious "cycle of fear."[5] What, then, can break the cycle of fear?

Only love. Which is why, in Christ, God took definitive action to cast out our fears with love—and make us courageous (1 John 4:18, ESV).

Act II: Redeemed by Love

But one day
we accepted the Lie:
"God is not Love, and you are not the Beloved."
We turned away from God to self.
We turned away from neighbor to self.
And then that self asked, "Am I my brother's keeper?"
We barely noticed our exchange of faith for fear:

fear of God, fear of death, and fear of one another.
So much fear.
Self-interest—born.
Beloved Community—broken.
But Love
launched a plan!
A plan to redeem and restore
Beloved Community
rebuilt on faith and sacrificial love.
And Love spread its arms as wide as the cross,
casting out fear
forever,
filling us with courage
and empowering us to rebuild Beloved Community
together.

The love that grounds God's beloved community *and* ours is love of a particular kind. The love of beloved community is **agape love:** the sacrificial, self-giving, supernatural love of God that casts out all fear (1 John 4:18). While our broken world pressures us to succumb to the slavery of self-interest, agape love frees us to be like Christ, to look not to our own interests but "to the interests of the others" (Philippians 2:4).

The ultimate goal of color-courageous discipleship, like all discipleship, is the expression of agape love. Consider this: Jesus taught plenty of former commands in new ways, but only once did he claim to establish a "new command." And that new command was about agape love: "A new command I give you: Love one another. As I have loved you, so you must love one another" (John 13:34). The disciples already knew that love was important—so what, exactly, made this command "new"?

What made it new was that Jesus was establishing *himself* as the standard of love. Jesus took agape love from an abstract concept to a concrete model—in himself. Jesus's new command was to love not in some abstract way but just like he loves. *My new command is this: Don't just love in some vague, unspecified way. Love in precisely the same way that I have loved you.*

Honestly, this command is terrifying. Jesus loved us by dying an excruciating death on the cross. He loved us by forgiving those who had hurt him. He loved us by suffering, sacrificing, and shedding streams of blood. That just doesn't sound like a recipe for living your best life. Yet the story doesn't end with the cross; Jesus loved us like this "for the joy set before him" (Hebrews 12:2).

As Jesus followers, we are not called to comfortable discipleship. We are called to cruciform discipleship. **Cruciform** discipleship is discipleship in the shape of the cross. We are called to *love like Jesus* with agape love, to suffer and sacrifice for the joy set before us.

God has promised to meet our every need according to the riches of his glory in Christ Jesus (Philippians 4:19). For this reason, we can practice agape love. We need not exhaust ourselves in self-interest; we can look to the interests of others. Still, sometimes it certainly doesn't *feel* like God is supplying our every need! That's why we can only love like Jesus by faith. If Christ did not rise from the dead, then our faith is futile (1 Corinthians 15:17). If Christ did not rise, then it makes sense to look out for number one. But Christ *did* rise. There is life beyond this life. As we set our minds "on things above, not on earthly things," we will be free to love like Christ loved (Colossians 3:2). Color-courageous disciples build beloved community *by faith*.

We are not called to comfortable discipleship. We are called to cruciform discipleship.

The enemy of our souls seeks to stymie beloved community by prompting us to answer no to Cain's perennial question: "Am

I my brother's keeper?" (Genesis 4:9). But our God whispers a different response: "Yes! A thousand times yes! It is by becoming your brother's keeper that you build beloved community *and* experience fullness of life."

One way to practice agape love in our journey toward beloved community is to create safe, courageous spaces where we can talk openly and honestly about our fears.[6] These spaces must be characterized by grace—spaces where people can connect without fear of judgment or reprisal. The ultimate goal? To lay the foundations for a beloved community, a community that by definition casts out fear with love.

Self-interest, rooted in fear, is normal and natural. But disciples are called to that which is supernatural. Color-courageous disciples, in a posture of agape love, look not only to our "own interests" but also "to the interests of the others" (Philippians 2:4).

As God's love pours into us by the power of his Spirit and overflows to others, we will find that beloved community begins to take shape. This is a beautiful parallel to Pentecost.

Act III: Called to Beloved Community

Behold: Pentecost!
Behold beloved community recreated
in fire and light.
Behold God's chosen ones, holy and beloved
from every tribe, tongue, people, and nation
now being transformed from glory to glory
delighting in difference, savoring the dance.
Behold the Body of Christ reincarnate,
empowered by the Spirit,
and entrusted with a Great and Colorful Commission:
You are blessed to love in living color!
You are blessed to go and build beloved community.

BUILDING BELOVED COMMUNITY

We are privileged to live now in the third act—the age of Pentecost. At Pentecost, God filled the disciples with his Spirit. This Spirit gives us the power to actually *become* beloved community. But what does that look like?

We can glean some wisdom on this from Paul's first letter to the Corinthians. The believers in Corinth formed a gifted and vibrant congregation, but it was also deeply divided. Paul addressed divisions of all kinds. He called out disunity and disorder relating to apostolic authority, gender, class, sexual ethics, worship preferences, and ethnicity. His letter was designed to address their multiple divisions and move them toward agape love. To get there, Paul used the beautiful poetic metaphor of the body of Christ (1 Corinthians 12)—and we can too.

In this metaphor, the Holy Spirit is key: Disciples are forged into the body of Christ *by the power of the Holy Spirit*. In Paul's words, "We were all baptized by one Spirit so as to form one body—whether Jews or Gentles, slave or free—and we were all given the one Spirit to drink" (1 Corinthians 12:13).

Before going further, let's clarify two things. First, color-courageous disciples do not build beloved community in our own power. Yet the language of building itself is biblical, as we see in Ephesians 4:16: "From [Christ] the whole body, joined and held together by every supporting ligament, grows and *builds itself up in love,* as each part does its work." Our desire is to see the Spirit of God work in and through disciples to build beloved community.

Second, a few interpretative comments: It is true that 1 Corinthians 12 is not narrowly about ethnic division—although both ethnicity and class divisions *are* mentioned in verse 13. Further, this passage was not written as social commentary. It was written to instruct a local congregation in the exercise of diverse spiritual gifts. Yet I agree with N. T. Wright on its broader applications:

Paul clearly has the life of the local congregation in mind. . . .
But we in our age have been given, through instant electronic
communication, a far more detailed picture of the worldwide
church than any previous generation has ever had. . . . Should
we not also rejoice with, or grieve with, all Christians around
the globe who celebrate or suffer?[7]

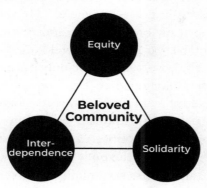

As we proceed now through the poetry of 1 Corinthians 12,
we will discover three timeless characteristics of the body of
Christ: biblical **solidarity,** biblical **interdependence,** and biblical
equity. So color-courageous disciples can build beloved community by engaging in these three paradigm shifts:

1. From separation to solidarity: "We are one body"
2. From independence to interdependence: "We need each
   other"
3. From equality to equity: "We love best when we love
   some people differently"

1. From Separation to Solidarity: "We Are One Body"

A body, by definition, is one. So it is ludicrous, of course, for
one part of the body to ignore the suffering of the other parts.
At best, this would signify dysfunction; at worst, it would be a

death sentence. It just makes sense for each member to "have equal concern for each other" (1 Corinthians 12:25). But what does "equal concern" look like?

Paul clarified: "If one part suffers, every part suffers with it; if one part is honored, every part rejoices with it" (verse 26). This is what Dr. King meant when he said that "injustice anywhere is a threat to justice everywhere."[8] He also said, "To the degree that I harm my brother, no matter what he is doing to me, to that extent I am harming myself. . . . If you harm me, you harm yourself. Love, *agape,* is the only cement that can hold this broken community together."[9]

This is where the concept of solidarity comes in. Entering into solidarity is about intentionally living into the reality that we are *already* profoundly connected. Although Paul was talking in 1 Corinthians 12 about the body of Christ, solidarity is vital for the health of any diverse community. Caring for one another just makes sense.

Members of a beloved community both acknowledge and own the suffering of their fellow members.

As time passes, we continue to uncover surprising new dimensions of our fundamental connectedness. In the brilliant book *The Sum of Us: What Racism Costs Everyone and How We Can Prosper Together,* Heather McGhee makes an evidence-based case for how racism hurts everyone—not just people of color—in tangible ways.[10] Society tends to incline toward a **zero-sum paradigm,** the idea that one group's gain comes at another group's loss. In reality, racial zero-sum thinking leads to measurable diminishment of life for all racial groups in nearly every sector, including education, housing, labor, public recreation, and the environment. McGhee advocates instead for the "Solidarity

Dividend: the benefits we gain when people come together across race to accomplish what we simply can't do on our own."[11] Similarly, in his book *Dying of Whiteness,* Jonathan Metzl demonstrates the counterintuitive ways in which racism has harmed White communities in healthcare and education.[12]

Just as a body naturally cares for itself, so a beloved community cares for itself. Members of a beloved community both acknowledge and own the suffering of their fellow members.

2. From Independence to Interdependence: "We Need Each Other"

Americans tend to chafe against the idea of needing anybody else in order to thrive. We must remember, however, that this American mindset does not reflect a biblical worldview, as 1 Corinthians 12 demonstrates. Robin DiAngelo, too, points out what extreme independence costs us when it comes to race:

> The most profound message of racial segregation may be that the absence of people of color from our lives is no real loss. Not one person who loved me, guided me, or taught me ever conveyed that segregation deprived me of anything of value. I could live my entire life without a friend or loved one of color and not see that as a diminishment of my life.[13]

The conviction that we lose nothing as we live segregated lives is a diabolical lie that diminishes our lives. As Paul said, "The eye *cannot* say to the hand, 'I don't need you!' And the head *cannot* say to the feet, 'I don't need you!'" (1 Corinthians 12:21). Independence has its place, but members of the body of Christ have the higher calling to *inter*dependence. It is a great mystery that "those parts of the body that seem to be weaker are indispensable" (verse 22):

There are different kinds of gifts, but the same Spirit distributes them. There are different kinds of service, but the same Lord. There are different kinds of working, but in all of them and in everyone it is the same God at work. *Now to each one the manifestation of the Spirit is given for the common good.* (verses 4–7)

The word translated *manifestation* in verse 7 is literally "revelation." I love that. The word *revelation* emphasizes this important truth: It is impossible to know in advance precisely how the gifts of each diverse member of the body will benefit the whole. This is something that only God knows and gradually reveals. What we do know is that the strong members of the body are blessed, often in unexpected ways, by those who are "weaker." In God's economy, it is the poor who are richly blessed—which paradoxically means that the so-called poor have much to share with the larger body (Luke 6:20). Jesus even taught that in caring for "the least of these," we have the opportunity to encounter him (Matthew 25:31–46).

Remember our definition of *ethnicity:* a God-ordained cultural identity that God delights in as a means for bringing glory to himself and enrichment to his kingdom. This is meant to be experienced in the diverse, interdependent body of Christ! How can we do more to delight in ethnic diversity as a means to bring greater enrichment to the whole body? Color-courageous disciples seek to dismantle racism so that we can all experience the riches of a colorful community.

Independence has its place, but members of the body of Christ have the higher calling to interdependence.

Of course, racial and ethnic categories are just one way of thinking about "stronger" and "weaker" members of the body of

Christ. In his writings, author Henri Nouwen reflected upon the riches he gained by moving from Yale to L'Arche, a community of people who are disabled. In the eyes of the world, this was an irrational decision. While Yale is one of the most prestigious institutions in the world, L'Arche represents a community of people who tend to be devalued and even despised by society. Nevertheless, Nouwen came to understand that the move was his gain: "L'Arche exists not to help the mentally handicapped get 'normal,' but to help them share their spiritual gifts with the world. The poor of spirit are given to us for *our* conversion. In their poverty, the mentally handicapped reveal God to us and hold us close to the gospel."[14] It was while he was at L'Arche that Nouwen learned many of his greatest spiritual lessons.

When we live in solidarity with "the least of these," we will be blessed in unexpected ways.

Let's be sure, though, to remember that the converse is also true. Just as the strong need the weak, so, too, do the weak need the strong. We all need each other. At times, people of color have become fed up with the status quo (justifiably) and embraced racial separatism movements. I'm not referring to healthy race-specific expressions of community but to a kind of independent separatism that is antithetical to God's ideal for the body of Christ:

Now if the foot should say, "Because I am not a hand, I do not belong to the body," *it would not for that reason stop being part of the body.* And if the ear should say, "Because I am not an eye, I do not belong to the body," it would not for that reason stop being part of the body. (1 Corinthians 12:15–16)

Regardless of our placement in the body—whether we consider ourselves weaker or stronger, more advantaged or less advantaged—we need the rich and surprising gifts that God grants to us only in and through one another.

3. From Equality to Equity: "We Love Best When We Love Some People Differently"

A common objection to antiracism is that it results in **reverse racism**. The objectors claim, for example, that antiracism initiatives simply exchange an unfair preference for Whites with an unfair preference for Blacks. This important concern needs addressing.

It is true that color-courageous disciples must be careful not to exchange one type of injustice for another type of injustice. At the same time, biblical equity does not preclude the need for *customized treatment* in all cases. We've already seen that **equality** emphasizes *sameness* while equity emphasizes *fairness.* To be clear, both have their place. At first glance, sameness seems appropriate for every circumstance. Everyone should receive the same treatment, right? In actuality, though, this logic works best in situations where everyone enjoys a similar starting point. Using this well-known baseball game illustration from the Interaction Institute for Social Change, it is clear that giving the same footstool to people of different heights does not make sense—at least not if the goal is for everyone to see the ball game![15]

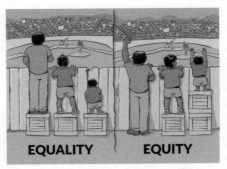

EQUALITY   **EQUITY**

Interaction Institute for Social Change
Artist: Angus Maguire

In this case, *equal* footstools result in vastly *unequal* experiences. What would be more helpful here is **equity**—a fair *opportunity* for everyone to watch the game. In our illustration, this would require a customized stool for each person.

Please note: In a biblical approach to equity, we are not talking about a Marxist state where everyone is forced toward the same outcomes *regardless of their efforts.* We are speaking of creatively seeking to provide everyone with *a fair opportunity to employ their efforts.* The reality, of course, is that even when people are granted fair opportunities, we will still observe widely different outcomes. First, there is the matter of individual effort. What an individual does with the opportunities they have been given will always vary, and biblical equity does not preclude the need for hard work and individual responsibility. What's more, individuals have unique interests and talents, which also contribute to a diversity of outcomes. All of this is true; it is *also* true that, given the stubbornly entrenched racial disparities of our society, seeking to provide more equity of opportunity is one way that we can move toward seeing everyone flourish.

Our baseball game illustration is not perfect, of course, and many have suggested other metaphors that you might prefer. This is just one winsome way to demonstrate that, at times, *equal concern is most constructively expressed through customized treatment.* Most important, this idea of customized treatment is not a new-fangled, secular concept. It is biblical to the core. Going back to our passage, notice the curious repetition of the word *special:*

> The parts that we think are less honorable we treat with *special* honor. And the parts that are unpresentable are treated with *special* modesty, while our presentable parts need no *special* treatment. But God has put the body together, giving *greater honor* to the parts that lacked it, so that there should be no division in the body, but that its parts should have *equal concern* for each other. (1 Corinthians 12:23–25)

The call to *special treatment* occurs here three times, and appearing once is the concept of giving *greater honor* to some—*precisely in order to express "equal concern for each other"* (verse 25). In Western culture, many have a negative knee-jerk reaction when a person or group receives so-called special treatment. Yet God's economy is countercultural, and here we find an example of that. The Scriptures teach that a healthy, fair, and caring community—a beloved community—actually necessitates "special treatment" and "greater honor" for some members at least some of the time (12:24).

At times, equal concern is most constructively expressed through customized treatment.

Some might ask, "When does it end? Must we now give people of color special treatment indefinitely? Isn't this just a form of reverse oppression?" This is a legitimate concern. We don't want to unwittingly set up a reverse caste system, simply changing the categories of who's permanently on top and who's permanently at the bottom. We have already explored how all human beings possess a sin nature, both individually and corporately, so there is always the possibility for a former victim to become a victimizer.

That is why we must keep our goal clearly before us. The goal is not a new caste system; the goal is biblical equity. When everyone enjoys fair opportunity, then theoretically, special treatment will no longer be needed. However, assuming that this goal *could* be reached in a broken world, it would undoubtedly take a very long time to get there—just as it has taken us a very long time to get to where we find ourselves now.

In one of his final speeches, Martin Luther King, Jr., directly addressed those who would make the argument that the Black community should not receive any special treatment to better their condition. He countered with this:

There is another myth that still gets around: *it is a kind of over-reliance on the bootstrap philosophy.* There are those who still feel that if the Negro is to rise out of poverty . . . if he is to rise out of discrimination and segregation, he must do it all by himself. . . . They never stop to realize the debt that they owe a people who were kept in slavery 244 years. In 1863 the Negro was told that he was free as a result of the Emancipation Proclamation. . . . But he was not given any land to make that freedom meaningful. . . . [Our nation] simply said, "You're free," and it left him there penniless, illiterate, not knowing what to do. And the irony of it all is that *at the same time the nation failed to do anything for the Black man—through an act of Congress it was giving away millions of acres of land in the West and the Midwest—* which meant that it was willing to undergird its white peasants from Europe with an economic floor. . . . It's all right to tell a man to lift himself by his own bootstraps, but *it is a cruel jest to say to a bootless man that he ought to lift himself by his own bootstraps.* We must come to see that the roots of racism are very deep in our country, and there must be something positive and massive in order to get rid of all the effects of racism and the tragedies of racial injustice.[16]

The American proclivity for the bootstrap mentality is in many ways admirable. I fully agree that color-courageous disciples should avoid fostering a mindset of never-ending victimhood and helplessness among people of color. That will not help anyone. Furthermore, we don't want to undermine the benefits of meritocracy—which, when functioning rightly, rewards people appropriately on the basis of merit and skill.

The issue, as King put it, is *overreliance* on the bootstrap mentality. As it turns out, God's usual way often provides for a community through the members' *mutual reliance on one another.* When there is a special need, some parts of the body may indeed benefit from special attention.

Maybe you now find yourself in agreement with the idea that it is good for disciples to willingly sacrifice for the sake of building beloved community. But what does that look like concretely? More is coming on this, especially in chapter 10 in our discussion on "true" fasting. There, we will look at tangible ways to willingly leverage or sacrifice the various forms of power that we have been given, for God's glory and for the sake of beloved community.

"GO AND DO LIKEWISE"

I have a friend who once conducted a survey of more than one hundred evangelical churches and organizations—most of them well-known—to compare their statements of faith. To his surprise, not one of them contained the language of love.[17] He reflects,

> We Evangelicals have not rejected love; we have just forgotten to include it in our conversations, mission plans, statements of faith, and theological reflections. That's unfortunate. To move forward, we need to put a priority on the presence of love. . . . It's not sufficient to *assume* that we love God, each other, and our global neighbors. We need to think about it, talk about it, preach it, practice it, and put it in the center in everything we do.[18]

Love is our beginning. Love is our way. Love must be the end of all our striving. And Jesus must be our inspiration *and* our model for love.

And—I find this fascinating—when Jesus was asked to illustrate love, he painted a cross-racial picture. When a Jewish expert in the law asked Jesus about loving one's neighbor, Jesus told a surprisingly scandalous story about the crossing of an ethnic divide (Luke 10:25–37). While both a Jewish priest and a Jewish scribe passed by a victimized man on the street, the Samaritan had "compassion," stopped to help, and loved the beaten man in tangible ways (Luke 10:33, ESV). To have compassion is to *suffer with: com-* ("with") plus *-passion* ("suffer").

That is the essence of beloved community: a colorful community whose members suffer *and* rejoice together by way of the courage that God provides. It is also why Jesus ended his surprising parable on cross-racial love with these simple words: "Go and do likewise" (Luke 10:37).

EFREM SMITH

PASTOR AND AUTHOR OF *THE POST-BLACK AND POST-WHITE CHURCH: BECOMING THE BELOVED COMMUNITY IN A MULTI-ETHNIC WORLD.*

Efrem Smith is co-lead pastor of Midtown Church in Sacramento, California. He has served as president and CEO of World Impact and is the author of numerous books.

How has God uniquely prepared you for color-courageous ministry?

I received Christ at an outreach where John Perkins preached on reconciliation. So right from the start, I understood that reconciliation was about reconciliation with God as well as racial reconciliation. As soon as I got home and told my mother that I had received Christ, she shared something with me for the first time. When she was pregnant with me, she'd had a prophetic dream that I would be a preacher—and not just *any* preacher. I was going to preach, specifically, to thousands of people of different races and backgrounds. Well, at the time, I was teenager with no clue that something supernatural was going on. I told her, "I'll be a Christian, but I don't want to be a preacher. I'm not doing that." You know how that turned out!

What, for you, does antiracism have to do with discipleship?

I believe that antiracism is an integral part of our cross-cultural mandate from Jesus to make disciples of all nations. In Acts, we see this being fulfilled as Jew and Gentile come together and the church is born. But soon after, we also see ethnic conflict emerge between Hellenistic and Hebraic widows in the distribution of food. Almost immediately, we see "systemic racism" at work that required an "antiracist" intervention. Cross-cultural disciplemaking can't be separated from antiracism. As we pursue unity in diversity, systemic challenges will emerge that we will need to overcome together.

Tell us about your vision for beloved community—and what does *beloved community* mean to you?

Beloved community is one practical way to talk about the kingdom of God. I've read many of the writings of Dr. Martin Luther King, Jr., and he was always making the case that the end goal was bigger than voting rights, civil rights, and the like. The goal was beloved community. The goal was the expression of agape love empowered by the redemption and reconciliation found in Jesus Christ. The church is called to build beloved community now, but we also need to equip people with cultural intelligence and the cross-cultural instincts they need to nurture beloved community.

How have you drawn closer to Jesus in the pursuit of antiracism?

My commitment to racial righteousness and reconciliation has always emerged from the overflow of my relationship with God. It is an overflow of my intimacy with God the Father, my identity in Christ, and the dwelling of the Holy Spirit in me.

What advice would you like to give to growing color-courageous disciples?

I'm concerned that there are many involved in racial reconciliation whose souls are wounded and damaged, and it's easy for this work to drown out rhythms of intimacy with God, intimacy that brings healing. For instance, the death of George Floyd was very traumatic for me. I realized my soul was wounded. I had to call my spiritual director; I had to temporarily put my own emotional and physical health ahead of my work. I had to resume the rhythms of getting into God's Word and having transparent conversations with Christian friends. As we continue to make disciples and dismantle racism, we must be sure to tend to our souls. It is vital that we take responsibility for our self-care and our intimacy with God—that's how we'll sustain the ministry that God has called us to.

FURTHER READING

I've Seen the Promised Land: Martin Luther King, Jr., and the 21st Century Quest for the Beloved Community by C. Anthony Hunt

The Sum of Us: What Racism Costs Everyone and How We Can Prosper Together by Heather McGhee

The Post-Black and Post-White Church: Becoming the Beloved Community in a Multi-Ethnic World by Efrem Smith

Welcoming Justice: God's Movement Toward Beloved Community by Charles Marsh and John Perkins

COLOR-COURAGEOUS SPIRITUAL PRACTICES

We have now come to an important juncture in our color-courageous discipleship journey, so let's take a step back to gain some perspective on where we've been and where we're going next.

In part 2, we recovered four discipleship paradigms that can help us more clearly comprehend how a color-courageous posture naturally proceeds from following Jesus Christ. To be specific, we took an in-depth look at how color-courageous discipleship rediscovers discipleship as awakening, wardrobe change, inner healing, and becoming beloved community.

Yet to grow as color-courageous disciples, we need not only paradigm shifts; we also need spiritual practices. We have said that at its core, racism is a spiritual problem that requires spiritual solutions. We can find those spiritual solutions with the help of spiritual practices, also known as spiritual disciplines. Notice, too, the relationship between the words *discipline* and *disciple*. Without spiritual disciplines, we disciples are left to dismantle racism in our own strength. But *with* spiritual disciplines, color-courageous discipleship can become an intimate journey with

Christ. Spiritual practices have always been the means of grace that God has provided that allow us access to his infinite strength.

In the end, spiritual practices enable us to be transformed so that we can transform the world. But here's the thing: For this transformation to happen, it's not enough to simply *do* spiritual practices; what matters even more is *how* we do them.

It's not enough to simply do spiritual practices; what matters even more is how we do them.

Consider the Pharisees: they were exceedingly faithful when it came to executing spiritual practices. Yet even as the Pharisees carried out these practices, *there was something about how they did them that served to perpetuate injustice rather than dismantle it*. This is what prompted Jesus to say: "Woe to you, teachers of the law and Pharisees, you hypocrites! You give a tenth of your spices—mint, dill and cumin. But you have neglected the more important matters of the law—justice, mercy and faithfulness. You should have practiced the latter, without neglecting the former" (Matthew 23:23). But how do we do it? What does it look like to "practice the latter, without neglecting the former"?

Consider also institutional slavery in America, the Holocaust in Germany, and apartheid in South Africa. All three of these legalized racist systems somehow thrived in well-established "Christian" cultures. How can this be? How is it possible to be deeply Christian yet also deeply racist—even genocidal? Faithful Southern Christian slaveholders read their Bibles, prayed, donated to the church, and faithfully worshipped at church every Sunday. So what happened? What went wrong?

Now consider a final example, this time from Rwanda. The Rwandan Civil War of 1994 was fundamentally a conflict between warring ethnic groups. In the aftermath of the conflict, this is what Ugandan-born theologian Emmanuel Katongole said when he came upon a decimated church baptismal font:

> [The altar] bears the scars of being hacked by machetes, and the church was littered with thousands of bones of people who were killed. You couldn't find a more strange and ironic and tragic image than that: a common baptism surrounded by killing in the name of Hutu and Tutsi.[1]

Yet again, we see this pattern. Rwanda is a primarily Christian country with more than 90 percent of Rwandans identifying as Christians. So how was it possible for ethnic and tribal hatred to so perniciously infect its people? Or as Rose Dowsett puts it, how could their spiritual practices be "so shallow that they left the blood of tribalism untouched by the water of baptism"?[2]

So we come full circle to this thought: What matters is not only *that we do* spiritual practices as followers of Jesus. What may matter even more is *how* we do them. Are we practicing spiritual disciplines in ways that

- inspire us to advance God's mission in holistic ways— through proclamation, demonstration, and reconciliation?
- open our eyes to the riches to be found in the technicolor text of the Scriptures?
- equip us to name the cultural presuppositions that we each bring to our Bible reading?
- encourage us to process pain and racial trauma well, especially through lament?
- prompt us to name and uproot the unconscious biases of our hearts?
- move us to cross geographic and cultural boundaries in curious, fully embodied ways?

- incline us toward empathy for others, especially those on the margins?
- influence us to identify our power so that we might better leverage or sacrifice it for others?
- empower us to carry the cross with Christ in every part of our lives, including race?
- foster within us the godly courage we need to dismantle racism and build beloved community for a lifetime?

Beloved friends, our spiritual practices have so much potential to cultivate color-courageous discipleship! *But if we want to realize that potential, we need to practice them differently.* That is why, in part 3, we will take a look at uncommon ways of practicing four spiritual disciplines that commonly appear in the Scriptures. Two of these practices are more familiar (Bible reading and prayer), while two may be less familiar to contemporary disciples (pilgrimage and fasting—not just any fasting, but fasting "for real").

Using these as case studies, we will seek to understand how we can live into all our spiritual practices in color-courageous ways. If we want to faithfully follow Jesus, dismantle racism, and build beloved community, we need spiritual practices that will truly transform *us*—heart, soul, and mind—as we seek to transform our world.

READ (IN LIVING COLOR)

Rediscover the Technicolor Text

I am not myself by myself.

—EUGENE PETERSON, *CHRIST PLAYS IN TEN THOUSAND PLACES*

When I first heard the news about Lausanne Cape Town 2010, I knew I had to be there despite still being quite young—and quite broke!

Founded by Billy Graham, the Lausanne Movement is known for its commitment to mobilizing "the whole Church to take the whole gospel to the whole world," and it has played a meaningful role in shaping global missions over the past century. Miraculously, my husband and I both applied, were accepted, and then swiftly raised the financial support we needed to go. With diaper bag and Snap-N-Go stroller in hand, we toted our wide-eyed eight-month-old right along with us.

In the end, Cape Town 2010 hosted more than four thousand leaders from 198 countries and was hailed as "the most representative gathering of Christian leaders in the 2,000 year history of the Christian movement."[1] My most vivid memories will always be of the opening night—an intercultural worship celebration beyond compare. I was stunned by the boundless breadth and depth of our gorgeously global church. *What would it look like to be enriched by our incomparably colorful church in my everyday discipleship practices too?* I wondered.

Our journey in Christ will be richer to the extent that it reflects this statement from the Nicene Creed: "We believe in one holy catholic and apostolic church." We are privileged to follow Jesus together with the church across time ("apostolic") and around the world ("catholic"). Yet most of us are missing out on this. Too often our discipleship consists of bland monochromatic snack food instead of the rich and colorful banquet God intends.

Though evangelicals have placed much emphasis on Bible reading, for example, we have not placed as much emphasis on reading the Bible with any cultural insight. Color-courageous disciples take a different approach: They seek to read the Bible in living color, both to glean more riches from the Word and to attain wisdom for bringing racial shalom to the world.

Reading the Bible in living color means acknowledging two realities. First, we acknowledge that we do not come to the Bible as a blank slate. Understanding this, we ask, *What cultural assumptions am I bringing to this text that may impact how I understand it?* We also acknowledge that the Bible is far more culturally complex than we can imagine. I mean that quite literally. Because we live thousands of years removed from biblical cultures and contexts, we have a terrible time imagining them with any accuracy.

This leads us to our second question. Reading the Bible in living color also means asking, *What cultural insights about this text might help me to understand it more deeply?* The truth is, the Bible is an intriguingly technicolor book. More precisely, it is a technicolor library of sixty-six books written by forty authors in multiple languages. Bible stories take place in a vast array of cultural contexts such as Mesopotamia (the patriarchs), Egypt (Exodus), Persia (Esther), Babylon (Daniel), Assyria (Jonah), and

Rome (Paul). The Bible also traverses vast cultural differences *within* a single place. Just as in the United States there are many distinct regional cultures (Southern hospitality, Midwest stoicism, East Coast urgency, West Coast laissez-faire), the same is true of Bible lands.[2] In Israel, for example, there were stark differences between life in the crowded metropolis of Jerusalem compared to life in the calm green hills of Galilee. Understanding differences like these will shed new and dazzling light on biblical truth and prevent us from painting all the Bible with the same brush.

Reading the Bible in living color means reading God's Word in a color-courageous way.

Reading the Bible in living color means reading God's Word in a color-courageous way. Rather than tainting our reading of Scripture with the racial and cultural assumptions that we bring to the text, we are free to better understand its original meaning and to enjoy more fully all the riches of God's Word.

DISCOVER YOUR OWN CULTURAL CONTEXT

Let's begin with our first question: What cultural assumptions am I bringing to this text that may impact how I understand it? When we open a book, we too often unwittingly treat it like a mirror; our default bias is to read our assumptions and experiences into the text. None of us is without culture. Given that we cannot remove our cultural lenses any more than we can remove our DNA, we can and should become more aware of what those lenses are.[3] When we don't, misreading the Bible is the inevitable result.

Sociologist Michael Emerson has unearthed three cultural

lenses of White evangelicalism. These three lenses go a long way in explaining why White evangelicalism has perpetuated rather than dismantled a racialized society. Here we will examine those lenses of White evangelical culture: individualism, relationalism, and antistructuralism.[4]

First, **individualism** understands the individual rather than the collective to be paramount. When a plural *you* appears in the Bible, we often misread it as a singular *you*. It isn't our tendency to consider what it looks like to resist racism not only as individuals but as a group. We rarely if ever think about what responsibility to dismantle racism the larger church has together as a collective. Unfortunately, in our individualistic culture, questions like these are often viewed with suspicion. Disciples in individualistic cultures tend to be flummoxed by stories like that of Achan, whose entire family was punished for one man's sin. As Tim Keller explains, "Achan's family (Joshua 7) did not do the stealing, but they helped him become the kind of man who would steal."[5] Individualistic cultures like ours tend to miss the collective nature of sin. Disciples in individualistic cultures often seek to address the problem of racism in a system, for example, by identifying and uprooting individuals—the bad apples— rather than identifying and addressing collective dysfunctions.

Next, the lens of Western evangelical **relationalism** attaches "central importance to interpersonal relationships."[6] This derives in part from our evangelical emphasis on having a personal relationship with Jesus Christ—which I believe is one of evangelicalism's greatest strengths. On the flip side, relationalism morphs into a weakness when it causes disciples to view most social problems as "rooted in poor relationships."[7] Evangelicals tend to see most societal problems as a failure to love others as we love ourselves, which is no doubt partially true. But absent from this "is the idea that poor relationships might be shaped by social structures, such as laws, the ways institutions operate, or forms of segregation."[8]

Disciples in relational cultures prefer conversations about racial *reconciliation* rather than racial *justice,* and they like to take relational countermeasures when it comes to resisting racism, countermeasures like getting people together, pursuing unity, or developing cross-racial friendships. But these gestures are often regarded as shallow offerings by those on the receiving end.

Finally, we'll consider **antistructuralism.** To resist racism in a truly restorative way, color-courageous disciples seek not only relational repair; they also creatively seek tangible and structural repair whenever possible. Take the story of Zacchaeus. After his encounter with Jesus, Zacchaeus showed true repentance because he not only apologized but made restitution. He exclaimed, "Look, Lord! Here and now I give half of my possessions to the poor, and if I have cheated anybody out of anything, I will pay back four times the amount" (Luke 19:8). *This act of spiritual repentance, generously demonstrated through tangible restitution,* is what prompted Jesus to proclaim with delight: "Today salvation has come to this house" (verse 9).

We find another example of a structural approach to inequity soon after the birth of the church: "In those days when the number of disciples was increasing, the Hellenistic Jews among them complained against the Hebraic Jews because their widows were being overlooked in the daily distribution of food" (Acts 6:1). This is deeply lamentable because at Pentecost, God had clearly demonstrated his fiery desire for a church of diverse disciples. Yet soon after, we see a painful example of cultural and ethnic conflict. Notice the difference here again between **intention vs. impact.** I would wager that it was not the *intention* of the Hebraic Jews to mistreat the Hellenistic Jews. These were all God-fearing people. Nevertheless, ethnic mistreatment was exactly the *impact* of their existing system, policy, and power structure. We can learn what color-courageous discipleship looks like by observing how the Twelve—all Hebraic Jews—responded when the Hellenistic Jews complained. They did not deny that there was a problem, drag their feet, blame the victims, or tell them to pull themselves up by their bootstraps. Instead, they took action to change the system itself so that biblical equity was the result. In fact, the Twelve changed the power structure itself, raising up Hellenistic leaders to oversee the food distribution. What was the result? "The word of God spread," and the "number of disciples in Jerusalem increased rapidly" (verse 7). That is the power of color-courageous discipleship at work!

As we have seen through our analysis of just three White evangelical cultural lenses—individualism, relationalism, and antistructuralism—culture has a profound impact on how we read, understand, and apply the Bible. If you think you don't have a culture—which is common among dominant-culture disciples—that's an urgent flag saying that you have work to do! *If your culture is dominant, you are more likely to be blind to what your culture actually is.* This is why White-culture disciples in particular can perhaps benefit more than anyone else from cultural self-reflection. That being said, color-courageous readers from all backgrounds must constantly work to grow in their awareness of the cultural biases they bring to the biblical text.

Reading through our cultural lenses also inclines us to read certain parts of the Bible more than others. I was reminded of this in a powerful way when I visited the innovative Museum of the Bible in Washington, D.C. The most memorable exhibit for me was in the museum's "African American Experience" wing. Behind a large pane of glass, I spotted a copy of the Slave Bible—a Bible produced specifically for use by slaves. Cut from the biblical text were passages that would have undoubtedly been among the slaves' favorites. The story of the Israelite slaves' exodus from Egypt is omitted, as are passages like Galatians 3:28 that emphasize equality between groups of people. The book of Revelation—which as we know depicts a diverse family of disciples standing before the throne of God—was also left out. This supposed "Bible" was not *holy* precisely because it was not *whole*. The slave *owners* might have possessed their own complete copies of the Bible, but the Slave Bible reveals that, in their cultural context, they clearly preferred certain parts of their Bibles to others.

As disciples, we are actually not so different today. We affirm the Bible as our foundation for discipleship, but we also prefer to spend most of our time in certain parts. Perhaps just like the publishers of the Slave Bible, we do this because there are parts of the Bible that we would rather avoid—they make us uncomfortable or challenge our way of life. This tendency to read selectively is culturally conditioned.

SELECT PARTS

OF THE

HOLY BIBLE,

FOR THE USE OF THE

NEGRO SLAVES,

IN THE

BRITISH WEST-INDIA ISLANDS.

London:
PRINTED BY LAW AND GILBERT,
St. John's Square, Clerkenwell.

1807.

Slave Bible, 1807

Now we move to our second question: What cultural insights about the Bible itself might help me to understand it more deeply?

DISCOVER THE BIBLE'S CULTURAL CONTEXT

It was a normal Sunday morning in Birmingham in September 1963 when four little girls clothed in colorful dresses made their way to services at Sixteenth Street Baptist Church. I imagine them, like most youngsters, there in the church basement, giggling and fidgeting during the Sunday school Bible lessons, gospel songs, and flannelgraph presentations. After class, they gather to change into their white choir robes. As they run back upstairs to bless the congregation with song, the last thing they see on this earth is a brilliant flash of burning light.

The Ku Klux Klan proudly took responsibility for the explosion of the nineteen sticks of dynamite that killed Addie Mae, Carol, Carole, and Cynthia—a blast so brutal that it decapitated one of the girls, mutilating her so badly that she could only be identified by her clothing. The bombing was a major galvanizing event for the Civil Rights Movement and mobilized momentum for the long-awaited passing of the Civil Rights Act in 1964, the very next year.

In the aftermath of that horrific event, people saw a very strange sight: At the time, Sixteenth Street Baptist Church was flanked by a series of beautiful stained glass windows. One of the most startling images to emerge from the wreckage was a damaged window that featured a faceless White Jesus, his visage seemingly blown away with eerie precision.

In Western contexts, when we read the narratives of Jesus in the Bible, we tend to imagine him with White skin. But how and when did Jesus "become" White?

Perhaps the most famous portrait of Christ was created in

Sixteenth Street Baptist Church,
Birmingham, Ala., Public Library Archives

1924 by the artist Warner Sallman, a member of my own denomination—the Evangelical Covenant Church, then known as the Swedish Covenant Church. Originally, Sallman created the charcoal portrait of Christ to grace the cover of our denominational magazine, the *Covenant Companion*. It resonated with many. In fact, the "popularity of the cover was so great that requests for reprints streamed in after all 7,000 copies of the magazine were sold."[9] Later, in 1940, Sallman was commissioned to paint this Jesus in full color as a gift from the graduating class of North Park Theological Seminary to their school. This resulted in the now-famous portrait of a European Christ with blue eyes and flowing hair looking heavenward. Some refer to the portrait as the "Swedish" Jesus. This is certainly understandable, given that the painting originated in a Swedish American cultural context.

Sallman's inspired work has brought joy and comfort to countless people, including scores of American servicemen who were given pocket-sized reproductions of Sallman's Christ during World War II.[10] The painting has been called "the best-known American artwork of the 20th century" and is ubiquitous around the world. There are more reprints of this White Jesus in circulation than there are people in the United States.[11] In fact, it's considered to be the most reproduced image ever, estimated to have been reprinted more than one billion times.[12]

We tend to imagine Jesus in our own racial and cultural image. We do this out of a desire to relate to Jesus—and that is a wonderful thing. You can now find images of Jesus portrayed in every ethnicity. At the same time, depicting Jesus in our image can have unintended consequences. In the words of my colleague Paul Robinson, executive minister of Love Mercy Do Justice for the Evangelical Covenant Church, Eurocentric depictions like these have caused many to "link the image of Jesus with the very real experience of racism at the hands of some white people and institutions."[13]

The Covenant Companion
cover, February 1924

What do we know about what Jesus looked like? We know that "the earliest depictions of Jews, which date from the 3rd

Century, are—as far as can be determined—dark-skinned. . . . 'The safest thing is to talk about Jesus as "a man of colour."'"[14] In *The Historical Jesus: An Essential Guide,* James H. Charlesworth writes that Jesus's skin was "most likely dark brown and sun-tanned."[15] Just imagine: What if the vast majority of our depictions of Christ—in books, flannelgraphs, posters, frescoes, and stained glass windows the world over—portrayed a more historically accurate brown-skinned Jesus? What difference might that make for our shared perception and treatment of Black and Brown people today?

> *Imagine: What if our depictions of Christ portrayed a more historically accurate brown-skinned Jesus? What difference might that make for our treatment of Black and Brown people today?*

Given the racial challenges that we face, it is vital to comprehend, not only with our *minds* but also with our *hearts,* that the main character of the Bible was not White. Jesus was Jewish, a marginalized and oppressed minority in the Roman empire, and most likely one with brown skin.

When we read Jesus in living color—as he actually was—we more deeply comprehend that "Jesus identifies with the oppressed and that the experience of marginalized people is not foreign to God."[16] I am proud that the Evangelical Covenant Church actually *excels* when it comes to multiethnic diversity, but it has taken us many years of intentionality to get here.

When we read the Bible in living color, we perceive Jesus (and all other Bible characters) in their full vibrance and reality, and as we do, new insights emerge that enrich our understanding of the text, our faith, and our capacity to build beloved community.

READ WITH COLORFUL COMMUNITY

For years my friend Dr. Max Lee, professor of New Testament at North Park Theological Seminary, has taught and refined a course called "Intercultural Readings of the Bible."[17] Originally prompted by students of color at the seminary, the course explores an **intercultural** approach to reading the Bible that results in mutual insight and transformation.

Although the Word of God does not change, the same text can result in fresh insights when read from different vantage points. This is an incredibly exciting proposition. Bible reading in colorful community enriches us as we exchange **community cultural wealth,** "the array of cultural knowledges, skills, abilities, and networks" that every culture possesses.[18] As we have learned, ethnicity is a God-ordained cultural identity that God delights in as a means of bringing glory to himself and enrichment to his kingdom. This is exactly what we see in the biblical vision of the new creation where every culture brings unique treasures into the kingdom of God (Isaiah 60:1–14; Revelation 21:24–26). Thankfully, we don't have to wait until the new creation to experience these riches.

Indigenous readers like Randy Woodley, for example, draw us to the connection between discipleship and creation.[19] Reconciliation not only with God and fellow humans but also with creation, brings shalom, well-being, and joy. Indigenous readings remind us that all creation is groaning under the weight of a curse of our own doing (Romans 8:22). Disciples become agents of holistic healing as we steward creation with care, let creation prompt worship as it did for the psalmists, and even learn directly from creation as Jesus modeled when he pointed to sparrows, lilies, vines, and water in his teachings.

James Cone, a Black reader of the Bible, has made striking connections between the cross and the lynching tree.[20] Like the countless Blacks who were lynched in America, Jesus was unjustly accused, falsely condemned, maliciously mocked, and hung on a tree to die. Yet he did so "for the joy set before him" (Hebrews 12:2). Many Black readers remind us that joy is an act of resistance.

My colleague Dominique Gilliard, author of *Rethinking Incarceration,* is another Black Bible reader who made eye-opening comparisons between criminal justice in the Bible and criminal justice today.[21] Jesus and the disciples suffered injustices within the criminal justice system, just as many people of color do today. Jesus was imprisoned by a biased judiciary. Although he was innocent, he received the death sentence. Don't forget that many of the apostles and disciples "did time"—entire books of the Bible were written by convicted criminals! Recalling these events prompts new questions: How are we identifying and addressing unfairness and bias in our criminal justice systems today? Do we paint all incarcerated people with the same brush? Are we making restorative investments in prisons, understanding them to be fertile fields and even launching pads for ministry? Did you know, for example, that incarcerated people are now partnering with free churches in creative and beautiful ways—making disciples and even planting churches behind bars?[22]

Latino readers have drawn attention to the fact that Jesus could be considered, in modern parlance, both an immigrant and a refugee.[23] Just as many immigrants attempt entry into the United States to flee violence or poverty, Joseph, Mary, and Jesus abruptly migrated to Egypt to escape violence in Israel. In fact, our generation has seen some of the largest refugee migrations in human history. To what extent can we recognize God in the immigrants among us, many of whom are Christian?

We receive even more insights from Scripture as we read with the global church. For example, Indian readers might help us see how Christianity can thrive in a pluralistic society or learn how to better share the gospel with people from other religions. For centuries, Christians in India have existed as a religious minority in an environment with significant populations of other religions, including Hindus, Muslims, Buddhists, Jains, Sikhs, and numerous folk religions. The British missionary and apologist Lesslie Newbigin, for example, is known for his insights after a long career in India about how the gospel can thrive in a pluralist society.[24] Sadhu Sundar Singh, who was raised as a Sikh but later experienced a miraculous conversion, was an Indian Christian missionary who authored a number of works, including reflections on reaching practitioners of other religions.[25]

There are so many more examples to share. African and Asian readers might help us understand what it means to live out our faith not only with our present community but also mindful of our community of faithful ancestors, the "great cloud of witnesses" that surrounds us (Hebrews 12:1).[26] South Korean readers, with that church's long tradition of intensive early morning prayer, can teach us to enjoy the benefits of awakening the dawn in worship (Psalm 57:8, 108:2) and "pray[ing] in the Spirit on all occasions" (Ephesians 6:18).[27]

Of course, it is important that we do not overgeneralize about racial and cultural groups. Every member of a group is unique, and no group is monolithic. The main takeaway here is that the wider and more diverse your reading community is, the richer and more accurate your understanding of the Bible will be. How diverse are the voices speaking into your life? For example, how colorful is your bookshelf?[28] You'll find many more colorful resource recommendations at https://michelletsanchez .com/colorcourageous.

Reading in colorful community highlights the importance of **decentering** one's own culture. Profound wisdom emerges as we move from an **ethnocentric** approach (my cultural perspective is central and most important) to an **ethnodiverse** approach (my cultural perspective is one among a rich tapestry of cultural perspectives). Ultimately, reading in colorful community is not

something we do to check off a box or jump on the latest politically correct bandwagon. Color-courageous disciples read in
living color to get more of God and to fulfill more of God's good
purposes in the world.

LOVE IN LIVING COLOR

When I worked on Wall Street, the hours were brutal. Under
my desk, I stored a pillow and blankets for snoozing at work. It
was challenging to maintain even a semblance of spiritual life,
but I was creative.

One day, for instance, I found an empty conference room and
started to pace and pray aloud vigorously. Suddenly, my friend
Maurice opened the door. He gave me a bemused look, shut the
door, and swiftly vanished. I chuckled, knowing I'd have some
explaining to do. Later he messaged me: "Hey, so . . . what were
you doing up there?!" My response: "Yup, you caught me. I'm
not crazy, I promise. I was just talking to the Man Upstairs!"

In the end, I was grateful for the kerfuffle because it launched
an ongoing spiritual conversation. Maurice had graduated first
in his class from Morehouse College, one of the most prestigious
of historically Black colleges and universities. He was gently in-
timidating and undeniably brilliant. He was also firmly opposed
to the Christian faith. At lunch one day he asked me point-
blank, "Michelle, how can you seriously believe this stuff? Don't
you get that Christianity has been an oppressive tool for hundreds of years?" As we have learned, there is truth to accusations
like these.[29] Christian "discipleship" for Blacks has included oppressive tools like the Slave Bible.

But as I prayed, a light bulb came on: *I'm going to shift from
sharing Jesus in a color-blind way to sharing Jesus in living color.* I said,
"Maurice, you're right. Christianity has been co-opted as a tool
of oppression, especially with the Black community. And that

breaks my heart. But you know what? I like to stay focused on Jesus himself—who he actually was, what he said, and what he did. He was a marginalized and oppressed minority. Most likely a Brown one. He can relate."

At that point I could see the lights turning on for Maurice; he couldn't hide the subtle sparks of curiosity about the true Jesus. It was a turning point in his willingness to reconsider the Christian faith.[30]

Reading the Bible in living color is vital for making disciples in today's diverse world. It's projected that by 2045, the majority of Americans will be people of color.[31] Our youngest generations have already surpassed this milestone. Reading and loving in living color will be key to reaching these future generations for Christ.

———

Many people have heard about the tragedy of the four little girls at Sixteenth Street Baptist Church, but far fewer have heard about what came after. Disciples of Jesus mobilized on a global level to restore what had been broken—including the stained glass windows.

Across the ocean in Wales, a Christian artist began to fashion a brand-new stained glass window as a restorative gift for the church. Now often ironically referred to as *The Wales Window,* it portrays a brown-skinned Jesus on a cross. And notice his hands: *His right hand is defiantly resisting injustice while his left hand is extending forgiveness.* It's the very posture of color-courageous discipleship: resisting racism while building beloved community. The window is accompanied by the words "You do it to me," based on Matthew 25:40. Today, Sixteenth Street Baptist Church lives on as a thriving community and a beacon for justice and hope.

The point is not that we'll fix all our racial challenges by replacing our images of a White Jesus with a Jesus who is African,

The Wales Window, Sixteenth Street Baptist
Church, Birmingham, Alabama, 2010

PHOTO BY CAROL M. HIGHSMITH, LIBRARY OF CONGRESS

Latino, or Native. The point is that when we revisit the Bible in living color—including Jesus himself—we will be blessed with new insight. We may be reminded, for example, that Jesus was a marginalized person and that he held up marginalized peoples as role models for us. No doubt, what we discover will impact how we engage marginalized communities today. As we read the Bible in living color, we see more clearly that God is at work in all cultures and peoples—and that we should honor everyone as exemplars of the royal image of God.

ESAU MCCAULLEY

NEW TESTAMENT PROFESSOR AND AUTHOR OF
READING WHILE BLACK

Esau McCaulley is assistant professor of New Testament at Wheaton College and a priest in the Anglican Church in North America. He completed his PhD in New Testament at the University of St. Andrews under the direction of N. T. Wright. He is the author of *Reading While Black: African American Biblical Interpretation as an Exercise of Hope.*

What spiritual practices have been particularly life-giving for you?

Fellowship is so important. My community keeps me accountable; I don't strive to be independent. And I enjoy fellowship not only with living saints but with the whole communion of saints, past and present. I am especially encouraged whenever I can read the stories of saints from our great cloud of witnesses. I also love to read the Bible—of course!

What prompted you to write *Reading While Black*?

I wrote it to help the emerging Black generation to understand that, yes, you can follow Jesus and pursue justice. I wrote it to show how Black Bible readers have always put these together.

Why is intercultural Bible reading—reading with a diverse group of disciples—important?

We need diverse voices because we have blind spots. Intercultural Bible reading can help us discover what those are. Also, disciples from other backgrounds have had experiences with God that I haven't had. They have asked questions of the text that I haven't asked. They can offer rich wisdom to the body of Christ that benefits everyone.

What are some insights that have emerged uniquely from Black readings of the Bible?

You know, I tell people that Black people actually saved Christianity in the West! I mean that! In the 1800s, some White Western Christians espoused a heretical Christian anthropology. Racism distorted White Christian theology to the extent that they actually believed that some humans reflected the image of God more than others. It was primarily Black disciples who, over time, pushed back and corrected that heretical idea. In Black readings of the Bible, the **imago dei** (image of God) has always been more than just an abstraction. The *imago dei* is about real dignity. The *imago dei* is a political idea with political implications. If we are all created in the image of God, that implies true political equality. Black readings of the Bible have always made clear connections between orthodoxy and orthopraxy. We see the ways in which theology has real-life, practical implications.

What are some unique contributions that the Black church can offer to the whole church?

In the Black church, kingdom theology is prominent. We understand the kingdom of God as a holistic, wide-reaching reality. We understand the implications of the fact that Jesus is king over everything. I must say that the existence of the Black church is also, in and of itself, a testament to hope. This gift of hope that we can contribute to the larger church is rooted in tragedy, of course. But we have learned what it means to hope in God and rely on his power in even the darkest of situations. Finally, I think we can show the church what it means to be a Christian when you're not in control, when you are not the one in power. We understand what that means, and we have followed Jesus anyway—and flourished.

FURTHER READING

Santa Biblia: The Bible Through Hispanic Eyes by Justo L. González

Reading While Black: African American Biblical Interpretation as an Exercise in Hope by Esau McCaulley

Many Colors: Cultural Intelligence for a Changing Church by Soong-Chan Rah

Misreading Scripture with Western Eyes: Removing Cultural Blinders to Better Understand the Bible by E. Randolph Richards and Brandon J. O'Brien

PRAY (IN THE RAW)

Lament Your Way to Faith, Hope, and Love

I am beginning to see that much of praying is grieving.
—HENRI NOUWEN, *THE RETURN OF THE PRODIGAL SON*

It's a Tuesday morning in September, and I'm at work, gearing up for the day. I look up from my desk and see a most curious thing out the window: a waterfall of white documents showering from the sky. They are fluttering every which way like a cadre of confused butterflies. I wonder to myself, *What is this? Has a Xerox machine exploded somewhere?*

In that moment, I was sitting on the seventeenth floor of my company's skyscraper in downtown Manhattan. After studying international business in college, I had landed a plum job as an investment banking analyst at Goldman Sachs. I launched my career at not only one of the most prestigious banks on Wall Street but also within one of its most prestigious divisions. Many of my classmates, upon hearing the news, simply raised their eyebrows in astonishment.

Frankly, I was astonished too. Because I am a woman of color, the odds had been undeniably stacked against me. Women of color, and Black women in particular, have long suffered abysmal rates of hiring, pay, and promotion in the corporate world. There were precious few people at Goldman Sachs who looked like me. Nevertheless, by God's grace, I had been invited to the table. After so many years of pain, I was finally reaping some significant rewards.

Summer training was done. The date was September 11, 2001—my second day on assignment. I had not been at my desk long that morning when paper started to rain down from the sky outside. Of course, we soon learned that much more was going on than an exploding photocopier. It was terrorism that had exploded into our world. Mayhem and confusion descended. In one moment, I was desperate to get out of there. Would our building be next? In the next moment, I was desperate to stay. Outside, the day had suddenly turned to night, and the air was choked with thick and putrid smoke.

At some point, we were given masks and urged to vacate the area. When I walked outside, it felt just like emerging from a spaceship. Everything was cloaked in ghostly white ash— buildings, cars, people. And it was quiet. . . . Everything was eerily quiet in the city that *never* sleeps: every phone cut off, no honking taxis, no screeching subways. People staggered around in silence. And the smell, I will simply never forget the stench— unnatural, metallic, and foul. I can smell it now.

At the time I lived in Brooklyn, miles away. Like everyone else, the only way for me to get home that day was to walk. So I started the trek—first in heels, then in bare feet. It was surreal to cross over the Brooklyn Bridge. I was just one dot in a sea of stunned people, and the city was still aflame behind us. I remember being terrified that a third or fourth plane would come. I imagined it smashing into the bridge and causing me to tumble to my death in the cold, dark water below. In that moment, this thought bolted into my mind: *If I had to meet God right now, would I be ready?* I had a relationship with Jesus, yes. Yet I had pursued many of my career choices primarily for me rather than for him. Much of my life had been blighted by bitterness about having *less.* Black women always seemed to have *less.* But I was determined that my story would be different. I had decided to chase after earthly treasures, come what may, as a means of finally having enough, of being enough, of quelling my insecurities once and for all.

To be clear, a financial career is absolutely a God-honoring career choice for many people. But, in my heart, I knew that banking was not for me. What would it look like for me to truly trust God not only with my career but also with my very identity?

On 9/11, I felt a clear nudge from God to go back to the drawing board of my life. But before I could even think about doing that, God directed me to go on a walk with him through the valley of the shadow of death. In the days that followed, I was haunted by trauma and beset by grief. It was the sheer randomness of it all that made the loss so disturbing. I was tormented by the endless loop on television of people jumping from the burning inferno of the Twin Towers to an unimaginably gruesome death. *Some of them, I was certain, had to be followers of Jesus.*

Imagine. One moment, you're at work, bright and early, groggily sipping your coffee and making plans for the day. In the blink of an eye, you are deciding between being burned alive or jumping from a window to your death. I just couldn't wrap my mind around it.

The towers were soon memorialized in an art installation called *Tribute in Light.* It features two towering shafts of light that reach straight up to the heavens. *But, really, what kind of God were they reaching out to? What kind of God was I reaching out to?*

I plunged into depression. I began meeting regularly with a deacon from my church. I shed countless tears. I was filled with rage as I considered not only this event but all the other horrific things that God had allowed to happen before and since. I ago-nized: *What kind of God allows pain like this?* I cried out to God and begged him to show me the way through because I couldn't see one. And then something happened.

I had a dream that I was running through a deep forest. I knew that I was on mission for Jesus in this place, but for some reason, I was being pursued by people who wanted to kill me. I was terrified. And I knew with clarity: "This is it. This is the end. I'm going to lose my life." Suddenly, a door appeared in midair. It opened to perfection, beauty, and warm, radiant light. Pastel flower petals burst from the door. Just as my at-tackers came upon me, I ran through the door, and the door vanished.

I woke up with a start, awash with a kind of relief that I had never felt before and haven't felt since. But in that moment I knew two things with complete certainty: One, my worst fear had come to pass. Going through that door meant that I had died. Two, God had saved me. Going through that door also meant I was home at last, safe and secure, about to launch a new adventure of life with God forever. My soul flooded with grati-tude and joy. *Okay, Jesus,* I thought. *I got the message. I'm always in your hands, no matter what.*

I share my 9/11 experience not because it is about race but because it is about pain. On 9/11 and throughout its after-math, I endured some of the most excruciating pain of my life. Antiracism, too, involves dealing with excruciating pain— personal pain as well as the pain of others. Color-courageous disciples must learn to grapple with racial pain rather than avoid it if we are to effectively dismantle racism and build be-loved community. But before we talk specifically about racial pain, let's first return to the Scriptures and understand some things about how pain works as well as the remedy for pain that God has provided.

GOD'S ANTIDOTE FOR PAIN

Pain is pervasive in our fallen world. When pain prompts us to become angry or resentful toward God, it distorts our relationship with him. And when we inevitably cause other people pain, it distorts our relationships with them. And when one racial group causes another racial group pain, it distorts the beloved community that God intends.

But here's the amazing thing: God has provided us with an antidote that can transform pain into a spiritual catalyst. That antidote is lament. In the cauldron of our suffering, God invites us to lament, to pray in the raw. At its heart, **lament** is a "prayer of pain that leads to trust."[1] Learning to lament is like learning a new language. It's the language that God has given disciples to talk to him about pain. The language of lament does not come easily, but as we become increasingly fluent, we will find that our pain increasingly becomes infused with redemptive possibility.

We are also seeing more clearly that there is acute racial pain all around us. Yet it is precisely because the contemporary church has tended to avoid pain that we have been ineffective in our racial reconciliation and racial justice efforts. In response, modern-day prophets urge the church to realize that lament is vital for long-lasting racial shalom. In this chapter, we will examine personal and corporate lament, as well as a third kind—divine lament—and explore how each brims with potential for healing and spiritual growth.

THE GIFT OF PERSONAL LAMENT

Our relationship with God deepens as we increasingly allow ourselves to bring our pain to him: unprocessed, real, and raw. We live in a desperately broken world, a fallen world teeming with pain. Lament is the gift that God has given us to talk to him about that pain. Our human default is to avoid pain, but in lament we learn to bring our pain to God.

Our relationship with God deepens as we increasingly allow ourselves to bring our pain to him: unprocessed, real, and raw.

Lament is how we infuse our pain with redemptive possibility. Lament is God's invitation for us to be honest with him and, ultimately, to trust him with our pain. But—and this is critical—we can't entrust our pain to God unless we've been real with him about it first. We can't entrust our pain to God unless we have taken the risk of being authentic with him about our anger at him and our disappointment in him for allowing that pain. We can't entrust our pain to God in prayer unless we pray in the raw.

The book of Psalms is the disciple's prayer book, teaching us what it means to pray in the raw. While most of the Bible is God's Word directed at us, the book of Psalms is our word directed at God. It shows us what it looks like to bring the full range of human emotion to God. The psalms come in all varieties—praise psalms, thanksgiving psalms, royal psalms, and more. But the largest number of psalms are psalms of lament.

The psalms of lament reveal a pattern for constructively bringing our pain to God. In *Dark Clouds, Deep Mercy,* Mark Vroegop writes about the devastating experience in grieving his stillborn child. He describes four movements that he discovered as he immersed himself in the psalms of lament: (1) Turn, (2) Complain, (3) Ask, and (4) Trust.[2] Let's take a brief look at each of these as they appear in Psalm 22.

Psalm 22 is attributed to King David, who wrote it during an experience of abandonment and despair. At some point, though,

David made a conscious decision to *turn* to God: "My God, my God, why have you forsaken me?" (verse 1). Three times in the first two verses, David insistently repeats, "My God." Even amid his pain, David turns to God.

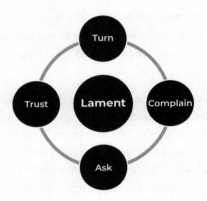

Next, we *complain* before God. We get real, as David does in Psalm 22: "I cry out by day, but you do not answer, by night, but I find no rest" (verse 2). God invites you to be brutally honest with him about your pain because God wants to meet you where you actually are. Think about it. Where else can he meet you? God's desire is to meet you where you are so that he can comfort you, heal you, walk with you, and guide you toward abundant life.

The third step in lament is to *ask*. David implored God for many things, some of which he had undoubtedly requested before: "Do not be far from me, for trouble is near"; "You are my strength; come quickly to help me"; and "Rescue me from the mouth of the lions" (verses 11, 19, 21). When we are in pain, God yearns for us to ask him for comfort, hope, and peace. Being honest about what we *really* want is another opportunity to present our true self to God and grow our relationship with him. In the process of asking, we often will also gain clarity about what would actually be best for us. And, of course, sometimes God will give us exactly what we ask for (Matthew 7:7; James 4:2).

The final frontier of lament is *trust*. Our trust in God is our highest expression of our love for him. David wrote, "In you our ancestors put their trust; they trusted and you delivered them" (Psalm 22:4). When David wrote prayers like these, his pain had not vanished. Nevertheless, he discovered profound peace—and even newfound praise—as he chose to trust in God's greater purposes for his life.

God can take our pain—including our racial pain—and repurpose it to form deep and unshakable faith in him.

In the life of Jesus, we discover a beautiful moment when his own prayerful ask blossomed into prayerful trust. In the Garden of Gethsemane, Jesus lamented. He turned to God and asked to be spared the cup of pain . . . but then he concluded with a declaration of trust: "I want your will to be done, not mine" (Matthew 26:39, NLT). Jesus trusted that if God allowed this pain into his life, then God would certainly work his good purposes through it.

Philip Yancey puts it this way: "Faith means believing in advance what will only make sense in reverse."[3] I do not understand why God allowed me to suffer merciless racial trauma as a little girl. I do not understand why God allows systemic inequity to persist. Nor do I understand why God allows heart-rending catastrophes like 9/11 to explode into our lives. What I *do* understand is that the only way forward is trust. God can take our pain—including our racial pain—and repurpose it to form deep and unshakable faith in him.

THE GRACE OF CORPORATE LAMENT

To the extent that we learn to process our personal pain through lament, we color-courageous disciples will be able to help others process their pain too. As we learned from our chapter on inner healing, healing from pain and trauma of all kinds is vital for the work of antiracism.

We are now ready for our next question: *How can lamenting together help us dismantle racism and build beloved community?* Lamenting together forges loving connection between members of a community and sometimes even between communities as we weep with those who weep and rejoice with those who rejoice. We have acknowledged that *solidarity* is vital to beloved community. Lamenting together is what makes solidarity happen. We cultivate solidarity as we feel the weight of other people's pain. In the process, we will discover that beloved community grows and a mutual longing for sustained change is born.

Lamenting together is what makes solidarity happen.

I believe one reason why efforts toward racial reconciliation in the church stall is that our communities resist lament. This is understandable because embracing lament means embracing pain. Many evangelicals prefer to *avoid* the pain of our racial challenges, while others attempt to immediately jump in and *fix* racism. Avoiding pain and fixing pain are preferred over entering into the harder work of solidarity. But true solidarity extends beyond the pursuit of "cheap diversity."[4] True solidarity pursues long-term lament, heartfelt repentance, and systemic transformation.

In our wealth and comfort, we evangelicals are more inclined to praise than to lament. Dr. Soong-Chan Rah reflects on how even though roughly 40 percent of the psalms are laments, a much tinier percentage of our contemporary songs of worship are laments. A recent survey of the top one hundred worship songs sung in churches revealed that only five of the songs could qualify as a lament. Most of the songs reflect themes of praise:

"Happy Day," "Glorious Day," "Marvelous Light," "How Great Is Our God," and "Victory in Jesus."[5]

Nothing is wrong with songs of praise, of course, but Rah reminds us that there has been an imbalance for some time. The contemporary church's resistance to pain and discomfort is one major reason that the church has been ineffective in the sustained pursuit of antiracism. *But we can only dismantle racism to the extent that we are willing to bear racial pain in solidarity with suffering people.* There are no easy fixes, no cut-and-paste solutions. It is through the process of bearing our neighbors' pain that we can best come to understand what is required for lasting change.

Earlier I mentioned how Mark Vroegop practiced sustained personal lament after the tragic passing of his stillborn daughter. This lament was key to his personal healing and reconnection with God. Later in Mark's ministry, God prompted him to pursue racial reconciliation within his own congregation. As Mark did, he made a life-changing connection with members of his church family.

The contemporary church's resistance to pain and discomfort is one major reason that the church has been ineffective in the sustained pursuit of antiracism.

Just as lament had been key to his personal healing after the loss of his daughter, he realized that lament could be key to the racial healing of his community. So he applied what he'd learned from personal lament to community lament, leading to his book *Weep with Me: How Lament Opens a Door for Racial Reconciliation.* Vroegop's story is a beautiful example of how personal lament and corporate lament intersect and enrich each another. This is a game-changing realization for color-courageous disciples: It can help empower our transformation so that we can transform the world.

There are many creative ways that church communities can lament together in our pursuit of beloved community. We can more frequently voice prayers of lament in our worship services—and not just after particularly tragic race-related events, but regularly. We can buck the trend and regularly sing songs of lament, and African American spirituals can be a rich resource. We can provide more education at church about the grievous history of racism and its continuing effects in our contemporary world. We can share stories of joy and pain. We can show up even when we don't fully understand one another . . . while also humbly promising to grow in our understanding.

In the end, lament may be the most powerful way to begin the journey toward beloved community, and lament may also be the most powerful way to sustain it.

Before moving on, let's briefly address three common questions about corporate lament.

Why so much talk about ongoing lament, and when can we move on?

Contemporary American disciples are inclined toward action, and the messiness of lament can make it feel "unproductive," even a waste of valuable time and energy. Nevertheless, as we mourn with those who mourn, God quietly works out his purposes through the process.

As long as some part of the body is suffering, God calls other parts of the body to co-suffer with it. Our unwillingness to suffer together has resulted in many of the racial challenges we now face. Of course, there is a difference between healthy, God-centered weeping and unhealthy, self-centered wallowing. Yet the fact remains that most disciples today are not in danger of lamenting too much.

It is only through sustained solidarity that sophisticated understanding and sustainable systemic solutions can emerge. Our

Savior calls us to carry our cross daily (Luke 9:23). The good news is, we are also called to rejoice daily (Philippians 4:4)! Like lamenting together, rejoicing together is an important means of expressing solidarity. Disciples mourn and disciples rejoice *together*. It's not either/or; it's both/and.

Disciples also understand that one purpose of the Scriptures is to connect us with the errors of the past so that we do not repeat them today. That is precisely the purpose of the book of Lamentations, which later served as a perpetual reminder for Israel to resist idolatry. As we lament the past and teach our children to do the same, we can move toward a different and more beautiful future.

Why should I lament for something I didn't do?

It is technically true that one individual cannot repent for the sins of another. Yet it is also true that the Scriptures portray numerous examples of corporate repentance and lament. Although it may be countercultural today, corporate lament was normative in Scripture. The truth is, "our participation may not be active or direct, but often we are complicit—at least in simply turning a 'blind eye.'"[6] At minimum, today's disciples can express remorse for unjust actions taken in the past that continue to impact the present. Today's disciples can lament their own silence about and passivity in the face of racial inequity. They can lament their indifference toward the pursuit of deeper understanding. And they can lament "the extent to which [they] have contributed to and been a part of a culture that allows, sanctions, or benefits from the sinful actions of others—both past and present."[7]

Corporate repentance has never implied that each individual in a collective is personally responsible. It may help to remember that *repent* means "to pivot." Repentance is most essentially about intentionally choosing to go in a different direction. When we

understand repentance in this way, it is clear that addressing corporate problems will require corporate repentance.

Does it make sense to lament if I'm not sure I understand or agree with the reasons for the lament?

There is only one place in the Bible where it says that "Jesus
wept," and I believe that moment can help us answer this question. After the death of Lazarus, Jesus returned to the home of
Mary and Martha.

> When Jesus saw [Mary] weeping, and the Jews who had come
> along with her also weeping, he was deeply moved in spirit and
> troubled. "Where have you laid him?" he asked.
>
> "Come and see, Lord," they replied.
>
> Jesus wept.
>
> Then the Jews said, "See how he loved him!" (John 11:33–36)

This, for me, is a curious account. Jesus was about to resur-
rect Lazarus, so what was the point of crying about his death?
Further, Jesus challenged the sisters to remember that he was
"the resurrection and the life," meaning that they had no ultimate cause for despair (verse 25). Nevertheless, upon seeing the
grief of the sisters and the rest of the people, Jesus did not judge
them. Instead, Jesus *wept with* them. And the people understood
his weeping to signify love (verse 36). I love how one pastor puts
it: "The Bible calls us to weep with those who weep. It doesn't
tell us to judge whether they should be weeping."[8]

So let us first mourn with those who mourn; then let us
commit to a more sophisticated understanding of the reasons for
that mourning. Friends do not approach other grieving friends

with interrogation. Friends begin by mourning together. Only *as friends* can we have constructive conversations about the nature of the problems we face—and how we might solve them together.

THE GLORY OF DIVINE LAMENT

Effective color-courageous discipleship involves growing in our ability to process pain. Like you, I would rather not deal with pain. If pain were an elective class, I would choose to skip it! Pain is disorienting and exhausting. Yet we know that as we persevere through pain in a posture of lament, we can forge a deeper connection with God as well as deeper shalom in the world.

As we persevere through pain in a posture of lament, we can forge a deeper connection with God as well as deeper shalom in the world.

But we're not done with lament yet. There is a third and even more mysterious type of lament that also has the power to transform our pain. It is divine lament, the lamentation of God himself. This is lament that we *behold*. Once we have eyes to see, we can find divine lament throughout the Scriptures, but we see it most clearly in Jesus.

The word *excruciating* derives from the Latin word *crux,* meaning "cross." Whenever I hear the word, it reminds me that at the beating heart of our faith, there is a God that bore upon himself the excruciating pain that was mine to bear. On the cross, Christ bore the harrowing pain of the whole world—thus defeating pain forever. And he did it with the help of lament.

Although Psalm 22 is a psalm of David, we can also understand it to be the divine lament of Jesus Christ. Jesus prayed this psalm on the cross: "My God, my God, why have you forsaken me?" (Matthew 27:46). Whenever I find myself feeling forsaken by God, I envision Jesus there on the cross, speaking these words, suffering with me. When I begin to shed fresh tears in another moment of despair, I look up—and behold!—I see a God there who is crying with me.

Like Christ, we can persevere through racial pain, and all pain, as we embrace God's gift of lament. And because of Christ, we can know that because he was forsaken in his pain, we never will be. As color-courageous disciples behold the cross together, we can cherish the dazzling display of how God has forever infused pain with redemptive possibility.

MICHAEL EMERSON

PROFESSOR AND AUTHOR OF *DIVIDED BY FAITH: EVANGELICAL RELIGION AND THE PROBLEM OF RACE IN AMERICA*

Michael O. Emerson is professor and head of the department of sociology at the University of Illinois at Chicago. His book *Divided by Faith* received widespread acclaim for its groundbreaking research on how White-culture evangelicalism perpetuates the racial chasm. Currently, Emerson is the principal investigator of the largest study of race and religion ever conducted in the United States, funded by the Lilly Endowment.

How has God uniquely prepared you for color-courageous ministry?

I attended a Promise Keepers men's event back in the 1990s. At the time I had zero awareness of or interest in race in America. I was a White boy who grew up in a tiny town full of White folks in central Minnesota. That was it. But at this event, I had a "Damascus moment." I don't know why, and I've never been the same. I underwent an awakening—although no one was using that term back then. And the message I heard from God was very clear: "Racism is real. It's hurting my people. And you must work to overcome it." My family also discerned a call—and this was the hard part—to live as a racial minority in all aspects of life.

How have you drawn closer to Jesus as you have pursued antiracism?

When that call came, my wife and I had young children. In fact, we were just about to have our third. Over time we relocated to a new neighborhood, church, and schools where we were the minority. We got so much negative feedback, questions like "How can you do this to our grandchildren?" Frankly, we worried about what it all meant for our kids. But I'll never forget how one day, when I was with John Perkins, he said, "God is going to honor your family because of the commitment you made." And you know what? He has. We've had no choice but to hold tightly to Jesus through the years. Our children held tightly to Jesus with us, too, and they have always walked closely with the Lord.

What spiritual practices have you found life-giving on your color-courageous discipleship journey?

Christian community comes to mind first. In our diverse community, my family's world expanded, and we really got a much fuller picture of who God is. We have also realized not only how much we really need one another but also how much we need a diverse community. We've learned so much from others. Bible study has been huge, of course. I also think of giving. We have been very intentional about giving to persons and organizations of color to further their work.

Why is lament important, and what role has it played in your own life?

Following Jesus entails turning, walking in a different direction, leaving something behind. And that can be painful. In the beginning, I came to realize how many things I had denied or just didn't know. I felt embarrassment, sadness, even anger: How did I not see this before? How did my community not see this before? And then to realize that I had also *contributed* to the mess—well, it was horrifying. I went through a period of deep lament, deep sadness. For me, it was like a washing, a cleansing. You can't stay there, of course, but you've got to start there.

What distinguishes a Christian approach to antiracism from a secular approach?

For me, it comes down to realizing that our battle is not against flesh and blood. We have to realize that we are not each other's enemy; we are not in competition with one another in some kind of grand zero-sum game. We are in this together, and we are up against principalities and powers. The enemy is *racism,* and as we defeat racism, we all win. As disciples of Christ, we've got to unite in prayer, fasting, and action. As we do, we will all experience greater freedom.

FURTHER READING

Dark Clouds, Deep Mercy: Discovering the Grace of Lament by Mark Vroegop

Disappointment with God: Three Questions No One Asks Aloud by Philip Yancey

Prophetic Lament: A Call for Justice in Troubled Times by Soong-Chan Rah

Weep with Me: How Lament Opens a Door for Racial Reconciliation by Mark Vroegop

PILGRIMAGE (FOR PERSPECTIVE)

Pursue Transformation Through Incarnation

> Jesus *had* to go through Samaria because that's
> where the path of discipleship leads: right into the places
> where historic, systemic racial conflicts have led
> to division and strife.
>
> —DAVID LEONG, *RACE & PLACE*

Jars upon jars in an endless array, stretching from floor to ceiling—a kaleidoscope of earth colors in tan, clay, cocoa, and black. . . . Standing here, I am startled and nauseated. Each jar brims with soil collected from the site of an American lynching. Each one represents priceless and unique lives, tragically lost. Each one echoes the ancient lament of our Lord: "What have you done? Listen! Your brother's blood cries out to me from the ground" (Genesis 4:10).

On this day, I am one of a group of pilgrims that has arrived at the Equal Justice Initiative in Montgomery, Alabama. This is a stop on a Sankofa Journey, a racial discipleship experience of the Evangelical Covenant Church. Before the journey, I had never heard of *Sankofa,* a word that is both beautiful and wise:

Lynching Jars, Equal Justice Initiative
PHOTO BY MICHELLE T. SANCHEZ

Sankofa is a word from the Akan tribe in Ghana. It means *San* (to return), *ko* (to go), *fa* (to fetch, seek, and take). The bird with its head turned backward taking an egg off its back embodies Sankofa's meaning. Sankofa attests that we must look backward (into our history), before we can faithfully move forward together, in the present and future. The Sankofa experience does just this, by exploring historic sites of the Civil Rights Movement, connecting the freedom struggle of the past to our present realities.[1]

Our journey has included stops like the hotel where Martin Luther King, Jr., was murdered as well as the Edmund Pettus Bridge over which the "Bloody Sunday" protestors marched. More than ever before, I have been able to draw a bold, straight line connecting the past to the present—from slavery, to lynching, to Jim Crow, to mass incarceration and beyond.

To be honest, the Sankofa journey was downright distressing for me. Looking back into the blight of our past is not fun. Centuries ago, my own ancestors purposefully

**Traditional
Sankofa Bird**

uprooted themselves from the South and relocated to the North—and didn't look back. Accordingly, for most of my life, I have dealt with race by striving to forget the past and move toward the future. There is merit to that approach, of course. The Scriptures do encourage us to "[forget] what is behind and [strain] toward what is ahead" (Philippians 3:13). Yet the Scriptures also encourage us to proactively remember the past for the sake of the present: "Remember the days of old; consider the generations long past. Ask your father and he will tell you, your elders, and they will explain to you" (Deuteronomy 32:7). Remembering is especially important where caring for others is concerned: "Continue to remember . . . those who are mistreated as if you yourselves were suffering" (Hebrews 13:3). Like most things in life, it is both/and—the most fruitful way to move toward the future is with transformational wisdom gleaned from the past. We must also get proximate to the pain of both the present *and* the past to become a healing balm for the future. In our contemporary landscape—where racial pain is too often segregated away in both time and space—becoming proximate to pain typically requires a literal journey.

The most fruitful way to move toward the future is with transformational wisdom gleaned from the past.

Journeys like Sankofa are not about tourism; they are about transformation. They pursue travel not for the sake of play but for the sake of perspective. Sankofa has provided hundreds of disciples with a fully embodied opportunity to understand that racial righteousness is a crucial component of discipleship in today's world. In this way, Sankofa has become a powerful contemporary expression of the ancient Christian spiritual practice of pilgrimage.

PILGRIMAGE AS A SPIRITUAL PRACTICE

A Christian **pilgrimage** is an intentional journey undertaken by disciples for the purpose of spiritual formation. While tourism centers on rest and recreation, pilgrimage centers on exploration and transformation. Although there are many types of pilgrimage, one characteristic common to them all is *movement*. The history of pilgrimage within the Christian church is long and rich:

> Although the words *pilgrim* and *pilgrimage* are absent from most English translations of the Bible, the image is a major one, encompassing some of the deepest meanings of what it means to be a follower and worshiper of God. . . . In both Testaments pilgrimage becomes a metaphor for the shape of the earthly life of anyone who is headed toward a heaven beyond this world.[2]

Our faith itself was born on pilgrimage when God told Abraham, "Go from your country, your people and your father's household to the land I will show you"—and Abraham went (Genesis 12:1). Now consider this: God could have worked in and through Abraham precisely where he was, right there in his hometown. All things are possible with God. But in his wisdom, God elected instead to work through pilgrimage.

Later, God sent Israel on a forty-year pilgrimage of purification in the wilderness. Echoing this, Jesus launched his ministry with a forty-day devotional pilgrimage in the Judean desert. The theme of pilgrimage continues throughout the New Testament. In the book of Mark, pilgrimage is "repeatedly emphasized by reminders of Jesus' final journey" and "becomes the dominant image of discipleship" (Mark 8–10).[3] Of course, Jesus ultimately identified himself as the "the pilgrim's path to the Father" (John 14:6).[4] And then, in the book of Acts, Christianity is first called "the Way" (for example, Acts 9:2, 19:9, 22:4).[5]

Pilgrims Leaving Canterbury, 1455–1462
COPYRIGHT © THE BRITISH LIBRARY BOARD

For centuries, Christian disciples have imitated these biblical models by embarking on pilgrimage as an intentional spiritual practice. Early Celtic *peregrini* set out "for the love of Christ" without having a particular destination.[6] Chaucer's fourteenth-century *Canterbury Tales*—one of the most significant early texts in the English language—takes us on an adventure with a motley group that is on pilgrimage from London to a shrine in Canterbury. In the Middle Ages, countless pilgrims made their way to the Holy Land. Among books originally written in English, the most widely printed and translated book of all time is *The Pilgrim's Progress* by John Bunyan, and it's a story about a religious pilgrimage.

Pilgrimage holds transformational potential because it engages disciples as fully embodied creatures.

Ironically, it is far more challenging for contemporary disciples to practice pilgrimage now. This may partially explain the decline of pilgrimage; as travel has become more commonplace, it has simultaneously become less meaningful.

When people think about pilgrimage today, the idea often has a medieval tinge. Many think about how, during the Middle Ages, a pilgrimage was a means of doing penance, earning tickets to heaven (indulgences), and currying magical favors by cozying up with relics and shrines. In reality, though, these are distortions of the promise of pilgrimage.

N. T. Wright's robust Protestant training had him convinced that it was frivolous to travel to "holy" places in search of transcendent experiences. This is of course true because God is everywhere, and no place is holier than any other. Yet over time—and due in part to Wright's extensive studies in Israel—he had a change of heart. He came to understand that pilgrimage holds transformational potential because it engages disciples as fully embodied creatures.

Since racism is a deeply embodied reality, color-courageous disciples would do well to pursue deeply embodied spiritual practices.

Wright's appreciation for pilgrimage grew as he turned away "from various forms of dualism, to which evangelicalism is particularly prone, and towards a recognition of the sacramental quality of God's whole created world."[7] As Protestant disciples, we excel at engaging faith with our minds, but we are comparatively lacking when it comes to engaging faith with our bodies. But teachers know that students learn faster and remember longer when they employ all five senses. This is also how Jesus, our greatest teacher, taught his disciples—educating them through a hearty meal of bread and fish or pointing to coins, fields, and fig trees as object lessons. Since racism is a deeply embodied reality, color-courageous disciples would do well to pursue deeply embodied spiritual practices—and that is where pilgrimage shines.

What is most powerful about pilgrimage is simply this: It spurs us to *move*. In *Sacred Travels,* Christian George jests that today's church suffers from a bad case of "Couch Potato Christianity."[8] We are far too comfortable for our own good, and we resist new dimensions of our call that would unsettle us—literally! It is therefore no surprise that, in so many ways, our faith has become flabby. Pilgrimage is one fully embodied spiritual practice that can get us moving again, a catalyst that can move us out of our comfort zones and into the adventure of color-courageous discipleship.

THE PILGRIMAGE JESUS HAD TO TAKE

Of all the travel that Jesus did with the disciples, his journey to Samaria stands out. No other trip he took is described in this way: "So he left Judea and went back once more to Galilee. Now he had to go through Samaria" (John 4:3–4). *Had to?*

Strictly speaking, he didn't have to. Faithful Jews took the long way around Samaria. It would have been far easier to make a straight shot through Samaria, but faithful Jews knew that was a no-can-do.

Not so with Jesus. Befuddling his disciples yet again, Jesus made clear that he was the kind of rabbi who went *through* Samaria—and he took his disciples right with him. Why?

Author David Leong tells us why in *Race & Place:* "Jesus had to go through Samaria because that's where the path of discipleship leads: right into the places where historic, systemic racial conflicts have led to division and strife."[9] Really? Has your path of discipleship taken you right into places of systemic racial strife? I will confess, that's not typically where my path of discipleship has taken me.

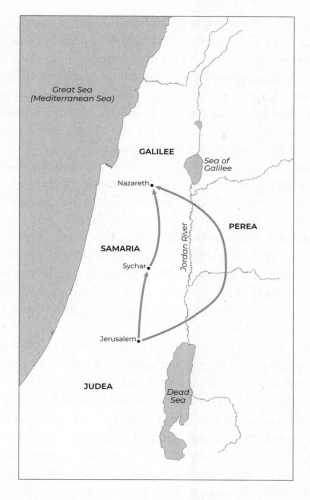

In the same way that the Twelve were flummoxed by the idea of a journey through Samaria, we are just as surprised when we are encouraged to visit—or even hang out in!—our own Samarias today. We especially do not know what to make of those pesky, social-justice-warrior-type disciples who make it sound like going to Samaria is still something that we all *have* to do. Says who?

Naturally, we still seek to "go around" any places that remain segregated by race, poverty, and culture, places blighted by historic and systemic pain. We set up our homes, our churches, and our hearts in neighborhoods that are safe and free of strife; we prefer to pilgrimage to places that are pretty. By default, we go around the places that remind us of hard history and inform us of the painful present. Of course we do! That's only natural. But Jesus calls his disciples to the *super*natural.

What's more, in this text Jesus wasn't leading his disciples to Samaria merely or even primarily to swoop in and save the Samaritans. Sure, the Samaritans needed to be transformed by Jesus—*but so, too, did the disciples.* Although they were committed to Jesus, the disciples remained blind to many dimensions of who Jesus was and what he was up to. Over the course of their pilgrimage through Samaria, the disciples came to a deeper appreciation of their Lord's longing to cross over boundaries of difference in a passionate pursuit to reconcile us both to God and to one another.

Jesus's longing for our reconciliation to God and to one another played out in *geographical* ways. Jesus's ministry centered in Galilee—known as Galilee of the Gentiles—because it was a thriving crossroads of Jewish and Gentile interaction. Then, after going through Samaria, Jesus took an even more scandalous journey to Tyre, a Gentile port city renowned for worldliness (Mark 7:24, NLT). It was in Tyre that Jesus engaged the Syrophoenician woman—a descendant of *Canaanites,* one of the most ancient enemies of the Jewish people (Matthew 15:21–28).[10] Jesus's message is clear: No kind of racial reconciliation is impossible for God. Throughout his life, Jesus crafted disciple-making in specifically geographic ways, culminating in his final words "You will be my witnesses . . . in Jerusalem, throughout Judea, in Samaria, and to the ends of the earth" (Acts 1:8, NLT).

Today's disciples are not called to the exact same locations as the original Twelve were, of course, but that doesn't mean that geography is no longer of any consequence to us. Discipleship has always had uniquely embodied, geographic dimensions; our task is to discern how those dimensions play out today. At the very least, it means posing questions that many others do not:

- Do I regularly consult God not just about *what* I do but also about *where* I do it?
- How did I come to live in this place?
- Who are my neighbors—or, put another way, what is the demographic makeup of my neighborhood and how did it come to be this way?
- What race-related trauma has happened in my area in the past—and what difference does that trauma continue to make today?
- Why do I travel, and how do I choose where I travel?
- Where, exactly, are the hard places I avoid going to (or have never gone to!) within a twenty-five mile to fifty-mile radius of home? Why?

Questions like these can be powerful catalysts for our growth as insightful and impactful color-courageous disciples.

RACE AND PLACE

We become more effective as color-courageous disciples when we learn to "think Christianly" about place, which means consistently asking not just *what* but *where.* Many of the most pressing racial crises that erupt in the news are associated with *place*—concrete locations on the map like Flint, Michigan, or Ferguson, Missouri. Place uniquely sheds light on race:

> What place and geography do . . . is provide a window into the systems and structures of race so that we can see more clearly

how racial issues . . . are not simply the result of "bad apples," or individual people with mean prejudices. Rather, the challenges of race that plague our cities are often rooted in how groups seek and maintain power (either implicitly or explicitly), how cultural patterns become physical structures, and how impersonal systems grow to protect the interests of those in power over time. In other words, geography reveals how race works systemically and not just individually.[11]

The demographic makeup of your neighborhood did not happen neutrally. Historic practices like redlining, predatory lending, discriminatory residential covenants, resistance to low-income housing, and outright scare tactics—to name just a few—have consistently segregated Americans by race. The result is that while the United States has become more diverse over time, segregation nevertheless persists.[12] More than sixty years after *Brown v. Board of Education,* most White people continue to live in majority-White neighborhoods, and most Black and Latino people live in majority-non-White neighborhoods.[13]

Most of us are so used to this segregated state of affairs that we rarely question it. Most probably don't think of it as a problem at all. After all, isn't it just proof that birds of a feather flock together? That is true to some extent, of course, but it belies the more foundational truth that contemporary residential segregation is a result of many painful years of systemic exclusion rather than personal choice. It also further masks the reality that separate still does not mean equal: "There are so many essentials to the American dream that are geographically constrained . . . good schools, proximate jobs, retail amenities, and parks."[14] A lower quality of life is the result in many communities of color because, quite simply, they have "worse access to education, employment opportunities, health care," and more.[15]

I believe that one reason why many disciples remain unmoved by racial inequity is that they literally *do not see it.* Many do not regularly come in contact with what writer, commentator, and political activist Michael Harrington called the "other America," the "invisible underclass that is largely isolated from the structures and opportunities of the dominant culture."[16] In *American Apartheid,* Douglas Massey and Nancy Denton add that "most Americans vaguely realize that urban America is still a residentially segregated society, but few appreciate [its] depth." [17] The fact is, many of today's most grievous injustices regarding both race and class have been relegated to our modern-day Samarias. And since they are out of sight, they are also out of mind—and heart.

Color-courageous disciples, however, come to understand that society remains segregated both literally and figuratively, and they seek to fight this segregation. We are literally segregated *in space* and so remain unaware of and unmoved by the true inequities of our society. We are further segregated *in time,* so we remain aloof from the racial trauma of the past, from the real pain that happened in real places and that continues to impact our world today. A racial discipleship pilgrimage has potential because it proactively protests our many segregations. It is a journey across the divides, a journey that pursues reconciliation in time and space.

PILGRIMAGE AS COLOR-COURAGEOUS DISCIPLESHIP

Prior to her first Sankofa journey, author and pastor Debbie Blue was apprehensive not so much about the journey but about what it would unearth in her own heart. "I was afraid of the anger," she recalls. "I didn't want to go there."[18] But "go there" she did, and it transformed her life.

For more than twenty years, the Evangelical Covenant Church has conducted Sankofa pilgrimages for more than one

Debbie Blue facilitates racial discipleship for a
bus full of sojourners on a Sankofa pilgrimage
PHOTO BY SARAH SWANSON

thousand participants—and counting. Over time, many have
asked about the reasons why the Covenant has flourished as a
multiethnic evangelical denomination. The Sankofa pilgrimage
is one reason. Although relatively few have taken the journey in
comparison to our total Covenant population, a fairly large pro-
portion of Covenant *leaders* have experienced the journey. In
this way Sankofa has had an outsized impact on our church's
unflagging commitment to multiethnic, antiracist ministry.

Originally pioneered by two Covenant leaders, one Black
(Harold Spooner) and one White (Jim Lundeen), Sankofa was
intended to provide our community with a truly immersive racial discipleship experience. The emphasis of Sankofa has been
the exploration of the Black/White experience in America primarily because—with the important exception of Indigenous
Americans—the Black/White story is longest, and the inequities remain greatest. Our decision to begin with the Black experience in America has provided us a firm foundation on which
to build a growing color-courageous engagement with *all* peoples, our ultimate goal.

At its heart, Sankofa is a Christ-centered journey that crosses
divides and enables travelers to connect with real *places,* real *peo-*

ple, and real *stories,* just as the disciples did on their pilgrimage to Samaria. A key component of the experience is that every person is assigned a partner for the journey, with at least one in every pair being a Black participant. The exact itinerary for each individual Sankofa journey has varied over time. Typically, the journey has started on a bus in Chicago followed by travels into the Deep South, taking time to make multiple stops at sites of major civil rights significance. Sankofa makes intentional connections between the *past* and the *present,* and therein lies its true transformational power: *Color-courageous disciples learn to discern the clear connecting lines between the racial inequities of the past and the racial inequities of the present.* If we can better understand those connecting lines, we may be better equipped to disrupt them.

Prior to Sankofa, I heard a lecture on mass incarceration at a pastors' conference, but it moved my heart only incrementally. Of course, lectures are absolutely vital for building awareness, and we have to start somewhere. Yet learning in a classroom setting will always have a limited impact. Embodied experience makes all the difference, and that's what Sankofa was for me. After viewing those jars of lynching soil, we sat in a small auditorium where a tall, soft-spoken gentleman began to tell his story. Anthony Ray Hinton, who grew up poor and Black in Alabama, spent nearly thirty years on death row for a crime he did not commit. His story was a case study of the bias that is still embedded within our criminal justice system. The point was clear: Racial inequity in the criminal justice system is an ongoing reality that stretches from the past to the present.[19] Suddenly, Hinton's story became part of my own.[20] What was I going to do about it?

Reflecting on his own Sankofa journey, Jim Oberg, a White pilgrim from a Covenant church in Owatonna, Minnesota, says that on Sankofa he came to realize that "Black history is everyone's history."[21] Now, whenever he encounters stories of racial challenge, he processes them differently: "Somehow they are now part of my story *because I have been there.*"[22] That is what pilgrimage does: It intertwines our multicolored stories into a beautiful and complex tapestry that has the potential to produce real transformation in oneself and in the world.

Pilgrimages like Sankofa also provide pilgrims of color a dynamic way to process racial identity and pursue healing. One woman of color from a Covenant church shares her experience:

> You can read about things, but experiencing them in relationship with other people is far more life changing. . . . [Sankofa] served as a catalyst to what God has called me to be as a reconciler, a bridge builder. Dealing with my personal identity is why I went on this journey and it has directed my life significantly. . . . I have the freedom to be who I am in Christ and not what others expect of me.[23]

So how was Debbie Blue's pilgrimage? Despite the grip of her apprehension, she chose to embark on the journey. As she courageously faced her fears, they lost their power. In their place, she gained something: a new confidence and a passion for helping others to be reconciled and to become reconcilers. After leading a number of Sankofa journeys herself, Debbie went on to become the first executive minister of compassion, mercy, and justice for the Evangelical Covenant Church, leading many others on pilgrimage as well.[24]

Sankofa pilgrims have moved on to multiply the impact of their experience by creating innovative racial discipleship pilgrimages across North America. Greg Yee, a Chinese American Covenant leader deeply impacted by Sankofa, launched a similar experience on the West Coast called *Journey to Mosaic (J2M)*. This pilgrimage takes the next step and explores racial dynamics beyond the Black/White divide. More recently, there have been conversations about crafting a Sankofa 2.0 experience as well as more targeted pilgrimages into the experiences and challenges of Indigenous Americans and Latino immigrants. Through pilgrimage, we can leverage the power of embodied experience for color-courageous discipleship.

EMBARK: PILGRIMAGE AFAR

After transitioning from her full-time role at the Evangelical Covenant Church, Debbie Blue continued on pilgrimage as an individual. For some time, she had been feeling compelled to go on pilgrimage to learn more about the Indigenous American experience. Over time, Debbie has now independently embarked with friends and colleagues on three journeys, including a pilgrimage on the Trail of Tears. Debbie's life bears witness to the fact that racial discipleship is truly a lifelong journey. In her own words, "The journey is not over!"

Whether undertaken as an individual or with a group, the spiritual practice of pilgrimage can have great impact, but either way, it takes initiative. If you find yourself in a position of ministry influence, you have a phenomenal opportunity to tailor a pilgrimage experience for your group. Mark Vroegop, whom we referred to in our previous chapter, tells the story of his own church in *Weep with Me:*

> For years our church had offered global vision trips to catch a vision for unreached people groups. Vision trips shaped the global-mission culture of our church as people saw firsthand the opportunity and the needs around the world. I was hoping for the same impact with racial reconciliation.
>
> I knew the trip would form new relationships between people from different ethnicities as they traveled together and processed their experience. . . .
>
> The trip became a pilgrimage.
>
> But not without risk. . . .
>
> Our journey was designed to bring change.[25]

So what does it take to design a pilgrimage? In *The Pilgrim Journey: A History of Pilgrimage in the Western World,* James Harpur offers five stages that have traditionally characterized pilgrimage throughout history. These traditional stages can be used to craft modern-day pilgrimages: preparation, departing journey, sacred rituals (which I will call "spiritual practices"), return journey, and reintegration.[26]

STAGE	KEY ELEMENTS
Preparation	Purpose Introductions Common Language
Departing Journey	Awareness Storytelling Relationship Building
Spiritual Practices	Exploration Commemoration Spiritual Disciplines
Return Journey	Reflection Group Processing
Reintegration	Envisioning Goal Setting Review

In *preparation,* it is important to establish a clear purpose and define hoped-for outcomes. Assign prework. Introduce the pilgrims in the group and the subject matter to be explored. (Before Sankofa, I made my way through a fairly extensive pre-assignment list.) Invite participants to an orientation to clarify common language, establish expectations, and answer questions.

The *departing journey* is the ideal time for storytelling, just as the pilgrims did in *The Canterbury Tales.* After all, the shortest distance between people—*and two communities*—is a story. On Sankofa, participants receive prompts and the opportunity to share their story with a partner of a different background. Pilgrims can take in more stories through both film and large-group sharing as well as through podcasts, magazines, audio tours, and live conversations with residents, tour guides, and museum staff.

Spiritual practices are essential; they are what distinguish a pilgrimage from mere tourism. You can design spiritual practices to engage God throughout the entire journey. Examples include lament, Scripture reading, prayer walks, intercession, fasting, feasting (breaking bread across boundaries of difference), financial giving, spiritual direction, and ceremonies of remembrance. Vroegop has focused on lament on his pilgrimages. After teaching the four elements of lament (turning, complaining, asking, and trusting), he encourages pilgrims to write their own psalm of lament along the way.[27]

The *return journey* is the time for processing one's experiences. Open-ended questions are most helpful for this stage: "What has been most impactful for me on this journey?" or "What do I consider my top three learnings—and why?" Responses can be processed both individually and as a group.

Finally, *reintegration* ensures that pilgrimage is not a one-time event but a catalyst for ongoing transformation. For a time, my Sankofa partner Cheryl and I followed up our pilgrimage with a monthly meeting for reflection and accountability. We knew that if we didn't, we could too easily slip right back into old patterns. Those conversations continue to bear fruit even for some of the content of this book. Perhaps the most important reintegration practice is to set specific goals and specify concrete next steps for color-courageous discipleship. For this, I highly recommend *How to Fight Racism: Courageous Christianity and the Journey Toward Racial Justice* by Jemar Tisby. This is the most practical resource I have seen that identifies concrete next steps in what he calls the "ARC of racial justice": awareness, relationship building, and commitment.[28]

Many parents have wondered how to do color-courageous discipleship as a family. Pilgrimage is an outstanding approach. My friend Erin Chan Ding, who is Chinese American, takes her children every year to the DuSable Museum of African American History in Chicago for Martin Luther King Day. It is a tradition for her family because when Erin was a child, her father took her to the museum every Martin Luther King Day as well. Those trips with her father have had a lasting impact.

When Erin's family travels, they also consider possibilities for pilgrimage "detours." On one trip, for example, Erin and her family stopped in Montgomery at the National Memorial for Peace and Justice and visited several other historic civil rights sites in Selma and Birmingham before dropping her son, Chandler, off at Space Camp in Huntsville, Alabama. Of course, as a mom to young kids, Erin is also realistic: Any family pilgrimage should include ample time for rest, connection, and fun. That's why her family pilgrimage with Chandler *also* featured stops for bubble tea!

Reflecting on these family experiences, Erin said, "I realized that kids process the heaviness of history in different ways. On one ninety-degree day, Chandler, who was nine years old, and I were standing in the sanctuary of the Sixteenth Street Baptist Church in Birmingham, where four girls lost their lives in a bombing by White supremacists in September 1963. Chandler looked at me, eyes wide, and said, 'Mommy, murders happened right here.' He paused, gazing at the stained glass windows, and then asked, 'Are we going to get ice cream?' Later, even as he licked his chocolate cone, I hoped that his physical presence at this site of tragedy and resilience would prompt the beginnings of a holistic understanding of history while building empathy and solidarity in his little heart."

Following Erin's example, I now have a goal of taking my

Erin Chan Ding's son, Chandler, gazes up at columns
at the National Memorial for Peace and Justice that
represent American counties where racial terror
lynchings took place

PHOTO BY ERIN CHAN DING

own children on pilgrimages designed to foster our color-courageous discipleship as a family. Washington, D.C., is an especially rich and accessible location for families given its plethora of cultural showcases designed to prompt conversations around diversity, citizenship, and equality for all peoples, including the United States Holocaust Memorial Museum, the National Museum of the American Indian, and the National Museum of African American History and Culture, to name a few.[29]

Perhaps one day your own pilgrimage will take you and your family across the globe. While my friend and colleague Lance Davis was still pastoring a local church, he designed a Sankofa pilgrimage to Ghana—home to some of the most infamous slave ports. His Ghana Sankofa itineraries have included sites such as the W.E.B. Du Bois Memorial Centre for Pan-African Culture in Accra, the River of the Last Bath (for those captured by slave trappers) at Assin Manso, and the coastal castles and slave dungeons at Elmina.[30]

The possibilities for pilgrimage are endless. Obviously, not everyone can go on costly, far-flung racial discipleship journeys. In different seasons of life, we each have constraints of various kinds—time, family responsibilities, money, or even limitations on travel itself, as we have so sadly witnessed throughout the Covid-19 pandemic. Surprisingly, though, there are still creative ways to take a racial discipleship pilgrimage at home.

FESTIVAL: PILGRIMAGE AT HOME

Here is a delightful truth: "Because the presence of God extends everywhere, even unto the very ends of the earth, pilgrimage can be practiced by anyone, anywhere, anytime."[31] Doing so, however, requires a shift in perspective:

> Pilgrimage, then, may refer to an inner—emotional, mental, and spiritual—journey as well as an outer, physical one: for Kempis [*The Imitation of Christ*] and Bunyan [*The Pilgrim's Progress*] it is possible for the pilgrim to remain in a cloister or a prison cell and yet go on a pilgrimage. Even so, inner pilgrimage, like its external counterpart, still implies *movement—toward a new spiritual state of being.*[32]

Let's explore a biblical approach to pilgrimage from home: the Jewish festivals or feasts. All Israelite men were required to go on a physical pilgrimage to Jerusalem during each of the festivals of Passover, Pentecost, and Tabernacles (Exodus 23:17; Deuteronomy 16:16). But for those who did not or could not go on pilgrimage—women, children, the elderly, and the infirm—God provided a replacement through multisensory festival celebrations. The biblical festivals were *fully immersive discipleship experiences* designed to forge vital links between the past and the present. For example, the Festival of Passover commemorates the

Hebrew nation's exodus from slavery in Egypt. The elements of the Passover feast (*seder*) symbolically tell the story. Bitter herbs represent the bitterness of bondage in Egypt; the lamb shank recalls the blood of the lamb on the doors; and unleavened bread (*matzah*) helps participants remember the swiftness of God's deliverance. During the weeklong Festival of Tabernacles, Israelites resided in *sukkoth,* temporary shelters meant to remind them of God's provision through their forty-year sojourn in the wilderness.[33]

When pilgrimage is not possible, immersive festivals can also catalyze color-courageous discipleship at home. The act of observing festivals with ethnic themes ideally serves a dual purpose. On the one hand, these festivals *foster multicultural appreciation.* We know that ethnicity is a God-ordained gift and that history will climax in a rich, multiethnic celebration—but why wait until then to enjoy the party? Festivals are meant to highlight the unique contributions, past and present, of each ethnic group. They are also fantastic opportunities to intentionally *foster color-courageous awareness and action.* Racism has prevented us from enjoying all that every ethnic group has to contribute, both to the church and to the larger society. So what has that looked like for each ethnic group—and what can we do about it now?

Here are some examples of what festivals have looked like for me. In the depths of the Covid-19 pandemic, when my family and so many others could not take a physical pilgrimage, we decided instead to celebrate the festival of Kwanzaa for the first time. **Kwanzaa** was established amid the Civil Rights Movement as a seven-day celebration of African American heritage. It was not originally a Christian holiday, but we infused it with Christian meaning. Since my husband is Colombian American, making my children Afro-Latino, we also expanded it to include their Latino heritage. Every day of Kwanzaa, we read a biography of a famous leader of color, reflected on all the challenges they overcame, and considered how we could make a difference as color-courageous disciples of Christ. We ate traditional foods, lit symbolic candles, engaged in conversation, and enjoyed festive music. It was a blast!

Another opportunity for an at-home pilgrimage is **Juneteenth,** a festival that has been commemorated by African Americans for more than 150 years in celebration of the emancipation of enslaved people in the United States. In addition, entire months honor communities of color. May, for instance, is Asian American and Pacific Islander Heritage Month and from September 15 to October 15 is National Hispanic American Heritage Month. To be clear, these commemorations can be observed by both the designated group as well as their allies and friends. After all, the whole point of something like Black History Month (February) is to invite *everyone* to appreciate Black cultures and contributions. Christian disciples and entire church communities can go one step further by infusing these multiethnic but secular observances with faith-based meaning.

INCARNATION: MAKING PILGRIMAGE PERMANENT

I would be remiss if I did not finish this discussion with an even more fundamental challenge: More of us should consider making pilgrimage a long-term or even permanent commitment. This happens, of course, when pilgrimage actually becomes *relocation* and *incarnation*. John M. Perkins, civil rights luminary and founder of the Community Christian Development Association, has long identified three pillars for high-impact community building: relocation, redistribution, and reconciliation. Foundational to them all is relocation: "Jesus relocated. . . . He didn't commute back and forth to heaven. . . . Relocation transforms 'you, them, and theirs' to 'we, us, and ours.'"[34]

In *The Power of Proximity,* Michelle Warren notes that "the most profound move you can make to address pain and injustice is to become proximate to it."[35] True transformation sees not only neighborhoods, but neighbors. My friend Dominique Gilliard encourages the church to "commission people to proximity." We need to get proximate to

> those people that the world has taught us to avoid. Those places and spaces that this world has taught us to do everything we can to actually go around. Those are the places I believe that we're actually called to be most intentional about going to, because when we go to those places, we actually get to see beyond the rhetoric, and we get to start to see that this is our brother and sister, this is our neighbor.[36]

As we disciples seek to live out our most important mandate from Jesus to love our neighbor, more of us should at least consider *becoming* neighbors to those most in need. For Jesus, the word *neighbor* was fundamentally a verb. So we would do well to routinely ask our Lord, "Jesus, where would you have me live? Where would you have me neighbor, and why?" Remember, these are not once-and-for-all decisions. People relocate multiple times throughout life. My husband and I now live in a calm suburb of Chicago, but we've also lived in the teeming metropolis of New York City and in an intentional community in a low-income Massachusetts neighborhood. Our journey continues—and who knows were God might direct us next?

NOT A PICNIC, BUT A PILGRIMAGE

As Billy Graham once quipped, Jesus "invited us not to a picnic, but to a pilgrimage."[37] God desires to open our eyes to important realities from the past and the present, and pilgrimage holds great potential for doing exactly that.

The disciples were clueless as to why Jesus took them on a pilgrimage through Samaria. They were even more clueless—shocked speechless, actually—when Jesus intentionally interacted with a low-class woman there. After she departed, the disciples tried to avoid the embarrassing incident entirely by offering Jesus some lunch. He refused: "My food . . . is to do the will of him who sent me and to finish his work. Don't you have a saying, 'It's still four months until harvest'? I tell you, open your eyes and look at the fields! They are ripe for harvest" (John 4:34–35).

Due to our color-blind reading of the Scriptures, we usually think of these words as referring to evangelism. Yet when we read these words in living color, we understand that Jesus was referring to a more comprehensive vision of reconciliation with God *and* with one another. On pilgrimage, Jesus sought to open his disciples' eyes to the urgent work of *harvesting holistic reconciliation*—both with God and across racial divides. As Leong prophetically enjoins,

> I believe Jesus is calling his church again, just as he did with the disciples that day in Samaria, to open our eyes and look. The fields around us have been blighted by racial conflict and cultural tensions, but they are ripe for reaping the fruit of reconciliation. By the Spirit, Jesus is continuing to move into our Samarias. I hope we will respond to Jesus' invitation to follow.[38]

The end of a pilgrimage is actually not an end, but a beginning: "a gateway into a new way of being, of seeing life afresh with spiritually cleansed eyes."[39] Jesus took the disciples on pilgrimage not only to open the eyes of the Samaritans but to open the eyes of the disciples as well.

GREG YEE

FOUNDER OF JOURNEY TO MOSAIC

Greg Yee serves as a superintendent with the Evangelical Covenant Church (ECC). He is the founder of the Journey to Mosaic, a multiethnic discipleship pilgrimage of the ECC's Pacific Northwest Conference. In 2020, the ECC awarded Greg the Irving C. Lambert Award, given annually to a leader who exemplifies a commitment to urban or ethnic ministry. Yee is the first Asian North American to receive the award in its thirty-nine-year history.

How has God uniquely prepared you for color-courageous ministry?

I grew up as a fifth-generation Chinese American in East Oakland, a predominantly Black neighborhood, so I have always been conscious of race and its effects. For most of my life, my Christian experiences were in predominantly Chinese churches and ministries. But when God called me to plant a church, I was invited to join the Evangelical Covenant Church, a vibrant multiethnic denomination. Eventually, I gained a vision for the multiethnic kingdom of God that we see so beautifully expressed in Revelation 7.

How have you grown closer to Jesus as you have pursued racial righteousness, and what spiritual practices have been particularly life-giving for you on the journey?

When I am in a diverse community, I get a bigger picture of God. No one culture captures all of God. Another life-giving spiritual practice for me has been hospitality. Even the simple practice of making eye contact with a person from a different ethnic background can warm a relationship and spark a connection. For me, longsuffering is also a deeply meaningful spiritual practice. This journey is hard. To both survive and thrive, we need to cultivate the spiritual disciplines of not despairing, suffering in hope, and awakening to the promise of the "already but not yet" kingdom of God.

Can you explain the Journey to Mosaic pilgrimage and how it came about?

I had been on the ECC's Sankofa Journey, which engages the Black/White racial experience. It was excellent, but as a person of color who is not Black, I wanted to expand the narrative. That's how I conceived of Journey to Mosaic. It's a multiethnic discipleship pilgrimage designed to raise awareness of the experiences of Latinos, Asian Americans, African Americans, and European Americans. Participants have toured sites like the Japanese American National Museum in Los Angeles; the reservation of the Yakama Nation in Toppenish, Washington; the Tacoma Chinese Reconciliation Park in Washington; Black Panther sites in Oakland, California; and a migrant farmworkers' camp in California's Central Valley. It's been an incredibly rich multiethnic discipleship experience.

Why is pilgrimage a helpful discipleship practice for us?

One reason is, it's embodied. I think we too often get stuck in our own minds, our own ideas, our own histories. Western civilization has always struggled with dualism—with the separation of our physicality from our spirituality and intellect. But we are holistic, embodied beings, and pilgrimage works because it is a deeply incarnational experience. Also, although pilgrimage can be done alone, it has traditionally been done in community. I believe there's a reason for that. My experience is that doing pilgrimage in life-on-life community—diving into one another's stories—is where the most stretching discipleship happens.

What advice would you like to give those thinking about crafting their own pilgrimage?

You definitely don't have to get it right on the first try. (I didn't!) Things won't go according to plan, and that's okay. You will learn. I also recommend investing the substantial resources that are needed to make the pilgrimage a quality discipleship experience. You will find that it's worth the investment.

FURTHER READING

Sacred Travels: Recovering the Ancient Practice of Pilgrimage by Christian Timothy George

Race & Place: How Urban Geography Shapes the Journey to Reconciliation by David P. Leong

A Family Guide to the Biblical Holidays: With Activities for All Ages by Robin Sampson and Linda Pierce

Weep with Me: How Lament Opens a Door for Racial Reconciliation by Mark Vroegop (appendix contains a sample pilgrimage itinerary)

FAST (FOR REAL)

Sacrifice Your Power to Build Beloved Community

Fasting ... is not mere self-denial, but rather
an earnest preparation for the feast
of beloved community.

—JONATHAN WILSON-HARTGROVE

So you might be thinking: *What in the world is the connection between fasting and color-courageous discipleship?* I'm so glad you asked, because fasting is precisely where this whole book has been leading.

Okay, but now you're wondering, *Is missing lunch really that important for antiracism?* The answer: nope. That's why I won't be talking too much here about missing lunch. What I *do* want to talk about is the disciple's call to self-sacrifice. **Fasting** has traditionally been about the denial of food, but in reality, it has always pointed to something more profound: the denial of self in order to build beloved community. I find it intriguing to see how the Scriptures make a clear connection between fasting and justice. Listen to what God says about it:

Is not this the kind of fasting I have chosen:
to loose the chains of injustice
    and untie the cords of the yoke,
to set the oppressed free . . .
    and not to turn away from your own flesh and blood?
    (Isaiah 58:6–7)

Fasting has always pointed to something more profound: the denial of self in order to build beloved community.

Since this kind of fasting is important to God, particularly when it comes to the formation of a just community, then it should be important to us too. In the end, color-courageous disciples will have maximum impact when they courageously choose to fast *for real*.

THE LORD'S CHOSEN FAST

The verses we just read come from the book of Isaiah and highlight the intriguing connection between fasting and justice. So let's go deeper with Isaiah. It has been called the Mount Everest of Hebrew prophecy; Isaiah's ministry spanned the reigns of four kings of Judah and lasted at least forty years. Isaiah's contemporaries exhibited fire for God through their rigorous spiritual practices. Ultimately, however, *all their personal piety was failing to build beloved community.* In fact, their piety obstructed beloved community. Isaiah's unenviable task was to deliver the message that God viewed the people's religious activities as a colossal exercise in missing the point.

Listen to God's own searing words on this: "The multitude of your sacrifices—what are they to me? . . . Stop bringing meaningless offerings! . . . I cannot bear your worthless assemblies. Your . . . appointed festivals I hate with all my being. They have become a burden to me. I am weary of bearing them" (Isaiah 1:11, 13–14).

I think we can agree: Worship that aggravates God isn't quite what we're going for, right? Actually, God is quite clear about what he'd like instead: "Learn to do good; seek justice, correct oppression" (Isaiah 1:17, ESV). What we learn here is that *spiritual practices that do not ultimately prepare us to do good, seek justice, and correct oppression in the real world become wearisome to God.* Back to Isaiah 58, which specifically applies this idea to the spiritual practice of fasting:

> Is not this the kind of fasting I have chosen:
> to loose the chains of injustice
>   and untie the cords of the yoke,
> to set the oppressed free
>   and break every yoke?
> Is it not to share your food with the hungry
>   and to provide the poor wanderer with shelter—
> when you see the naked, to clothe them,
>   and not to turn away from your own flesh and blood?
> Then your light will break forth like the dawn,
>   and your healing will quickly appear;
> then your righteousness will go before you,
>   and the glory of the LORD will be your rear guard.
>   (verses 6–8)

In the surrounding context of this passage, we find wordplay with the Hebrew *ḥāpēṣ,* which means "delight." Apparently, the people delighted to know God's ways (verse 2, ESV), and they delighted to draw near to God (verse 2, ESV). Yet God was not delighting in any of their sacrifices, offerings, incense, assemblies, feasts, festivals, or even their prayer (Isaiah 1:11, 13–15). He rebuked his people: *You are seeking your own delight as you do religion—not mine.* The people's religious practice had majored on navel-gazing—it was more about self-fulfillment than about fulfilling God's dream for beloved community.

This Scripture does not do away with traditional fasting. Fasting from food continues to have powerful transformational potential. But, in the end, God desires that all our spiritual practices—including fasting—will impact both us *and* our world.

FAST TO TRANSFORM YOUR WORLD

With the passing of years, I have increasingly realized that trying to change the world is usually folly. The list of people who have measurably changed the entire world is quite short. Nevertheless, I can seek to change *my* world—my unique sphere of influence—on a daily basis.

This is precisely where fasting comes in. Just as God taught us in the book of Isaiah, you can creatively reimagine fasting as *the practice of making tangible sacrifices in order to transform your world.* And when it comes to antiracism, the sacrifice of power may be the most important sacrifice that color-courageous disciples can make. Our model for sacrificing our power is Christ: "Having loved his own who were in the world, he loved them to the end. . . . Jesus knew that the Father had put all things under his power . . . so he . . . began to wash his disciples' feet" (John 13:1, 3–5). After this, Jesus then called his own disciples to imitate him by sacrificing power for the sake of love (verses 12–17).

My guess is that most disciples do not think of themselves as powerful or go around musing about how powerful they are (although I know that some probably do!). So let's reframe *power.* The truth is, within our spheres of influence, we *all* enjoy different types of power to different degrees. Let's consider four types of power that are vital for color-courageous disciples: (1) **privilege,** (2) **position,** (3) **platform,** and (4) **prosperity.**

Power Audit Practice

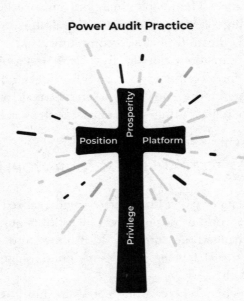

Brothers and sisters, if there is only one next step you take after reading this book, please make it a **power audit**—the ongoing practice of identifying the different types of power that you hold so that you can leverage those powers for good. The first step of a power audit is to discern what each of these four types of power looks like in your own life at any given time. The second step is to identify tangible sacrifices you can make in each of the four areas for the sake of building beloved community. Consider arranging—as I do—the four types of power into the shape of the cross. Ultimately, I pursue these sacrifices as a means of taking up my cross daily in love (Luke 9:23). For a free handout that you can use for your power audit practice, please visit https://michelletsanchez.com/colorcourageous.

This practice will be even more transformational and effective as you share your power audit practice with other color-courageous disciples who can provide accountability and encouragement as you continue the journey. Consider the very word *encouragement*—to give courage. We were never meant to pursue the color-courageous discipleship journey alone but to encourage one another in communities of love (Hebrews 10:25).

When it comes to antiracism, the sacrifice of power may be the most important sacrifice that color-courageous disciples can make.

Although we may not find the phrase *power audit* in the Bible, I believe we see each of the four sacrificial practices in the life of Queen Esther. She is, for me, a stunning portrayal of what it means to be color-courageous. Let's turn to her story now.

As the story opens, we find a Jewish community living in Persia as a marginalized ethnoreligious minority. King Xerxes and his wife, Vashti, had a major falling out, so he kicked her to the curb. There was no eHarmony in those days, so the king announced a beauty pageant so he could pick a new queen. Esther, a young Jewish orphan, saw this as her Cinderella moment: She hid her ethnic identity, won the pageant, and was ushered into royalty.

Unfortunately, her story didn't end here with a happily-ever-after. Haman, the king's right-hand man, despised the Jews and eventually convinced the king to slaughter them all on a specific date. Now pay attention: Esther responded to this grievous situation with fasting not only from food but also from power. At the possible cost of her own life, Esther finally revealed her ethnic identity to the king and successfully advocated for the lives of her people. In a stunning reversal, the king put Haman to death, and the entire Jewish community was saved. To this day, Jews celebrate this remarkable turn of events with the festival of Purim (Esther 9).

Now here's a curious thing: Fasting is the only spiritual practice named in the book of Esther. This is highly unusual for a book of the Bible. In the past, some have even questioned whether the book of Esther should be included in the Bible at all. Not even worship or prayer are mentioned—or clearly practiced—anywhere in the story. That makes me wonder: *Perhaps other spiritual practices aren't mentioned in the book of Esther because we're meant to pay special attention to fasting—fasting for real.* As noted above, Esther fasted from food, yes. But more important, she fasted from *power.* She willingly sacrificed privilege, position, platform, and prosperity to love her community. Let's take a closer look at each.

1. Privilege: How are you sacrificing or leveraging your unearned advantages for good?

Privilege is simply a way of referring to unearned advantage. There are many types of privilege, but we are concerned here with **racial privilege.** Most, if not all, societies harbor an invisible hierarchy in which some races, ethnicities, or cultures have historically held greater status than others. Although there is of course nothing inherently beneficial about being born White, our socially constructed hierarchy in America often bestows Whiteness with advantages. In America, "White" has been equated with "better" for hundreds of years. Those navigating this reality have generated a whole new lexicon with terms such as **White supremacy** and *White privilege.* I understand that not all White people *feel* privileged or somehow experience everything easier in life. In fact, plenty of White people find themselves worse off than many people of color—and, for that matter, worse off than many other Whites. In these cases, it can help to understand privilege as *the relative absence of disadvantage*. I like how David Swanson, who is a White pastor, puts it: "This is not to say that white people in America do not face injustices, even systemic ones—only that we don't face them *because of our race*."[1]

That being said, *privilege is not something that only White people have.* Unearned advantage comes in countless varieties. Esther's story is a wonderful case study for this. Her story begins by drawing attention to Esther's stunning beauty, which is a "privilege" in that she did nothing to earn or deserve it. She still had to decide, though, how to leverage that beauty—whether for selfish purposes or for some greater purpose.

As a Black woman I have always thought of myself as disadvantaged, but I have come to understand I have privilege too. In fact, I have lots of it. I did nothing to be born into a middle-class family and raised in a neighborhood with well-resourced schools. And these realities bestow real advantages upon me in life, advantages that many others do not have.

The tool of **intersectionality** helps us identify and leverage the unique privileges we hold due to overlapping identities in different, ever-shifting contexts. When we view Esther's story through the lens of intersectionality, we can identify her disadvantages as a woman and an ethnic minority. We can also identify her stunning beauty as the advantage that allowed her access to the most powerful people and resources in the land. We still read about Esther today because she chose to sacrificially leverage her privilege for the sake of her community.

Jesus did exactly the same with his own "privilege." Jesus enjoyed the lifelong status of equality with God, yet Jesus "did not consider equality with God something to be used to *his own advantage*" (Philippians 2:6). Instead, he lovingly relinquished his personal advantage to save our lives and make us whole.

2. Position: How are you sacrificing or leveraging your positional power? In what ways are you making space for others to have positional power?

Position is about your roles and the spheres of influence that come with them. We all have clear spheres of influence both through relational roles (mother, spouse, brother, friend, pastor, coach, small-group leader) as well as organizational roles (PTA member, elder board appointee, work supervisor, interview committee member, event planning team member, etc.).

The power of position can be overt, but more often it is quiet and unseen. As Hamilton put it in the musical, having power means being "in the room where it happens."[2] Position is what grants you access to the room where it happens. In a family, that room may be the dining room; in an organization, it's the boardroom.

The real climax of Esther's story is the moment she realized that she must decide, *What will I do with my position? Will I use my position to preserve my own life? Or will I use it to help my people and possibly lose my position and even my life as a result?* Notice that Esther ultimately processes these questions not by herself, but in community, with her cousin Mordecai. Mordecai encourages Esther—that is, he prompts her to have courage. Despite the risks entailed, he challenged Esther to intervene: "Who knows but that you have come to your royal position for such a time as this?" (Esther 4:14). I love this question for so many reasons. Most of all, I love it simply because it is a *question*. Mordecai prompted Esther to wonder about a question that all color-courageous disciples should consider: *How might God be inviting us to leverage our position for his glory?* After all, that is precisely why we have been blessed with our position in the first place.

Color-courageous disciples can *leverage* position by using position to make a difference in our sphere of influence. Parents can engage their children in racial discipleship, and Sunday school teachers can ensure that racial discipleship is included in the curriculum. A member of an interview committee can ensure that the search pool is diverse and draw attention to forms of unconscious bias that might taint an interview process. A missions committee member at a local church can point out opportunities to partner with ministries in local disinvested communities of color.

Other times, it may be best to voluntarily *relinquish* position. For many years, the Evangelical Covenant Church has had a commission, now called the Mosaic Commission, whose purpose has been to advocate for our constituencies of color. And, for as many years, the Mosaic Commission had been chaired by the president of the Covenant—which, as of this writing, has always been a White person. But soon after assuming his new role as Covenant president, John Wenrich chose to relinquish his de facto position as chair. While still remaining a member, John stepped aside so that a leader of color could assume the position of chair of the Mosaic Commission for the first time. I can testify that since John relinquished this position, the Covenant has continued to make pacesetting progress when it comes to racial diversity, biblical equity, and inclusion.

Keep in mind that most of the positions we will hold in life are actually temporary, so the time to act is now. You have God-given opportunities *right now* to dismantle racism, and these opportunities will not last forever. What would it look like for you to make the most of your positional influence . . . for such a time as this?

3. Platform: In what ways are you publicly advocating with your voice? How are you elevating or amplifying other voices?

While the power of position is often exercised quietly, platform is about taking a public stand. Anyone who has a voice has a potential platform, and you can leverage your platform whenever you advocate for antiracism.

Advocacy is a vital practice for the people of God. **Advocacy** is the practice of standing up and speaking out for what is right on someone else's behalf. God commands us to "defend the weak and the fatherless; uphold the cause of the poor and oppressed" (Psalm 82:3) and to "speak up for those who cannot speak for themselves" (Proverbs 31:8, NLT). Advocacy is a vital part of building beloved community:

> We reflect God's love when we call on leaders to protect the most vulnerable and marginalized people in our communities. As Christians we work toward a just world in which structures and institutions give every person the opportunity to thrive. . . . Providing direct assistance to people in need is vital, but it is also important to guard against policies that oppress, to partner with marginalized communities for long-term change, and to *speak up for policies that empower all people.*[3]

Notice that advocacy often comes down to addressing *policies.* A policy is simply a high-level plan. Systemic racism persists through policies that continue to produce racial inequity over time, whether intentionally or unintentionally. Esther was color-courageous in that she utilized her platform to oppose an unjust ethnic policy. The Jewish people were suddenly confronted with an unjust *policy* of ethnic genocide—and they certainly did not have the power to speak for themselves. But Esther *did* have the God-given power of voice. So Mordecai implored her to not "remain silent" and to use her voice in advocacy (Esther 4:14).

Now, anyone who approached the king unbidden faced a potential death sentence. Nevertheless, Esther made her choice: "Go, gather together all the Jews who are in Susa, and fast for me. . . . I and my attendants will fast as you do. When this is done, I will go to the king, even though it is against the law. *And if I perish, I perish*" (Esther 4:16).

I love how the Latin word *vox* ("voice") and the word *vocare* ("to call") are related. Whenever you are called (*vocare*) to be courageous, it will typically involve raising your voice (*vox*) in some way. Doing so comes with consequences—both positive and negative. Nevertheless, color-courageous disciples are called to the risk of raising their voice. Will there be pushback? For sure. This is what Jemar Tisby says about pushback in *How to Fight Racism:*

> There will be those who question why "you're making this about race." Others will want to argue endlessly about a particular turn of phrase or one part of your actions rather than attending to the general thrust of what you're trying to say. Some will disavow you. . . . But you should be prepared for positive reactions too. . . . No matter the reaction or the ratio of positive to negative responses, using your platform to promote racial justice is simply the right thing to do.[4]

When it comes to platform, you can also consider *how you might step back to create access for other voices.* Some Christians, however, have understood Proverbs 31:8—"Speak up for those who cannot speak for themselves"—to mean that they should perpetually use *their own* voice to speak for "voiceless" people. But this mindset quickly becomes problematic:

> An Indigenous leader once confronted church leaders who wanted to take part in Indigenous justice work. . . . He said to them, *With respect, I'm not voiceless; you are deaf.* Voicelessness is rare and justice advocates must take the time to listen before acting. Listening includes a commitment to working directly with people who experience injustice in order to confront the injustice together.[5]

In her viral article "The Case for Diversity on Your Conference Stage," Helen Lee counsels: "Whenever people of color see a Christian conference demonstrating a complete lack of awareness or willingness to present a full picture of God's kingdom, we hear the following messages: *You are not welcome here. Your perspective is not needed here. Your voice is not one we want to hear.*"[6] In reality, we all are interdependent in Christ: We need one another's gifts, perspectives, and voices to reach the full stature of Christ together. Lee urges leaders to platform more voices of color— not so that we will be "politically correct" but so that as the body of Christ, we all might experience deeper transformation and a fuller taste of the kingdom of God.

4. Prosperity: How are you giving generously of your resources to advance biblical equity?

Prosperity takes many forms, so it helps to first identify the different types of resources we have at our disposal. An oft-utilized framework for thinking about resources is time, talent, and treasure. Remember, too, that our resources usually do not remain static over the course of our lives. As we move through different life stages or in and out of different positions, our resources change. Young people are rich in time; tradespeople are rich in skill; many professionals are rich in assets. We are all rich in different ways at any given time.

Color-courageous disciples seek to steward the resources they have at their disposal in order to level the scales. Undoubtedly some people will wonder if "leveling the scales" is really a veiled case for socialism. The short answer is no. *Capitalism* is the private ownership of resources (*you own your money*), and *socialism* is the public ownership of resources (*the State owns your money*). In reality, most societies fall somewhere in between. As stated previously, a Christian approach to antiracism is not about any particular economic system; it is about biblical equity and justice in every economic system. Biblical justice is concerned with **stewardship,** the conviction that all resources belong to God (*God owns your money*). We are responsible for stewarding the resources that God has given us with both wisdom and generosity (1 Chronicles 29:14; 1 Corinthians 4:7).[7]

A Christian approach to antiracism is not about any particular economic system; it is about biblical equity and justice in every economic system.

Whatever the economic setting, biblical justice is concerned for biblical equity. As Paul put it, "For I do not mean that others should be eased and you burdened, but that as a matter of fairness" (2 Corinthians 8:13, ESV). Biblical justice is also concerned with restoration and repair. It's one thing to say "I'm sorry" for a wrong committed; it's entirely another to make the wrong, right. This is the essence of **reparations.** As Malcolm X made clear: "If you stick a knife in my back nine inches and pull it out six inches, there's no progress. [If] you pull it out all the way, that's not progress. The progress is healing the wound that the blow made."[8]

Much contemporary conversation relates to the idea of providing national reparations for American descendants of slavery. There is precedent for this: "Germany has paid about $50 billion to Holocaust survivors and their families. Japanese-Americans confined to internment camps during World War II received an apology from the government and $20,000 per victim."[9] A growing number of resources—including from a Christian perspective—make a compelling case for what reparations could look like.[10]

Yet tangible repair is not something that only governments can engage in. Color-courageous disciples also have power to practice *everyday* reparations with the resources God has given them:

1. Time: *Where can you, your community, or your family carve out regular time for antiracism?* Nothing happens without our investment of time. As Tisby insists, "Getting serious about fighting racism entails auditing how you spend your time. . . . Just as you have to revise your financial budget so you can make an important investment, you may have to shuffle your time and priorities to make investments in racial justice."[11] Incidentally, some of your time allotment can and should go to continued antiracism learning.

2. Talent: *What specialized skills could you or your community offer pro bono?* Many minority-led or antiracist-focused ministries and nonprofit organizations are under-resourced when it comes to human capital. What skills do you have—including graphic design, grant writing, accounting, food preparation, or beyond—that may be of value to others?

3. Treasure: *How can you financially support underfunded minority-led and/or antiracism-focused nonprofit organizations?* Think about this both individually and corporately. Does your church financially partner with minority-led organizations? Does your ministry patronize minority-led businesses? My friend Dave Ferguson, founder of Exponential, recently took up this challenge through #JusticeDeposits, a challenge to "churches, businesses, and individuals to . . . open checking or savings accounts as a way to safely but intentionally help Black-owned Banks, making funds more accessible to Black and minority families and businesses."[12] There are abundant possibilities.

Despite her royal status, Esther was fully dependent on others—and she did not have her own private bank account. Nevertheless, she figured out how to leverage the resources that she did have at her disposal, resources that came simply by virtue of being queen. Through a series of lavish banquets that she invited the king to and hosted, she exercised skillful hospitality as well as effective advocacy.

Granted, there were many forms of power that Esther did not have. But her story is a brilliant illustration of identifying the power that one *does* have—and sacrificially using it for good.

THE COURAGEOUS EMBRACE OF THE CROSS

And so we discover where the journey of color-courageous discipleship—like all discipleship—has been leading us: to the courageous embrace of the cross. We usually associate courage with valiant exploits, but the kingdom of God is upside-down in that things are often the opposite of what we expect. Jesus demonstrated with his own life that it is more courageous to rely on God than to defy God, to turn the other cheek rather than lash out, to serve rather than be served, to share rather than hoard, to sacrifice oneself rather than fixate on oneself. All of this requires us to take the courageous risk of trusting God with our lives.

Will you experience hardship, loss, or pain in your pursuit of color-courageous discipleship? Yes—that's pretty much guaranteed. Why else would you need courage? Yet, remember this: Every cross is temporary, and on the other side of that cross, there is joy and new life that can be found no other way. Thankfully, Jesus has gone before us: "For the joy set before him he endured the cross, scorning its shame, and sat down at the right hand of the throne of God. Consider him . . . so that you will not grow weary and lose heart" (Hebrews 12:2–3). Recall that *heart* is at the core of what courage is all about. As we focus on Jesus Christ, we will survive and thrive as color-courageous disciples, becoming more like him. We will experience the surprising presence of Jesus at work in and through us to transform our world. I love how C. S. Lewis described this Christ-transformation: "Every Christian is to become a little Christ. The whole purpose of becoming a Christian is simply nothing else."[13]

Esther is a beautiful example of what a "little Christ" looks like. You may be aware that the phrase *Christ figure* refers to a character whose life parallels the life of Jesus Christ, especially in that the character chooses a sacrificial death. Although people typically think of Christ figures as male, in my estimation, Esther is one of the most extraordinary Christ figures in all of Scripture. Just as Jesus began his ministry by fasting in the wilderness, so too did Esther begin with a fast. Also, like Jesus, she ultimately relinquished much more than food. She relinquished her claim to her God-given privilege, position, platform, and prosperity— *and was even willing to relinquish her very life*—for other people. Her willingness to take these courageous and sacrificial risks resulted in the salvation of her entire Jewish community. It is simply breathtaking.

Like Esther, we too can take color-courageous action in God's power and experience the promise of Isaiah 58: "If you do away with the yoke of oppression . . . then your light will rise in the darkness" (verses 9–10). As God's light shines through us in the darkness, people will see it and rejoice. Color-courageous disciples have the beautiful potential to not only build beloved community but also save lives and see new disciples made in the process.

Now, of course, we have an even more brilliant model than Esther: Jesus Christ our savior, who not only inspires us but also empowers us through his Spirit. This reminds me of the occasion in the Scriptures where eager crowds surrounded Jesus and asked: "What must we do to do the works God requires?" (John 6:28). That is, more or less, the question we've been asking: *When it comes to racism, what is the work that God requires?* Jesus's answer to us now is the same as it was then: "The work of God is this: to believe in the one he has sent" (verse 29). There is a Savior—and, thankfully, it's not us.

Jesus launched his ministry with a forty-day sacrifice of food. He concluded his ministry by sacrificing his reputation, his communion with his Father, and his very life. In sacrificing not only his *power* but *life itself,* Jesus made the way for us to enjoy God's beloved community forever. Now, Jesus invites color-courageous disciples to become "little Christs" and follow in his steps: "I have set you an example that you should do as I have done for you" (John 13:15).

May God bless you from here and make his face to shine upon you, now and always, as you pursue new adventures on your color-courageous discipleship journey.

EUGENE CHO

PRESIDENT AND CEO OF BREAD FOR THE WORLD

Eugene Cho is president and CEO of Bread for the World, a Christian advocacy organization dedicated to the eradication of world hunger. He is also the visionary behind One Day's Wages, a movement to alleviate poverty. For eighteen years he pastored Quest Church, a multicultural church in Seattle, and he is the author of numerous books including *Thou Shalt Not Be a Jerk: A Christian's Guide to Engaging Politics.*

How has God uniquely prepared you for color-courageous ministry?

I was born in South Korea. When I was six years old, my family emigrated to the United States after having experienced extraordinary hardship in Korea. Arriving in the United States was a jarring experience. When I got off the plane in San Francisco, I actually saw White people for the very first time! School was tough. Kids asked me: "Why do you look like that? Why do you talk like that? Why are your eyes like that?" It was definitely traumatic, but it was also deeply formative. When I started learning more about Jesus, I could relate to him. I was fascinated by his solidarity with the poor, the oppressed, the suffering, the marginalized, the forgotten. I could not help but see a constant thread of Jesus's inclination for people on the margins, and he understood what it meant to be marginalized too.

What, in your view, does antiracism have to do with discipleship?

Let's reframe this question. What does antiracism *not* have to do with discipleship? Antiracism is a newer term, a buzz word. But Jesus has always been at work reconciling us to God and to each other. I don't worship justice; I worship a just God. I don't worship antiracism; I worship a Savior who is going about the work of racial reconciliation. For me, discipleship is about seeking first the kingdom of God.

What spiritual practices have been life-giving for you?

When I pursue justice and live in a way that dignifies every human being, I feel more alive. It's life according to God's design. But Sabbath has helped me to sustain the work. I have wrestled at times with a personal messiah complex, which is why I need Sabbath to remind me that I am not God and that God is enough.

For me fasting is, at its heart, about making God-inspired sacrifices for the sake of others. What do you see as the place of sacrifice in Christian discipleship?

I think that we need a better imagination—a Christian imagination—about sacrifice. The kingdom of God is an upside-down kingdom. If you lose your life, you will find it. So for me, in the kingdom of God, sacrifice is actually about how we can become wealthy. Sacrifice is the true and lasting way to become rich.

You've been involved in advocacy work for some time. How do advocacy and discipleship relate?

Some think that sin is just a heart issue. But the reality is, broken people create broken systems and broken structures. Changing hearts, by itself, cannot reverse generations of systemic inequity. That is why politics matters—not because politics is the answer but because politics shapes policies and policies impact people. Advocacy acknowledges the importance of transforming policies for the sake of people. The Bible encourages us to speak up on behalf of the marginalized not because they don't have a voice, but because sometimes, with our broken systems, not everyone's voice can be heard.

What advice do you have for growing color-courageous disciples?

If we truly understand how radical Jesus is, the rest will follow. *Disciple* literally means "learner." Let's keep the emphasis on discipleship and commit ourselves to being lifelong learners of Jesus.

FURTHER READING

Cruciformity: Paul's Narrative Spirituality of the Cross by Michael J. Gorman

How to Fight Racism: Courageous Christianity and the Journey Toward Racial Justice by Jemar Tisby

Fasting: Spiritual Freedom Beyond Our Appetites by Lynne M. Baab

Subversive Witness: Scripture's Call to Leverage Privilege by Dominique DuBois Gilliard

Overrated: Are We More in Love with the Idea of Changing the World Than Actually Changing the World? by Eugene Cho

AFTERWORD

by Jemar Tisby

work sporadically and at unusual times of the day. I'm a writer, so I have the blessing and the tyranny of making my own schedule. All the most prolific and experienced writers advise novices to write a little each day, usually in the morning, and to relentlessly guard this time of productivity. That's what makes a wise writer. I'm not there yet.

My writing tends to happen after the football game on TV or when I finally roll out of bed after staying up until 2 A.M. doom scrolling on Twitter. At this point, well after the sun has arisen and closer to when most people are thinking about their mid-morning break, I crack open the laptop and start to peck away at the keyboard.

My less-than-disciplined writing habit cannot happen and does not happen without a dose of caffeine. But chemical motivation lasts only so long. Before the hour is up, I'm already slowing down. I feel my attention start to drift, and I begin thinking I really should read that article I've had open on a tab in my web browser for the last six months. The solution to my sloppy attempts at writing, of course, is to get a good night's sleep and maintain a consistent schedule. I'd get a lot more done with seven or eight hours of shut-eye than I ever could by relying on caffeine and energy drinks. I wouldn't artificially generate intense periods of productivity only to deal with the inevitable crash that follows. In other words, to write consistently and well I need sustainable practices.

I'm convinced that we often take an energy drink approach to racial justice rather than a sustainable practices approach. Instead of developing healthy spiritual habits that give us the strength to work for justice in the world, our commitment to justice relies on external factors such as the news cycle or other people's encouragement to kick into action.

What Michelle Sanchez does in *Color-Courageous Discipleship* is replace our energy drink approach to racial justice with a sustainable practices approach. She provides the practical methods we need to fight racism as a lifetime practice and not an occasional obsession.

In my antiracism work, one of the hardest parts is keeping people focused. The cell phone video of a White police officer with his knee on the neck of George Floyd in 2020 grabbed people's attention. It was even part of what led to a historic racial justice uprising that year. Even though I believe that period of the struggle was vital, people quickly turned their attention to other matters of both national and personal importance.

Racism is a deeply rooted weed in the soil of society. It's the kind you can't just pull up; you must dig it up. That takes ongoing effort. But people have jobs, bosses, reading for school, children to raise, other justice matters to consider, and a pandemic to navigate. It's easy to see how most people's commitment to racial justice entails sharing someone else's post on social media and ordering (though not always reading) the occasional book on the topic.

But to fight racism we'll need a sustained commitment to dismantling the ideologies, structures, and habits that lead to inequality. We can't transition from moment to movement without color-courageous disciplines.

People often ask me, "What keeps you going? How can you continue to engage in the work of racial justice?" The answer is a regular habit of enriching my mind, body, and soul through intentional actions.

As Sanchez has explained in this book, forms of lament are necessary when fighting racism. How can the suffering of so many image bearers of God *not* move us to sorrow? What do we do with that grief? We take it to God, and we weep and we wail. It's all right. God can take it. What's more, it's healing. It's cathartic. Lament lets out the wrenching pain that grabs us whenever injustice seems to win.

For most of my adult life, I've lived in the Mississippi Delta (Arkansas side), and it's been like an eighteen-year pilgrimage. You can't walk five steps down here without practically tripping over some significant aspect of our nation's racial past. It's the site of the Civil War. It's the theater of much of the Civil Rights Movement. It's the cotton country where you can practically see the ghosts of the ancestors wafting in the humid Delta air. The color-courageous discipline of pilgrimage lets us touch, taste, hear, smell, and see the material effects of racism and compels us to work for change.

Despite the color-courageous discipleship practices available to us, the longer I am on this journey of racial justice, the more I realize that not many people will stay on the path. Some will sojourn with you briefly, others for longer. Some may not get on the path at all. Others will even try to block the path. I have chosen to continue the fight against racism. I want the work of justice to figure prominently in my short time on this side of life.

The only way to stay on this racial justice journey for a lifetime is to realize that justice *is* the journey. Justice is not something separate from our faith—it is integral to it. As long as we see the work of racial justice as a distraction from our everyday life, then we will always be reactive and uneven in our efforts. Only when we realize that following Jesus means pursuing justice at the same time will we be able to make color-courageous discipleship a whole life orientation rather than a set of isolated actions.

Everyone could use an energy drink at some point. Life is hard. We don't always get the sleep we need or stick to the schedules we plan. But there's no replacement for disciplines that consistently prepare us for the work ahead. *Color-Courageous Discipleship* reminds us that just as we have been discipled into certain racist practices, we can be discipled into antiracist practices.

This is a lifelong commitment. But be encouraged. Your commitment to color-courageous discipleship is sustained by the One who remains committed to you.

—*Jemar Tisby*
The New York Times bestselling author of
How to Fight Racism and *The Color of Compromise*

CHAPTER 1: INVITATION TO A RACIAL DISCIPLESHIP JOURNEY

1. Color-courageous discipleship is actually about *rediscipleship,* about recognizing how you have already been discipled and choosing to be discipled again. Discuss the idea of rediscipleship. How might you have already been discipled in matters of race, whether intentionally or unintentionally?

2. What do you understand so far about the difference between being *not racist* and being *antiracist*? In what ways does this difference matter?

3. In what ways is the distinction between *race* and *ethnicity* helpful?

4. Do you know anyone who has been on a racial discipleship journey and experienced transformation in some way? (It could be someone you know personally or someone you know about, like Bonhoeffer.)

5. What are your concerns about embarking on this racial discipleship journey? What are your hopes? How might you experience Jesus more deeply along the way?

CHAPTER 2: A CHRIST-CENTERED APPROACH TO ANTIRACISM

1. What does it mean to you to be "Christ-centered"? Where in your life could you be centered more on Christ?

2. When, if ever, have you experienced an event that prompted you to explore issues of race more deeply? What motivates you to explore issues of race more deeply now?

3. When have you seen or experienced racial brokenness on any of the four levels of creation: individual, interpersonal, systemic, and cosmic? Which level(s) would you like to learn more about and why?

4. When, if ever, have you tried to be an ambassador of racial reconciliation? What has that looked like? What went well? And what didn't?

5. What questions about reconciliation do you have that this journey might address?

CHAPTER 3: DISCIPLESHIP AS AWAKENING

1. Why do you think the Bible urges people who are already committed to Jesus to wake up or stay awake?

2. The concept of waking up to racial inequity has been around as far back as Abraham Lincoln. Why do you think this idea of racial awakening has resonated across the ages?

3. Explain in your own words what the "myth of equality" is all about.

4. Review the seven symptoms of systemic racism. Which one(s) stand out to you and why?

5. Discuss the significance of this verse for you: "Wake up, sleeper, rise from the dead, and Christ will shine on you" (Ephesians 5:14).

CHAPTER 4: DISCIPLESHIP AS WARDROBE CHANGE

1. Review the seven categories of unconscious bias. Which one(s) stand out to you and why?

2. When have you observed one or more of these unconscious biases in yourself? In others? What interventions would you like to try?

3. Explain what it means to move from being color-blind to color-brave. Why would we want to do that, and what is there to be brave about?

4. Share about a time when adopting a mindset of humility made a real difference in your discipleship journey.

CHAPTER 5: DISCIPLESHIP AS INNER HEALING

1. Martin Luther King, Jr., said, "Only through an inner spiritual transformation do we gain the strength to fight vigorously the evils of the world in a humble and loving spirit." How would you explain this quote to someone?

2. Why is it important to understand the racial trauma that people have experienced, past and present? Why does understanding one another's trauma help us to love?

3. Review the many types of racial trauma experienced by both people of color and White people. What strikes you? Have you or someone you know experienced any of these? What would it look like to pursue healing?

4. Why is it important to replace the false stories in our heads and hearts with true stories? What differences does the truth make? What false stories would you like to replace, and how might you do that?

5. How might God repurpose trauma that you have experienced into a redemptive force for the future?

CHAPTER 6: DISCIPLESHIP AS BELOVED COMMUNITY

1. Discuss these words of Martin Luther King, Jr.: "I do not think of political power as an end. Neither do I think of economic power as an end. They are ingredients in the objective that we seek in life . . . the creation of the beloved community."

2. What are your thoughts at this point about the differences between a Christian approach and a secular approach to anti-racism?

3. Beloved community is characterized by solidarity. Since we all are already profoundly connected, caring for one another just makes sense. Furthermore, there is evidence that racial inequity tangibly diminishes the quality of life for everyone in nearly every sector, including education, housing, labor, public recreation, the environment, and more. What are your thoughts about why racism persists even when it hurts us all? What makes us so prone to zero-sum thinking, and what can we do to counter that mindset?

4. Beloved community is characterized by *interdependence:* We all need each other's gifts. Tell of a time when you have been unexpectedly blessed by someone from another race or culture.

5. Beloved community is characterized by *biblical equity.* In your own words, explain the difference between *equity* and *equality.* Why does the difference matter?

CHAPTER 7: READ (IN LIVING COLOR)

1. When have you experienced Christianity in a culture different from yours? What was that like? What did you learn or experience?

2. How would you explain this statement to someone? "If your culture is dominant, you are more likely to be blind to what your culture actually is."

3. In works of art, Jesus has overwhelmingly been portrayed as White. What difference do you think it makes for people of all races when they fully comprehend that Jesus was not White?

4. If you could study the Bible with disciples of a different ethnic or cultural background from your own, whom would you choose to study with and why?

5. What can you do to ensure that you have a colorful reading community on your bookshelves? What authors of color or global authors would you recommend and why?

CHAPTER 8: PRAY (IN THE RAW)

1. What is it like for you to pray in the raw, to bring your whole, unpolished self to God? When is this kind of praying easy for you—and when is it difficult? When has praying in the raw made a difference for you, whether with regard to race or some other area?

2. When have you grown spiritually or drawn closer to God as a result of pain? What current life challenges offer you opportunities to deepen your trust in God?

3. The word *excruciating* derives from the Latin word *crux,* meaning "cross." How could more often calling to mind the fact that Jesus suffered help you in your own suffering?

4. When, if ever, have you lamented together with people of other races? What about lament binds people together and builds beloved community?

CHAPTER 9: PILGRIMAGE (FOR PERSPECTIVE)

1. How would you explain the symbol of the Sankofa bird to someone else? Why is it important to go back before we go forward?

2. In what ways is Christian discipleship more like a pilgrimage than a picnic?

3. We've learned that a pilgrimage is an intentional journey undertaken by disciples for the purpose of spiritual formation. Where would you be interested to go on a racial pilgrimage? Why?

4. What festival(s) would you like to celebrate in order to better appreciate other cultures and diverse racial experiences?

5. According to David Leong, "Discipleship leads us right into the places where historic, systemic racial conflicts have led to division and strife." When, if ever, have you had such an experience? Would you be open to doing this kind of discipleship in the future? If so, what might that look like?

CHAPTER 10: FAST (FOR REAL)

1. At its heart, fasting isn't about food; it's about sacrifice. That's what we mean by fasting "for real." Describe the true fasting that God desires from us.

2. Using the framework of intersectionality, identify some ways you are advantaged and some ways you are disadvantaged relative to other people.

3. What do you find most inspiring or interesting about Esther's story?

4. Use the power audit cross to consider what next steps you can take to help build beloved community. Be specific about what sacrificing or leveraging your privilege, position, platform, and/or prosperity might look like.

5. Where would you like your color-courageous discipleship journey to take you from here?

ACKNOWLEDGMENTS

have dreamed of becoming an author ever since I was a little girl. What a beautiful surprise that it is happening now, earlier than expected, and for the sake of the church that I love. I give all praise and thanks to our Lord and Savior Jesus Christ, first and forever.

Mom and Dad, thank you so much for all you have invested in our family over all these years. I had a golden childhood nurtured by your wisdom, grace, and reams of unconditional love. I appreciate it all—increasingly so as the years go by. May your investments of love continue to bear kingdom fruit for generations to come.

Mickey, we are living the dream! Right now, before our very eyes, God is answering those prayers we lifted up on our knees at NYU more than two decades ago. Thank you for marrying me. It has been the joy of a lifetime to pursue our God-given mythos together. Your countless gifts of time, encouragement, and sacrificial love have been pivotal to seeing our dreams come true.

Color-courageous discipleship is a years-long journey. There are so many who have mentored me through their friendship, work, and ministry. I can thank only some of them here: Tim Keller, my pastor in New York City for many years, for grounding my faith in the gospel and for his writings that unpack how to apply the gospel to our racial challenges; David Swanson, for opening my eyes to the need for racial rediscipleship; Dominique Gilliard and Soong-Chan Rah, for many years of prophetic witness in the Covenant Church and beyond; Gary Walter, Dick Lucco, Harold Spooner, Greg Yee, and John Wenrich, and so many others, for modeling color-courageous denominational leadership; Michael Emerson, for his trailblazing racial equity research on behalf of the church as well as the generous personal wisdom he extended to me; Al Tizon, for his well-articulated vision for holistic mission in *Whole and Reconciled,* the most beautiful call to the whole gospel that I have read; Erin Chan Ding, for constantly modeling in new ways how to disciple a color-courageous family; Cheryl Lynn Cain, my Sankofa partner, for our many conversations about how to depict holistic redemption and for drawing my attention to the gorgeous reconciliation song of Colossians; Max Lee, for teaching students, including me, to read the Bible interculturally; Alex Gee, for his trailblazing advocacy work for Black communities and especially his "Black History for a New Day" course; and Rick Richardson, for strengthening within me the connections between evangelism, spiritual formation, and racial reconciliation.

I have been richly inspired by Mellody Hobson's TED Talk "Color Blind or Color Brave?," which prompted me to emphasize *courage* in the journey of racial discipleship.

Upon moving to Chicago, I am so grateful to have found New Community Covenant Church, formerly pastored by Peter Hong and now led by an incredibly dynamic staff. You have formed my family through your gospel-centered, color-courageous preaching. New Community continues to provide me with sweet friendship and fellowship (I'm thinking especially of you, Emily, Sue, and Jacqueline). I am richly blessed to be part of this community that is courageously forming a community of reconciled reconcilers in Chicago and beyond.

Heartfelt thanks to Dave Swaim, Meghan DeJong, and the leadership at Highrock Covenant Church in the Boston area for the privilege of serving on the Revelation 7 team and for exploring together creative approaches to color-courageous discipleship in the local church.

I am exceedingly grateful to all those who read early draft chapters of this book and offered valuable feedback: among them Brian Dietz, Jesse Slimak, Paul Robinson, Kevin Smallacombe, David Swanson, and Al Tizon. Thank you for the priceless gifts of your time, perspective, and wisdom.

Thank you to all whom I learned from and interviewed (both officially and unofficially) while writing this book. I could only recount some of the gems from our conversations in this work, but you all provided boundless treasures to me, which I will continue to carry with me: Debbie Blue, Sheila Wise Rowe, Greg Yee, Eugene Cho, Esau McCauley, Lisa Rodriguez-Watson, Cecilia Williams, Efrem Smith, Christina Edmonson, Sarah Shin, Michelle Clifton-Soderstrom, Beth Maynard, Mark Dirksen, Robert Chao Romero, Evelyn Johnson, Terry Wildman, Daniel Hill, and Michael Emerson.

My years at Gordon-Conwell Theological Seminary were some of the best of my life. I could never author works like this without the solid, stellar theological education I received there. Special thanks to all who poured into me, especially in the areas of spiritual formation and multicultural mission: among them Moonjang Lee, Tim Tennent, Grace May, Gwenfair Adams, David Currie, Susan Currie, and Roy Ciampa.

Thanks to those not yet mentioned who also provided wisdom, encouragement, and advice on publishing my very first book: Tish Harrison Warren, Trillia Newbell, Kevin Harney, Jemar Tisby, Ken Shigematsu, Angela Yee, and Stan Jantz.

All my love to Lissa Levy, Nikki Frey, and Carrie McCormack for sharing my love for books and for being my most enthusiastic fans in the neighborhood! (And, Lissa, for that surprise cup of coffee!)

With this three-book color-courageous project, I am so grateful to launch a fruitful creative relationship with Susan Tjaden and the WaterBrook and Multnomah / Penguin Random House team. Kudos to my enterprising agent, Don Gates, who made it happen!

Words cannot express my joy in having the opportunity to serve as a denominational leader for the Evangelical Covenant Church, my own cherished beloved community. Serving such a colorful and vibrant fellowship of churches has been the honor and adventure of a lifetime.

Finally, heartfelt thanks to the many who have prayed for me and for this project, including my best friend, Athena Lew. Thanks as well to faithful prayer teams led over the years by two Covenant pastors, Darren Olson and Chuck Wysong. I have no doubt that the prayers you two facilitated have been precious wind beneath my wings. Thank you eternally.

Solo Dei gloria.

AAPI. Asian American and/or Pacific Islander.

Advocacy. The practice of standing up and speaking out for what is right on someone else's behalf. (Chapter 10)

Agape Love. The self-giving, sacrificial, supernatural love of God that casts out all fear. Beloved community is characterized by agape love between people of all ethnicities. (Chapter 6)

Ambassadors of Reconciliation. All disciples have been appointed by God to be agents of God's reconciliation to the world (2 Corinthians 5:11–21). Disciples can foster reconciliation on every level of creation—personal, corporate, systemic, and cosmic. (Chapter 2)

Antiracism. The practice of becoming aware of and uprooting personal racial prejudice and bias *plus* working to dismantle systemic practices by institutions that lead to racial inequities in society. (Chapter 1)

Antistructuralism. A disinclination to consider structural or systemic factors, usually in favor of emphasizing individual or interpersonal factors instead. (Chapter 7)

Assimilation. The downplaying of one's ethnic distinctiveness in order to better fit in with the dominant group. (Chapter 5)

Attribution Error. A cognitive bias that causes people to attribute blame in lopsided ways. *Ultimate attribution error,* for example, causes us to blame a community or people group for their plight rather than adequately taking situational factors into account. (Chapter 4)

Beloved Community. A phrase popularized by Martin Luther King, Jr., to describe a loving, diverse society. A community grounded in Christlike, agape love for God and for one another across boundaries of difference. Beloved community is characterized by solidarity, interdependence, and biblical equity. (Chapter 6)

Bias Blind Spot (see **Truth Distortion**). The tendency of people to believe that they are less biased than other people. (Chapter 4)

BIPOC. Black, Indigenous, and People of Color. This term draws attention to the fact that Black and Indigenous people historically have been at a greater systemic disadvantage in North America than other people of color.

Black. Generally refers to people of African descent.

Black Lives Matter. A decentralized movement comprised of people of all racial backgrounds that is dedicated to raising awareness and inspiring change regarding the racial inequity experienced by Black people.

Blame (category **Unconscious Bias**). The human inclination to blame a person's behavior on their character rather than their circumstances or any other mitigating factors. Examples of blame bias include *puritanical bias* and *ultimate attribution error.* (Chapter 4)

Brown. An overarching term that refers to people of color with "brown" skin who are not Black, including people of Latino, Indigenous, Middle Eastern, or South Asian descent.

Chinese Exclusion Act. A nineteenth-century federal law that prohibited the immigration of Chinese people. (Chapter 4)

Cognitive Bias. A misperception of the mind; an unconscious bias. (Chapter 4)

Color-Blind. The belief that racism can be overcome by not seeing color and treating everyone the same. Unfortunately, those who cannot see color also tend to overlook racial disparity. (Chapter 4)

Color-Brave. The opposite of color blindness; those who are color-brave choose to see color (race and ethnicity) for the sake of cultivating racial equity. (Chapter 4)

Color-Courageous Discipleship. The courageous, lifelong journey of following Jesus, dismantling racism, and building beloved community. (Chapter 1)

Colorism. The prejudice that assigns higher value and beauty to lighter skin tones. (Chapter 4)

Community Cultural Wealth. The uniquely rich contributions that each culture can make to the world; includes knowledge, values, skills, artifacts, wisdom accumulated from common experiences, and more. (Chapter 7)

Confirmation Bias (see Truth Distortion). The tendency to see what we want to believe, even when it is not true. (Chapter 4)

Crabs-in-a-Bucket Effect. One crab in a bucket can escape without a problem. But a group of crabs in a bucket will drag down individual ones that try to escape, irrationally ensuring the demise of the whole group. Similar dynamics have been observed in marginalized communities. (Chapter 5)

Criminalization (category **Unconscious Bias**). A category of unconscious bias in which certain ethnic groups are seen to be more dangerous, guilty, or worthy of censure. (Chapter 4)

Critical Race Theory (CRT). A framework for processing and understanding the many complex dimensions of how race impacts systems and society as whole. (Chapter 1)

Cruciform. Taking the shape of the cross. Like all disciples, color-courageous disciples are called to cruciform discipleship. (Chapter 6)

Decentering. The process of moving from an *ethnocentric* approach (my cultural perspective is central) to an *ethnodiverse* approach (my cultural perspective is one among a rich tapestry of cultural perspectives). (Chapter 7)

Defensive Othering. The practice of distancing oneself from one's own racial or cultural group. (Chapter 5)

Dehumanization (category **Unconscious Bias**). Humans tend to assume that those who are not like us share our humanity to a lesser degree. When a person or group is considered to be less than human, it becomes easier to mistreat them. (Chapter 4)

Disciple (or **Discipleship**). Jesus extended this invitation to his first disciples: "Follow Me, and I will make you fishers of people" (Matthew 4:19, NASB). A disciple (1) follows Jesus, (2) is transformed by Jesus, and (3) is on mission with Jesus. (Chapter 1)

Discrimination (or Racial Discrimination). The act of treating people from different racial groups differently, resulting in some racial groups receiving worse treatment than others. (Chapter 2)

Divine Racial Trauma. Racial trauma that negatively impacts one's relationship with God. (Chapter 5)

Environmental Racism. A form of racial inequity in which communities of color are disproportionately exposed to pollutants or denied the high-quality municipal services that others enjoy. (Chapter 5)

Epigenetics. A field of scientific inquiry that studies inheritable changes in gene expression like those changes observed in transgenerational racial trauma. (Chapter 5)

Equality. Equality emphasizes sameness; for example, we are all equal in that we all possess the same image of God. In conversations about race, those who emphasize equality tend to advocate for same treatment regardless of whether or not the starting points are equal (contrast with **Equity**). (Chapters 3 and 6)

Equity (or Biblical Equity). Equity emphasizes fairness. The goal of biblical equity is not to force particular outcomes but to provide everyone with fair opportunities to exercise their God-given gifts. In conversations about race, those who emphasize equity typically acknowledge that people have different starting points; they therefore seek a customized approach to achieve fair opportunity (contrast with **Equality**). (Chapters 3 and 6)

Ethnicity. A God-ordained cultural identity which God delights in as a means of bringing glory to himself and enrichment to his kingdom. (Chapter 1)

Ethnocentrism. The belief that one's ethnic group is normative and/or superior to others. (Chapter 1)

Ethnodiverse (or **Ethnorelative**). The understanding that one's cultural perspective is not central but is instead one culture among a rich tapestry of human cultures. (Chapter 7)

Evangelical. Christians of all ethnic backgrounds who take the Bible seriously and believe in Jesus Christ as Savior and Lord.

Fasting. Traditionally, abstaining from food or drink for a purpose. A Christian approach to fasting can also entail abstaining from other resources such as *privilege, position, platform,* or *prosperity* for the sake of beloved community. (Chapter 10)

Gospel. The gospel is the good news that Jesus Christ is Lord and Savior. Through his crucifixion and resurrection, Jesus provided the free gift of salvation to sinners and is reconciling all creation to himself. (Chapter 2)

Hate Crime. A crime, typically involving violence, that is committed on the basis of prejudice. As recently as 2019, hate crime in America rose to levels not seen in a decade. (Chapter 5)

Ideology. A system of ideas. You can often recognize an ideology by its *-ism* ending (social*ism*, capital*ism*, liberal*ism*, conserva*tism*). Most ideologies are not harmful in themselves, but problems can arise when disciples lose perspective and allow their commitment to an ideology to compete with their commitment to Christ. Of course, that risk is also a possibility with antiracism. Even the well-intentioned pursuit of antiracism can compete with our commitment to Christ. (Chapter 2)

Idolatry. Worship of a false god; any competing loyalty to the supremacy of Jesus Christ in our hearts and lives. Idolatry is often taking a good thing and making it the supreme thing.

Imago Dei. Latin term meaning "image of God." Color-courageous disciples recognize that all people are equally created in God's royal image, which implies that we must treat everyone with dignity and resist dehumanization of all kinds. (Chapter 7)

Implicit Association Test (IAT). The IAT measures the strength of associations between concepts (Black people, White people) and evaluations (good, bad) or stereotypes (athletic, smart, dangerous). Analysis of IAT results reveal that a significant majority of Whites, Asians, and Latinos show anti-Black bias. (Chapter 4)

Implicit Bias. Another name for **Unconscious Bias.** (Chapter 4)

Individualism. A cultural lens that understands the individual, rather than the collective, to be paramount. (Chapter 7)

Intention vs. Impact Dilemma. Names the reality that our intentions do not always have the impact that we desire. For example, while a person might intend to treat people of all races equally, unconscious bias may still cause that person to negatively impact others through unequal treatment. (Chapters 4 and 7)

Intercultural. Intentional engagement between cultures that results in mutual insight and transformation. (Chapter 7)

Interdependence. The state of being dependent on one another, as are members of the body of Christ. Regardless of our placement in the body of Christ, we are inescapably connected, and we need the rich and surprising gifts that God grants us through one another. (Chapter 6)

Internalized Racism (also, **Internalized Oppression**). Racism that is not external but internal; internalized racism happens when marginalized racial groups internalize society's negative narratives about themselves. (Chapter 5)

Intersectionality. A framework for understanding the dynamics of overlapping identities in whatever context we might find ourselves. (Chapter 10)

Juneteenth. A U.S. holiday observed on June 19 that celebrates the emancipation of slaves in the United States. Juneteenth does not commemorate the date that Abraham Lincoln issued the Emancipation Proclamation (September 22, 1862); rather, Juneteenth commemorates the date that slaves in Texas were finally liberated by the Union Army upon the close of the Civil War (June 19, 1865). Juneteenth has been celebrated by many African Americans in the United States for more than 150 years. In 2021, Juneteenth was declared a U.S. federal holiday. (Chapter 9)

Kingdom of God. All-encompassing term for the rule of Jesus Christ on earth; includes every dimension of creation. (Chapter 6)

Kwanzaa. A seven-day celebration of African American heritage, culture, and pride observed from December 26 to January 1. The term *Kwanzaa* is Swahili for "harvest." Each day celebrates a value deemed important for Black community-building. (Chapter 9)

Lament. A prayer of pain that leads to trust, the key steps of which are turn, complain, ask, and trust. Lament can be personal, corporate, and divine. (Chapter 8)

Magis. A Latin word that means "more" or "greater." The Ignatians (Society of Jesus) have used the concept of *magis* as a reminder that Jesus continually invites his disciples to more. Color-courageous disciples seek to abide in Christ more deeply so that we might bear Christ's fruit more abundantly. (Chapter 4)

Majority. A synonym for **White** people. The term is waning in usage because the United States is projected to soon have a majority of **People of Color.** (Chapter 1)

Mass Incarceration. The disproportionate incarceration of a group of people relative to the population. (Chapter 3)

Minority. A synonym for **People of Color.** The term is waning in usage because the United States is projected to soon be minority White. (Chapter 1)

Moral Disengagement. The human tendency to mistreat people that we dehumanize; the tendency to mistreat those seen as sharing our humanity to a lesser degree. (Chapter 4)

Noetic Effect of Sin. *Noetic* means "relating to mental activity or the intellect." The noetic effect of sin means that sin has compromised the human ability to process information, discern truth, and perceive the world accurately. One example of this in race relations is **Unconscious Bias.** (Chapters 2 and 4)

People of Color (POC). An overarching term for non-White people that typically includes African Americans, Native Americans, Asian Americans, Latino Americans, and Arab Americans. (Chapter 1)

Perpetration–Induced Traumatic Stress (PITS). A form of PTSD that emerges after a person traumatizes someone else. (Chapter 5)

Pilgrimage. A journey taken for the purpose of spiritual transformation; involves intentional immersive experiences such as relocation, encounter, reflection, and the opportunity to engage in community across boundaries of difference. (Chapter 9)

Platform (category **Power Audit**). Platform is about utilizing one's voice and taking a public stand; it is also about elevating the voices of other people. (Chapter 10)

Position (category **Power Audit**). A role that bestows a sphere of influence. We have access to spheres of influence both through relational roles (mother, spouse, brother, friend, pastor, coach, small-group leader) as well as organizational roles (PTA member, elder board appointee, interview committee member). (Chapter 10)

Post-Traumatic Growth. The positive transformation that can be experienced as a result of one's struggle with a traumatic event. (Chapter 5)

Power Audit. The ongoing practice of identifying the different types of power that one holds so that these powers can be leveraged for good. (Chapter 10)

Powers and Principalities. The Scriptures reveal that larger forces of evil are at war against God; these include deceptive and destructive human ideologies like racism. As disciples, we are called to—in God's power—identify and prayerfully resist the powers and principalities of the world. (Chapter 2)

Prejudice. Derived from the roots *prae* ("in advance") and *judicium* ("judgment"), *prejudice* means "making a judgment prior to having sufficient facts; a preconceived opinion." In conversations about race, prejudice implies having a negative preconceived opinion about another race. Prejudice often leads to **discrimination.** (Chapter 1)

Privilege. An unearned advantage. (Chapter 10)

Prosperity. Resources of time, talent, and treasure. Color-courageous disciples seek to act as stewards and give a portion of their prosperity to foster biblical equity. (Chapter 10)

Pro-White Preference (category **Unconscious Bias**). Many people harbor a preference for Whiteness and a corresponding aversion to Blackness. Tragically, almost half of African Americans also harbor anti-Black bias themselves. (Chapter 4)

Race. A man-made system used to stratify humans into artificial categories based on visible characteristics such as skin color, typically for purposes related to power, division, and hierarchy. (Chapter 1)

Racial Privilege. Most societies, if not all, operate according to an invisible hierarchy in which some races, ethnicities, or cultures have historically held greater status than others. This invisible hierarchy confers unearned advantage to those racial groups at the top of the hierarchy. (Chapter 10)

Racial Profiling. The utilization of race as a grounds for suspected wrongdoing or criminal behavior. An example: Studies show that Black drivers are more likely to be pulled over than White drivers. (Chapter 4)

Racialized Society. A society in which race matters profoundly for differences in life experiences, life opportunities, and social relationships. This term was popularized in *Divided by Faith: Evangelical Religion and the Problem of Race in America* by Michael O. Emerson and Christian Smith. (Chapter 2)

Racial Supremacy. The conscious or unconscious conviction that one race is superior to others. Disciples are called to replace all forms of racial supremacy with the supremacy of Jesus Christ. (Chapter 2)

Racism. Personal racial prejudice, bias, and systemic practices of institutions that lead to racial inequities in society. (Chapter 1)

Reconciliation. The process of making broken things whole again. Since creation is broken on every level—individual, interpersonal, systemic, cosmic—it requires reconciliation on every level. God's plan is "to reconcile to himself all things" through Christ (Colossians 1:20). God also assigns to disciples of Jesus the ministry of reconciliation (2 Corinthians 5:17–21). (Chapter 2)

Rediscipleship. The process of being discipled again; rediscipleship is needed because all people have to some extent been unconsciously "discipled" by the racial narratives of the world. (Chapters 1 and 4)

Redlining. A once-legal discriminatory lending practice that limited mortgage financing opportunities for people of color. (Chapter 3)

Relationalism. A cultural lens of White evangelicalism that attaches central importance to interpersonal relationships and tends to neglect systemic realities. (Chapter 7)

Reparations. Tangible acts of restitution and repair. (Chapter 10)

Reverse Racism. In common parlance, the exchange of one unfair racial preference for another unfair racial preference. (Chapter 6)

School-to-Prison Pipeline. Once Black children enter the criminal justice system, often beginning with minor school disciplinary measures, they are far more likely than White children to be sentenced as adults. (Chapter 3)

Shalom. Often translated as "peace" in the Bible, *shalom* is the way things ought to be. It describes the experience of wholeness and flourishing in our relationships with God, with one another, and with all creation. (Chapter 1)

Shame. The intensely painful feeling that one is unworthy of love and belonging. (Chapter 5)

Sin. Any action that is contrary to God's design, including choosing our own will instead of God's will. The Bible says that "all have sinned and fall short of the glory of God" (Romans 3:23) and that the penalty of sin is death (Romans 6:23), which is why we need the Savior, Jesus Christ. (Chapter 2)

Solidarity. The experience of being united as one body in common life and purpose; the voluntary sharing of joys and challenges as an expression of unity. (Chapter 6)

Status Quo Bias (category **Unconscious Bias**). The human tendency to resist changes to the status quo even when those changes are shown to be beneficial. (Chapter 4)

Stereotype Threat (category **Unconscious Bias**). A phenomenon in which a person's anxiety about confirming a negative stereotype leads to underperformance. (Chapter 4)

Stewardship. The understanding that God owns all resources and that we have been entrusted to manage our God-given resources on his behalf. (Chapter 10)

Syncretism. The amalgamation of different and often contradictory religious beliefs and practices. Christians engage in religious syncretism when they combine their loyalty to Jesus with competing loyalties. (Chapter 2)

Systemic Racism. Persistent patterns of racial inequity that characterize systems, policies, and institutions as a whole, whether intentionally or unintentionally. (Chapter 1)

Truth Distortion (category **Unconscious Bias**). A category of unconscious bias that happens when the human mind distorts what is true. Examples include **confirmation bias,** the ostrich effect, and the **bias blind spot.** (Chapter 4)

Unconscious Bias (or Implicit Bias). The biases we unconsciously hold that create a gap between our intentions and our impact when it comes to the fair treatment of others and biblical equity. (Chapter 2)

Vicarious Trauma. The trauma that results when a person of color witnesses someone else's racial trauma either directly (firsthand) or indirectly (secondhand or thirdhand). (Chapter 5)

White. Refers to those who are not people of color, particularly people of European descent. (Chapter 1)

White Supremacy. A type of racial supremacy that understands the White race to be normative and/or superior to others. (Chapter 10)

Woke. Aware of and attentive to important social issues, particularly matters related to racial injustice. More recently, the term has taken on negative connotations, referring to extreme political correctness; this is a deviation from the term's original intent. (Chapter 3)

Zero-Sum Paradigm. The conviction that one racial group's gain comes at another group's loss. In reality, racial zero-sum thinking in America has led to the diminishment of life for everyone in nearly every sector, including education, housing, labor, public recreation, and the environment. (Chapter 6)

NOTES

CHAPTER 1: INVITATION TO A RACIAL DISCIPLESHIP JOURNEY

1. David W. Swanson, *Rediscipling the White Church: From Cheap Diversity to True Solidarity* (Downers Grove, IL: IVP, 2020).

2. Cornelius Plantinga, *Not the Way It's Supposed to Be: A Breviary of Sin* (Grand Rapids, MI: Eerdmans, 1999), 10.

3. "In the authoritative *Greek-English Lexicon of the New Testament and Other Early Christian Literature* the primary definition of the word *ethnos* is a body of persons united by kinship, culture, and common traditions." Another rendering for *ethnos* is "a large group of people based on various cultural, physical, or geographical ties." Given this more expansive understanding, I believe we have good reason to translate *ethnos* as "people group, culture, caste, tribe, ethnicity, ethnic group," and so on. See Luis Bush, "The Meaning of Ethne in Matthew 28:19," *Mission Frontiers,* September–October 2013, www.mission frontiers.org/issue/article/the-meaning-of-ethne-in-matthew-2819.

4. God is like a lion (Hosea 5:14; Revelation 5:5) and a lamb (John 1:29; Revelation 5:12). God is most often referred to in Scripture in male terms but also has female characteristics (for example, in Deuteronomy 32:18 God is said to have given birth; in Isaiah 49:15 God is compared to a nursing mother). God is both living water (Jeremiah 17:13) and a consuming fire (Hebrews 12:29).

5. Ta-Nehisi Coates, *Between the World and Me* (New York: Spiegel & Grau, 2015), 7.

6. See, for example, Ibram X. Kendi, *Stamped from the Beginning: The Definitive History of Racist Ideas in America* (New York: Nation Books, 2016) and Tiffany Jewell, *This Book Is Anti-Racist: 20 Lessons on How to Wake Up, Take Action, and Do the Work* (Minneapolis: Frances Lincoln Children's Books, 2020).

7. Jewell, *This Book Is Anti-Racist,* 154.

8. His fifth group, *Monstrosus,* applied to people with visible disabilities. Jewell, *This Book Is Anti-Racist,* 154.

9. Kendi, *Stamped,* 82. Somewhat strangely, he also added that peoples of the White race are "covered by tight clothing"!

10. Kendi, *Stamped,* 82.

11. Kendi, *Stamped,* 82.

12. Quoted in Ibram X. Kendi, *How to Be an Antiracist* (New York: One World, 2019), 9.

13. Kendi, *Antiracist,* 9.

14. Erin N. Winkler, "Children Are Not Colorblind: How Young Children Learn Race," *PACE: Practical Approaches for Continuing Education* 3, no. 3 (2009): 1–8.

15. Winkler, "Children Are Not Colorblind."

16. Matt Bruenig, "The Top 10 Percent of White Families Own Almost Everything," *The American Prospect,* September 8, 2014, https://prospect.org/power/top-10-percent-white-families-almost-everything.

17. See, for example, Sarah Mervosh, "How Much Wealthier Are White School Districts Than Nonwhite Ones? $23 Billion, Report Says," *The New York Times,* February 27, 2019, www.nytimes.com/2019/02/27/education/school-districts-funding-white-minorities.html. Also Dana Goldstein, "How Do You Get Better Schools? Take the State to Court, More Advocates Say," *The New York Times,* August 21, 2018, sec. U.S., www.nytimes.com/2018/08/21/us/school-segregation-funding-lawsuits.html.

18. George Yancey, *Beyond Racial Gridlock: Embracing Mutual Responsibility* (Downers Grove, IL: IVP, 2006), Kindle.

19. My children's book, *God's Beloved Community,* is designed to illustrate this colorful and captivating dream of beloved community that God calls us to as color-courageous disciples. Michelle T. Sanchez, *God's Beloved Community* (Colorado Springs, CO: WaterBrook, 2022).

20. Lexico.com (Oxford Dictionaries), s.v. "adventure," www.lexico.com/en/definition/adventure.

21. *Merriam-Webster,* s.v. "courage," www.merriam-webster.com/dictionary/courage.

22. William H. Frey, "The US Will Become 'Minority White' in 2045, Census Projects," Brookings (blog), March 14, 2018, www.brookings.edu/blog/the -avenue/2018/03/14/the-us-will-become-minority-white-in-2045-census -projects.

23. Joseph R. Barndt, *Understanding and Dismantling Racism: The Twenty-First Century Challenge to White America* (Minneapolis: Fortress, 2007), Kindle, emphasis added.

24. Advocates for the term *people of color* say it's the most respectful and inclusive term available and is preferred over *non-white* or *minority* for a number of reasons. See, for example, Luke Visconti, "Is 'People of Color' Offensive," DiversityInc (blog), May 22, 2007, www.diversityinc.com/is-people-of-color -offensive.

25. See, for example, Nancy Coleman, "Why We're Capitalizing Black," *The New York Times,* July 5, 2020, www.nytimes.com/2020/07/05/insider/capitalized -black.html; David Bauder, "AP Says It Will Capitalize Black but Not White," AP News, July 20, 2020, https://apnews.com/article/entertainment-cultures -race-and-ethnicity-us-news-ap-top-news-7e36c00c5af0436abc09e051261ffff1f.

26. A modified version of this section appeared in *Outreach* magazine at Michelle Sanchez, "Bonhoeffer's Black Jesus," OutreachMagazine.com (blog), September 14, 2020, https://outreachmagazine.com/features/leadership/58837 -bonhoeffers-black-jesus.html. Used with permission.

27. Quoted in Reggie L. Williams, *Bonhoeffer's Black Jesus: Harlem Renaissance Theology and an Ethic of Resistance* (Waco, TX: Baylor University, 2014), 23.

28. Williams, *Bonhoeffer's Black Jesus,* 45.

29. Dietrich Bonhoeffer, *Theological Education Underground: 1937–1940,* ed. Peter Frick, Dietrich Bonhoeffer Works, vol. 15 (Minneapolis: Fortress, 2011), Kindle.

30. Bonhoeffer, *Theological Education,* Kindle.

31. Williams, *Bonhoeffer's Black Jesus,* 34.

CHAPTER 2: A CHRIST-CENTERED APPROACH TO ANTIRACISM

1. Steven S. Skiena and Charles Ward, *Who's Bigger? Where Historical Figures Really Rank* (New York: Cambridge University, 2013).

2. Skiena and Ward, *Who's Bigger?*

3. John S. C. Abbott, ed., *Confidential Correspondence of the Emperor Napoleon and the Empress Josephine* (New York: Mason Brothers, 1856), 359, 361. This additional reflection from Napoleon is noteworthy: "Such is Christianity, the

only religion which destroys sectional prejudice, the only one which proclaims the unity and the absolute brotherhood of the whole human family" (360).

4. Daniel Motley, "C. S. Lewis' Ingenious Apologetic of Longing," The Logos Blog (blog), September 17, 2018, https://blog.logos.com/2018/09/c-s-lewis -ingenious-apologetic-longing-new.

5. This is why, in the classic Dante's *Inferno,* the culmination and climax of the journey through heaven is the *visio beatifica* or "beatific vision"—the beautiful vision of the face of God.

6. One of today's most helpful thought leaders on the subtle and insidious nature of White supremacy, and how it can be dismantled, is Daniel Hill. For more, see Daniel Hill, *White Awake: An Honest Look at What It Means to Be White* (Downers Grove, IL: IVP, 2017) and Daniel Hill, *White Lies: Nine Ways to Expose and Resist the Racial Systems That Divide Us* (Grand Rapids, MI: Zondervan, 2020).

7. John M. Perkins, *Dream with Me: Race, Love, and the Struggle We Must Win* (Grand Rapids, MI: Baker, 2017), 80.

8. George Yancey, *Beyond Racial Gridlock: Embracing Mutual Responsibility* (Downers Grove, IL: IVP, 2006), Kindle, emphasis added.

9. I have long envisioned the multilayered reconciliation that our world needs as a series of concentric circles, and it seems that numerous other thinkers have embraced a similar vision. For example, Lisa Sharon Harper has drawn circles that include self, gender, family, creation, governing structures, and nations in *The Very Good Gospel: How Everything Wrong Can Be Made Right* (Colorado Springs, CO: WaterBrook, 2016), 34. In a school paper, my friend Cheryl Lynn Cain labeled these circles as personal, interpersonal, systemic, and all creation, with everything holding together in God. I also thank Cheryl for highlighting that the Christ-hymn of Colossians 2 is a beautiful *song* of reconciliation.

10. Michael O. Emerson and Christian Smith, *Divided by Faith: Evangelical Religion and the Problem of Race in America* (New York: Oxford University, 2001), 7.

11. For more on the nature of powers and principalities in the world, see chapter 8, "Denouncing the Powers and Principalities," in Brenda Salter McNeil and Rick Richardson, *The Heart of Racial Justice: How Soul Change Leads to Social Change* (Downers Grove, IL: IVP, 2000). See also "Practice #5: Duel with the Devil" in Daniel Hill, *White Lies.*

12. This is a poetic Scripture paraphrase taken from Matthew 14:27; 28:20; and Revelation 22:13.

PART 2: COLOR-COURAGEOUS PARADIGM SHIFTS

1. Edward J. Blum and Paul Harvey, *The Color of Christ: The Son of God and the Saga of Race in America* (Chapel Hill, NC: University of North Carolina Press, 2012), Kindle.

CHAPTER 3: DISCIPLESHIP AS AWAKENING

1. Josephine Sedgwick, "25-Year-Old Textbooks and Holes in the Ceiling: Inside America's Public Schools," *The New York Times,* April 16, 2018, www .nytimes.com/2018/04/16/reader-center/us-public-schools-conditions.html.

2. Ken Wytsma, *The Myth of Equality: Uncovering the Roots of Injustice and Privilege* (Downers Grove, IL: IVP Books, 2017).

3. This section is modeled on the outstanding and frequently updated "7 Ways We Know Systemic Racism Is Real," Ben & Jerry's (blog), www.benjerry .com/whats-new/2016/systemic-racism-is-real.

4. Neil Bhutta et al., "Disparities in Wealth by Race and Ethnicity in the 2019 Survey of Consumer Finances," U.S. Federal Reserve System, September 28, 2020, www.federalreserve.gov/econres/notes/feds-notes/disparities-in-wealth -by-race-and-ethnicity-in-the-2019-survey-of-consumer-finances-20200928 .htm.

5. Jenna Ross, "The Racial Wealth Gap in America: Asset Types Held by Race," Visual Capitalist (blog), June 12, 2020, www.visualcapitalist.com/racial -wealth-gap.

6. Matt Bruenig, "The Top 10 Percent of White Families Own Almost Everything," *The American Prospect,* September 8, 2014, https://prospect.org /power/top-10-percent-white-families-almost-everything.

7. Gail MarksJarvis, "Why Black Homeownership Rates Lag Even as the Housing Market Recovers," *Chicago Tribune,* July 21, 2017, www.chicagotribune .com/business/ct-black-homeownership-plunges-0723-biz-20170720-story .html.

8. "The Racial Disparity in Homeownership Rates Persists," Joint Center for Housing Studies of Harvard University, www.jchs.harvard.edu/son-2020 -homeownership-gap.

9. MarksJarvis, "Why Black Homeownership Rates Lag."

10. Jenny Schuetz, "Rethinking Homeownership Incentives to Improve Household Financial Security and Shrink the Racial Wealth Gap," Brookings (blog), December 9, 2020, www.brookings.edu/research/rethinking-homeownership -incentives-to-improve-household-financial-security-and-shrink-the-racial -wealth-gap.

11. "The Future of Fair Housing," National Commission on Fair Housing and Equal Opportunity, December 2008, https://lawyerscommittee.org /wp-content/uploads/2015/08/The-Future-of-Fair-Housing-National -Commission-on-Fair-Housing-and-Equal-Opportunity.pdf.

12. See chart "Denial Rates for Home Loan Applications by Race," in Shayanne Gal et al., "26 Simple Charts to Show Friends and Family Who Aren't Con-

vinced Racism Is Still a Problem in America," *Business Insider,* July 8, 2020, www.businessinsider.com/us-systemic-racism-in-charts-graphs-data-2020-6.

13. Drew DeSilver, "Black Unemployment Rate Is Consistently Twice That of Whites," Pew Research Center (blog), August 21, 2013, www.pewresearch .org/fact-tank/2013/08/21/through-good-times-and-bad-black-unemploy ment-is-consistently-double-that-of-whites.

14. Janell Ross and National Journal, "African-Americans with College De-grees Are Twice As Likely to Be Unemployed as Other Graduates," *The At-lantic,* May 26, 2014, www.theatlantic.com/politics/archive/2014/05/african -americans-with-college-degrees-are-twice-as-likely-to-be-unemployed-as -other-graduates/430971.

15. Robert Manduca, "How Rising U.S. Income Inequality Exacerbates Racial Economic Disparities," Equitable Growth (blog), Washington Center for Eq-uitable Growth, August 23, 2018, www.equitablegrowth.org/how-rising-u-s -income-inequality-exacerbates-racial-economic-disparities.

16. Sarah Mervosh, "How Much Wealthier Are White School Districts Than Nonwhite Ones? $23 Billion, Report Says," *The New York Times,* Febru-ary 27, 2019, www.nytimes.com/2019/02/27/education/school-districts -funding-white-minorities.html.

17. Rose French, "Study: White Students Favored over Blacks in Gifted Pro-grams," *The Atlanta Journal-Constitution,* www.ajc.com/news/local-education /study-white-students-favored-over-blacks-gifted-programs/ns6XS6kgfW 8falN1YSybUK. *Civil Rights Data Collection Data Snapshot: School Discipline* (Washington, D.C.: U.S. Department of Education Office for Civil Rights, March 2014), www2.ed.gov/about/offices/list/ocr/docs/crdc-discipline -snapshot.pdf.

18. Phillip Atiba Goff et al., "The Essence of Innocence: Consequences of De-humanizing Black Children," *Journal of Personality and Social Psychology* 106, no. 4 (2014): 526–45, www.apa.org/pubs/journals/releases/psp-a0035663 .pdf.

19. Kim Farbota, "Black Crime Rates: What Happens When Numbers Aren't Neutral," *HuffPost,* September 2, 2016, www.huffpost.com/entry/black -crime-rates-your-st_b_8078586.

20. Jennifer L. Eberhardt, *Biased: Uncovering the Hidden Prejudice That Shapes What We See, Think, and Do* (New York: Penguin, 2019), 129–31.

21. "Racial Bias in the Justice System," Innocence Project, September 17, 2009, https://innocenceproject.org/racial-bias-in-the-justice-system.

22. Farbota, "Black Crime Rates."

23. "Criminal Justice Fact Sheet," NAACP, May 24, 2021, https://naacp.org /resources/criminal-justice-fact-sheet.

24. "Introduction to COVID-19 Racial and Ethnic Health Disparities," Centers for Disease Control and Prevention, Decembeer 10, 2020, www.cdc.gov /coronavirus/2019-ncov/community/health-equity/racial-ethnic-disparities /index.html.

25. Samantha Artiga et al., "Health Coverage by Race and Ethnicity, 2010–2019," KFF (blog), July 16, 2021, www.kff.org/racial-equity-and-health-policy /issue-brief/health-coverage-by-race-and-ethnicity.

26. Christen Linke Young, "There Are Clear, Race-Based Inequalities in Health Insurance and Health Outcomes," Brookings (blog), February 19, 2020, www.brookings.edu/blog/usc-brookings-schaeffer-on-health-policy/2020 /02/19/there-are-clear-race-based-inequalities-in-health-insurance-and -health-outcomes.

27. Khiara M. Bridges, "Implicit Bias and Racial Disparities in Health Care," *Human Rights Magazine* 43, no. 3 (2018), www.americanbar.org/groups/crsj /publications/human_rights_magazine_home/the-state-of-healthcare-in -the-united-states/racial-disparities-in-health-care.

28. Dayna Bowen Matthew, Edward Rodrigue, and Richard V. Reeves, "Time for Justice: Tackling Race Inequalities in Health and Housing," Brookings (blog), October 19, 2016, www.brookings.edu/research/time-for-justice -tackling-race-inequalities-in-health-and-housing.

29. Mathieu Rees, "Racism in Healthcare: What You Need to Know," *Medical News Today*, September 17, 2020, www.medicalnewstoday.com/articles/racism -in-healthcare.

30. Austin Frakt, "Bad Medicine: The Harm That Comes from Racism," *The New York Times*, January 13, 2020, www.nytimes.com/2020/01/13/upshot /bad-medicine-the-harm-that-comes-from-racism.html.

31. Xingyu Zhang et al., "Trends of Racial/Ethnic Differences in Emergency Department Care Outcomes Among Adults in the United States from 2005 to 2016," *Frontiers in Medicine* 7 (2020): 300, https://doi.org/10.3389/fmed .2020.00300.

32. Frakt, "Bad Medicine."

33. Richie Zweigenhaft, "Fortune 500 CEOs, 2000–2020: Still Male, Still White," *The Society Pages*, October 28, 2020, https://thesocietypages.org /specials/fortune-500-ceos-2000-2020-still-male-still-white. Allana Akhtar, "Corporate America Is Seeing a Spike in the Age of CEOs Being Hired—and Yes, They're Overwhelmingly White Men," *Business Insider*, November 1, 2019, www.businessinsider.in/strategy/news/corporate-america-is-seeing-a -spike-in-the-age-of-ceos-being-hired-and-yes-theyre-overwhelmingly -white-men/articleshow/71856494.cms. Also, Gal et al., "26 Simple Charts to Show Friends and Family Who Aren't Convinced Racism Is Still a Problem in America."

34. Gal et al., "26 Simple Charts."

35. Aaron Zitner, "The U.S. Has Elected Only Two Black Governors. Why That Might Change," *Wall Street Journal*, September 1, 2020, www.wsj.com/articles/black-candidates-are-now-winning-in-mostly-white-districts-opening-path-to-higher-office-11598980352.

36. Denise Lu et al., "Faces of Power: 80% Are White, Even as U.S. Becomes More Diverse," *The New York Times*, September 9, 2020, www.nytimes.com/interactive/2020/09/09/us/powerful-people-race-us.html.

37. Nicholas Kristof, "We're No. 28! And Dropping!" *The New York Times*, September 9, 2020, www.nytimes.com/2020/09/09/opinion/united-states-social-progress.html.

38. *Merriam-Webster*, s.v. "woke," www.merriam-webster.com/dictionary/woke.

39. "Stay Woke: The New Sense of 'Woke' Is Gaining Popularity," *Merriam-Webster*, www.merriam-webster.com/words-at-play/woke-meaning-origin.

40. Martin Luther King, Jr., *Where Do We Go from Here: Chaos or Community?* (Boston: Beacon, 2010), 181.

41. Jemar Tisby, *The Color of Compromise: The Truth About the American Church's Complicity in Racism* (Grand Rapids, MI: Zondervan, 2019), Kindle.

42. King, *Where Do We Go from Here,* 10.

43. Barry Beckham, *Garvey Lives!: A Play,* 1972.

44. *The NIV Exhaustive Bible Concordance,* 3rd ed. (Grand Rapids, MI: Zondervan, 2015).

45. James Martin, "Magis," Ignatian Spirituality (blog), July 13, 2018, www.ignatianspirituality.com/magis. As James Martin, SJ, writes, "The unofficial motto of the Society of Jesus is *Ad Majorem Dei Gloriam:* For the Greater Glory of God. The fundamental idea is that we try to do the more, the better, the greater, for God. Not for ourselves." *Magis* is also a beautiful concept in that it encourages disciples to do what is *more beneficial* for the common good. See Fr. Barton T. Geger, "What Magis Really Means and Why It Matters," *Jesuit Higher Education* 1, no. 2 (2012): 16–31.

46. Daniel Hill, *White Awake: An Honest Look at What It Means to Be White* (Downers Grove, IL: IVP Books, 2017), 4.

CHAPTER 4: DISCIPLESHIP AS WARDROBE CHANGE

1. See, for example, Friedrich Försterling, *Attribution: An Introduction to Theories, Research, and Applications* (New York: Psychology Press, 2001).

2. David W. Swanson, *Rediscipling the White Church: From Cheap Diversity to True Solidarity* (Downers Grove, IL: IVP, 2020).

3. I am grateful to Christina Edmonson, long-time dean of intercultural student development at Calvin College, for first drawing my attention to this idea.

4. John Powell and Rachel Godsil, "Implicit Bias Insights as Preconditions to Structural Change," *Poverty and Race Journal* 20, no. 5 (October 2011): 3, https://prrac.org/implicit-bias-insights-as-preconditions-to-structural-change-by-john-powell-rachel-godsil-sept-oct-2011-pr-issue.

5. "About the IAT," Project Implicit, https://implicit.harvard.edu/implicit/iatdetails.html.

6. Alexis McGill Johnson and Rachel D. Godsil, *Transforming Perception: Black Men and Boys* (Perception Institute, March 2013), 8, http://perception.org/wp-content/uploads/2014/11/Transforming-Perception.pdf.

7. Katherine L. Milkman, Modupe Akinola, and Dolly Chugh, "What Happens Before? A Field Experiment Exploring How Pay and Representation Differentially Shape Bias on the Pathway into Organizations," *Journal of Applied Psychology* 100, no. 6 (November 2015): 1678–712, www.apa.org/pubs/journals/releases/apl-0000022.pdf.

8. Dolly Chugh, Katherine L. Milkman, and Modupe Akinola, "Opinion | Professors Are Prejudiced, Too," *The New York Times,* May 9, 2014, www.nytimes.com/2014/05/11/opinion/sunday/professors-are-prejudiced-too.html.

9. As of this writing, a variety of free online implicit association tests can be taken at https://implicit.harvard.edu.

10. Jacques-Philippe Leyens et al., "Psychological Essentialism and the Differential Attribution of Uniquely Human Emotions to Ingroups and Outgroups," *European Journal of Social Psychology* 31, no. 4 (July/August 2001): 395–411, https://doi.org/10.1002/ejsp.50. "People attribute more uniquely human characteristics to the ingroup than to the outgroup."

11. Jennifer L. Eberhardt, *Biased: Uncovering the Hidden Prejudice That Shapes What We See, Think, and Do* (New York: Viking, 2019), 149.

12. Eberhardt, *Biased,* 145.

13. Johnson and Godsil, *Transforming Perception,* 8.

14. See German Lopez, "A New Study Shows Even 5-Year-Olds Can't Escape Racism," *Vox,* June 29, 2017, www.vox.com/identities/2017/6/29/15893172/study-racism-innocence-black-girls and Phillip Atiba Goff et al., "The Essence of Innocence: Consequences of Dehumanizing Black Children," *Journal of Personality and Social Psychology* 106, no. 4 (2014): 526–45, https://doi.org/10.1037/a0035663.

15. See, for example, Civil Rights Data Collection, *An Overview of Exclusionary Discipline Practices in Public Schools for the 2017–2018 School Year* (U.S. Depart-

ment of Education, Office for Civil Rights, June 2021), https://ocrdata.ed.gov /assets/downloads/crdc-exclusionary-school-discipline.pdf. Also Johnson and Godsil, *Transforming Perception*, 10.

16. Christopher Ingraham, "You Really Can Get Pulled over for Driving While Black, Federal Statistics Show," *The Washington Post,* September 9, 2014, www.washingtonpost.com/news/wonk/wp/2014/09/09/you-really-can -get-pulled-over-for-driving-while-black-federal-statistics-show.

17. *Social Science Literature Review: Media Representations and Impact on the Lives of Black Men and Boys* (The Opportunity Agenda, October 2011), https://bit.ly /blackmenboys, 24.

18. "When They See Us: Improving the Media's Coverage of Black Men and Boys," The Opportunity Agenda, 2019, www.opportunityagenda.org/explore /resources-publications/when-they-see-us-media.

19. Steve Stroessner and Catherine Good, "Stereotype Threat: An Overview," Femmes et Mathématiques, https://femmes-et-maths.fr/wp-content/uploads /2021/01/stereotype_threat_overview.pdf.

20. "Empirically Validated Strategies to Reduce Stereotype Threat," Stanford, https://ed.stanford.edu/sites/default/files/interventionshandout.pdf.

21. Gordon Hodson, "System Justification: Why People Buy Into Social Inequality," *Psychology Today,* February 16, 2017, www.psychologytoday.com/us /blog/without-prejudice/201702/system-justification-why-people-buy -social-inequality. "Taking action against a powerful advantaged group can result in retaliation or an unstable situation, both of which can be undesirable for the weaker party."

22. "The Ostrich Effect: Why and How People Avoid Information," *Effectiviology,* https://effectiviology.com/ostrich-effect.

23. Eberhardt, *Biased,* 217. See also Philip J. Mazzocco, *The Psychology of Racial Colorblindness: A Critical Review* (New York: Palgrave Macmillan, 2017).

24. Mazzocco, *The Psychology of Racial Colorblindness,* 174.

25. Mellody Hobson, "Color Blind or Color Brave?," March 2014, TED, www .ted.com/talks/mellody_hobson_color_blind_or_color_brave.

26. Johnson and Godsil, *Transforming Perception,* 11. "Studies also show that people will act according to egalitarian values when conscious that race may affect their decision-making." See also Lily Zheng, "Practice Reduces Prejudice," SPARQ, https://sparq.stanford.edu/solutions/practice-reduces-prejudice and K. Kawakami et al., "Just Say No (to Stereotyping): Effects of Training in the Negation of Stereotypic Associations on Stereotype Activation," *Journal of Personality and Social Psychology,* 78, no. 5 (2000): 871–88.

CHAPTER 5: DISCIPLESHIP AS INNER HEALING

1. Ibram X. Kendi, *How to Be an Antiracist* (New York: One World, 2019), 129. Kendi acknowledged: "To be antiracist is to see ordinary White people as the frequent victimizers of people of color *and* the frequent victims of racist power" (emphasis added).

2. Michael Balsamo, "Hate Crimes in US Reach Highest Level in More than a Decade," AP News, November 16, 2020, https://apnews.com/article/hate -crimes-rise-FBI-data-ebbcadca8458aba96575da905650120d.

3. "Bullying Statistics," National Bullying Prevention Center, last updated November 2020, www.pacer.org/bullying/info/stats.asp.

4. "Bullying Statistics."

5. "When Black Death Goes Viral, It Can Trigger PTSD-like Trauma," PBS NewsHour, July 22, 2016, www.pbs.org/newshour/nation/black-pain-gone -viral-racism-graphic-videos-can-create-ptsd-like-trauma.

6. Nora Chavez, "Shouldering Grief: Validating Native American Historical Trauma," NM Cares Health Disparities Center, https://hsc.unm.edu/programs /nmcareshd/docs/story_heart.pdf.

7. Chavez, "Shouldering Grief."

8. Chavez, "Shouldering Grief."

9. Resmaa Menakem, *My Grandmother's Hands: Racialized Trauma and the Pathway to Mending Our Hearts and Bodies* (Las Vegas: Central Recovery, 2017), 39–40.

10. Menakem, *My Grandmother's Hands,* 40.

11. Menakem, *My Grandmother's Hands,* 56.

12. Menakem, *My Grandmother's Hands,* 40–56.

13. Vann R. Newkirk II, "Trump's EPA Concludes Environmental Racism Is Real," *The Atlantic,* February 28, 2018, www.theatlantic.com/politics/archive /2018/02/the-trump-administration-finds-that-environmental-racism-is -real/554315.

14. Melissa Denchak, "Flint Water Crisis: Everything You Need to Know," NRDC, November 8, 2018, www.nrdc.org/stories/flint-water-crisis-everything-you -need-know.

15. Malcolm X and Alex Haley, *The Autobiography of Malcolm X: As Told to Alex Haley* (New York: Ballantine, 1999), 3. First published October 1965.

16. Malcom X and Haley, *Autobiography of Malcom X,* 5–6.

17. Michael Beschloss, "How an Experiment with Dolls Helped Lead to School Integration," *The New York Times,* May 6, 2014, www.nytimes.com/2014

/05/07/upshot/how-an-experiment-with-dolls-helped-lead-to-school
-integration.html.

18. In her short 2005 documentary film *A Girl Like Me,* Kiri Davis replicated the doll test and showed that the majority (fifteen out of twenty-one) of Black children continued to "choose the white dolls over the black, giving similar reasons as the original subjects, associating white with being pretty or good and black with ugly or bad." *A Girl Like Me* (film), Wikipedia, https://en .wikipedia.org/wiki/A_Girl_like_Me_(film).

19. Rebecca Rangel Campón and Robert T. Carter, "The Appropriated Racial Oppression Scale: Development and Preliminary Validation," *Cultural Diversity & Ethnic Minority Psychology* 21, no. 4 (October 2015): 497–506, https://doi.org /10.1037/cdp0000037; Dawne M. Mouzon and Jamila S. McLean, "Internalized Racism and Mental Health Among African-Americans, US-Born Caribbean Blacks, and Foreign-Born Caribbean Blacks," *Ethnicity & Health* 22, no. 1 (February 2017): 36–48, https://doi.org/10.1080/13557858.2016.1196652.

20. You can find the Racial Slur Database at www.rsdb.org. See also Kat Chow and Gene Demby, "Overthinking It: Using Food as a Racial Metaphor," NPR, September 14, 2014, www.npr.org/sections/codeswitch/2014/09/12 /348008432/overthinking-it-using-food-as-a-racial-metaphor.

21. The 2011 documentary *Dark Girls* (directed by D. Channsin Berry and Bill Duke) poignantly explores colorism. The sequel, *Dark Girls 2* (directed by D. Channsin Berry and released in 2020), delves deeper into colorism on an international level.

22. Jennifer L. Hochschild and Vesla Weaver, "The Skin Color Paradox and the American Racial Order," *Social Forces* 86, no. 2 (2007): 2.

23. Hochschild and Weaver, "The Skin Color Paradox," 2.

24. Menakem, *My Grandmother's Hands,* 271, emphasis added.

25. Brené Brown, "Shame vs. Guilt," Brené Brown (blog), January 15, 2013, https://brenebrown.com/articles/2013/01/15/shame-v-guilt.

26. One recent work on the intersection of racism and shame is Tarana Burke and Brené Brown, eds., *You Are Your Best Thing: Vulnerability, Shame Resilience, and the Black Experience* (New York: Random House, 2021).

27. Dana Brownlee, "This Therapist's Message to White Men: Become an Agent of Change or a Victim of Progress," *Forbes,* May 12, 2021, www.forbes.com /sites/danabrownlee/2021/05/12/this-therapists-message-to-white-men become-an-agent-of-change-or-a-victim-of-progress.

28. Andrew Horning, *Grappling: White Men's Journey from Fragile to Agile* (Carson City, NV: Lioncrest Publishing, 2021). See also Robin J. DiAngelo, *White Fragility: Why It's So Hard for White People to Talk About Racism* (Boston: Beacon, 2018).

29. Stacy Weiner, "Bryan Stevenson: It's Time to Change the Narrative around Race and Poverty," AAMC, November 8, 2019, www.aamc.org/news-insights /bryan-stevenson-it-s-time-change-narrative-around-race-and-poverty.

30. Brené Brown, *Rising Strong: How the Ability to Reset Transforms the Way We Live, Love, Parent, and Lead* (New York: Spiegel & Grau, 2015), xx.

31. Brown, *Rising Strong*, 39.

32. Brené Brown, *I Thought It Was Just Me (but It Isn't): Making the Journey from "What Will People Think?" to "I Am Enough."* (New York: Gotham, 2007), introduction, Kindle.

33. Henri J. M. Nouwen, *Life of the Beloved: Spiritual Living in a Secular World* (New York: Crossroad, 2002), 43–45.

34. Nouwen, *Life of the Beloved*, 30–33.

35. "What Is PTG?," Posttraumatic Growth Research Group (blog), January 16, 2013, https://ptgi.uncc.edu/what-is-ptg.

36. Shelley H. Carson, "From Tragedy to Art: Meaning-Making, Personal Narrative, and Life's Adversities," *Psychology Today*, June 18, 2010, www.psychology today.com/us/blog/life-art/201006/tragedy-art-meaning-making-personal -narrative-and-life-s-adversities.

37. Desmond Tutu, *No Future Without Forgiveness* (New York: Image Classics, 2000).

38. Miroslav Volf, *Exclusion and Embrace: A Theological Exploration of Identity, Otherness, and Reconciliation* (Nashville, TN: Abingdon, 1996), 124.

39. Martin Luther King, Jr., *Strength to Love* (Minneapolis: Fortress, 2010), 44–45.

40. Volf, *Exclusion and Embrace*, 80.

41. King, *Strength to Love*, 50.

42. Volf, *Exclusion and Embrace*, 81.

43. Henri J. M. Nouwen, *The Wounded Healer: Ministry in Contemporary Society* (London: Darton, Longman & Todd, 2004), 82–83.

CHAPTER 6: DISCIPLESHIP AS BELOVED COMMUNITY

1. "The King Philosophy—Nonviolence365," The King Center, https://theking center.org/about-tkc/the-king-philosophy. According to the site, the quote originated in a July 13, 1966, article in *Christian Century Magazine*.

2. John Perkins, *Dream with Me: Race, Love, and the Struggle We Must Win* (Grand Rapids, MI: Baker, 2017).

3. Ibram X. Kendi, *How to Be an Antiracist* (New York: One World, 2019), 230, emphasis added.

4. George Yancey, *Beyond Racial Gridlock: Embracing Mutual Responsibility* (Downers Grove, IL: IVP Books, 2009), Kindle, emphasis added.

5. Yancey, *Beyond Racial Gridlock*.

6. Yancey, *Beyond Racial Gridlock*.

7. N. T. Wright, *Paul for Everyone: 1 Corinthians,* The New Testament for Everyone (Louisville, KY: Presbyterian Publishing Corporation, 2015), 165.

8. Martin Luther King, Jr., "Letter from Birmingham Jail," The Martin Luther King Jr. Research and Education Institute, https://kinginstitute.stanford.edu /king-papers/documents/letter-birmingham-jail.

9. Martin Luther King, Jr., and Clayborne Carson, *Stride Toward Freedom: The Montgomery Story,* The King Legacy Series (Boston: Beacon, 2010), 127–28.

10. Heather McGhee, *The Sum of Us: What Racism Costs Everyone and How We Can Prosper Together* (New York: One World, 2021).

11. *The Sum of Us* (Amazon book description), Amazon.com, https://amazon.com /Sum-Us-Everyone-Prosper-Together-ebook/dp/B0871KZQ3G/ref=sr_1 _2?crid=22CJBYEHGPS76&dchild=1&keywords=the+sum+of+us+what +racism+costs&qid=1612633510&s=books&sprefix=the+sum+of+racism %2Caps%2C162&sr=1-2.

12. Jonathan M. Metzl, *Dying of Whiteness: How the Politics of Racial Resentment Is Killing America's Heartland* (New York: Basic Books, 2019).

13. Robin J. DiAngelo, *White Fragility: Why It's So Hard for White People to Talk About Racism* (Boston: Beacon, 2018), 67–68.

14. Arthur Boers, "What Henri Nouwen Found at Daybreak," *Christianity Today,* October 3, 1994, www.christianitytoday.com/ct/1994/october3/4tb028.html, emphasis added.

15. Lawrence Barriner II and Danielle Coates-Connor, "Using #the4thbox: Play and Political Imagination," Interaction Institute for Social Change, June 23, 2016, https://interactioninstitute.org/using-the4thbox-play-and -political-imagination.

16. Martin Luther King, Jr., "Remaining Awake Through a Great Revolution," *A Testament of Hope: The Essential Writings and Speeches of Martin Luther King, Jr.,* ed. James Melvin Washington (San Francisco: HarperSanFrancisco, 2003), 268–78, emphasis added. King delivered this address at the National Cathedral, Washington, D.C., on March 31, 1968, and it was entered into the *Congressional Record* on April 9, 1968.

Dr. King was likely using sweeping language to illustrate a wider point. The United States Homestead Acts transferred more than 270 million acres of land to individuals in the decades following the Civil War. Black people were technically eligible to receive land under these acts, and some certainly did. Nevertheless, for a variety of reasons, Black homesteading recipients were the exception rather than the rule; in reality, "almost all" of the ultimate beneficiaries were White. "Indeed, the Homestead Acts excluded African Americans not in letter, but in practice—a template that the government would propagate for the next century and a half." Keri Leigh Merritt, "Land and the Roots of African-American Poverty," Aeon, March 11, 2016, https://aeon.co /ideas/land-and-the-roots-of-african-american-poverty. See also Larry Adelman, "Background Readings," Race—The Power of an Illusion, PBS, www.pbs .org/race/000_About/002_04-background-03-02.htm.

17. Mark Russell et al., *Routes & Radishes: And Other Things to Talk About at the Evangelical Crossroads* (Grand Rapids, MI: Zondervan, 2010), 128.

18. Russell et al., *Routes & Radishes,* 128–29, emphasis added.

PART 3: COLOR-COURAGEOUS SPIRITUAL PRACTICES

1. Emmanuel Katongole, "From Tower-Dwellers to Travelers," interview by Andy Crouch, *Christianity Today,* July 3, 2007, www.christianitytoday.com /ct/2007/july/9.34.html.

2. Rose Dowsett, *The Cape Town Commitment,* Study Edition (Carol Stream, IL: Tyndale, 2012).

CHAPTER 7: READ (IN LIVING COLOR)

1. "Cape Town 2010: The Third Lausanne Congress on World Evangelization," Lausanne Movement, www.lausanne.org/cape-town-2010-the-third-lausanne -congress-on-world-evangelization.

2. A fascinating resource that analyzes the United States as a nation of eleven distinct regional cultures is Colin Woodard, *American Nations: A History of the Eleven Rival Regional Cultures of North America* (New York: Viking, 2011).

3. Some excellent contributions to this discussion are E. Randolph Richards and Brandon J. O'Brien, *Misreading Scripture with Western Eyes: Removing Cultural Blinders to Better Understand the Bible* (Downers Grove, IL: IVP Books, 2012) and E. Randolph Richards and Richard James, *Misreading Scripture with Individualist Eyes: Patronage, Honor, and Shame in the Biblical World* (Downers Grove, IL: IVP Academic, 2020).

4. Christian Smith and Michael O. Emerson, *Divided by Faith: Evangelical Religion and the Problem of Race in America* (Oxford: Oxford University Press, 2000), 76.

5. Tim Keller, "A Biblical Critique of Secular Justice and Critical Theory," *Life in the Gospel,* https://quarterly.gospelinlife.com/a-biblical-critique-of-secular -justice-and-critical-theory.

6. Smith and Emerson, *Divided by Faith,* 76.

7. Smith and Emerson, *Divided by Faith,* 78.

8. Smith and Emerson, *Divided by Faith,* 78.

9. Greg Asimakoupoulos, "A Head of His Time: How One of the Most Recognizable Images of Jesus Came to Be," *Covenant Companion,* February 8, 2016, https://covchurch.org/2016/02/08/a-head-of-his-time.

10. Asimakoupoulos, "A Head of His Time."

11. Mark Rosen, "Much-Beloved, Much-Maligned 'Head of Christ' Has Graced Many Walls—and Now a Dallas Museum," *The Dallas Morning News,* July 14, 2018, sec. Visual Arts, www.dallasnews.com/arts-entertainment/visual-arts /2018/07/15/much-beloved-much-maligned-head-of-christ-has-graced -many-walls-and-now-a-dallas-museum.

12. Asimakoupoulos, "A Head of His Time."

13. Paul Robinson, "We Can't Cancel 'White Jesus,' but We Can Keep Telling Our Church's Story," Religion News Service, June 29, 2020, https://religion news.com/2020/06/29/we-cant-cancel-white-jesus-but-we-can-keep -telling-our-churchs-story.

14. Giles Wilson, "So What Colour Was Jesus?," BBC News Online Magazine, October 27, 2004, http://news.bbc.co.uk/2/hi/uk_news/magazine /3958241.stm.

15. James H. Charlesworth, *The Historical Jesus: An Essential Guide* (Nashville, TN: Abingdon Press, 2008), 72.

16. Emily McFarlan Miller, "How Jesus Became White—and Why It's Time to Cancel That," Religion News Service, June 24, 2020, https://religionnews .com/2020/06/24/how-jesus-became-white-and-why-its-time-to-cancel -that.

17. Dr. Max Lee tells the story of the course's creation, development, and hoped-for outcomes in Max J. Lee, "Reading the Bible Interculturally: An Invitation to the Evangelical Covenant Church and Evangelical Christianity," *The Covenant Quarterly* 73, no. 2 (August 24, 2015): 4–14.

18. Tara Yosso's original definition of *community cultural wealth* applies specifically to communities of color as the "array of knowledges, skills, abilities and contacts possessed and utilized by Communities of Color to survive and resist racism and other forms of oppression" (Trina M. Valdez and Catherine Lugg, "Community Cultural Wealth and Chicano/Latino Students," *Journal of School Public Relations* 31, no. 3 (2010): 224–37, ERIC, https://eric.ed.gov/?id= EJ916875). See also R. Tolteka Cuauhtin, "We Have Community Cultural Wealth! Scaffolding Tara Yosso's Theory for Classroom Praxis" in *Rethinking Ethnic Studies* (Milwaukee: Rethinking Schools, 2019) and Stephanie Carrillo, "Summary of All the Wealth We Cannot See: Cultural Assets and Community Capital" (PoCC 2019 Presentation, December 7, 2019).

19. For example, Randy Woodley, *Shalom and the Community of Creation: An Indigenous Vision,* Prophetic Christianity Series (Grand Rapids, MI: Eerdmans, 2012).

20. James H. Cone, *The Cross and the Lynching Tree* (Ossining, NY: Orbis Books, 2011).

21. See Dominique DuBois Gilliard, *Rethinking Incarceration: Advocating for Justice That Restores* (Downers Grove, IL: IVP Books, 2018).

22. For more on these inspiring prison ministry movements, see Jonathan Sprowl, "The Church Inside: A New Movement in America's Prisons," Outreach Magazine.com (blog), July 31, 2019, https://outreachmagazine.com/features /discipleship/44484-the-church-inside-a-new-movement-in-americas -prisons.html and Troy Rienstra, "Partners in the Gospel: The Church Behind Bars," *The Christian Century,* October 3 2006, www.christiancentury.org /article/2006-10/partners-gospel.

23. See, for example, Albert L. Reyes, "I Was a Stranger: Jesus and the Undocumented Immigrant," in *Immigration: Christian Reflection,* A Series in Faith and Ethics, ed. Robert B. Kruschwitz (The Center for Christian Ethics at Baylor University, 2008), 63–67.

24. Lesslie Newbigin, *The Gospel in a Pluralist Society* (Grand Rapids, MI: Eerdmans, 1989).

25. Sadhu Sundar Singh, *The Search After Reality: Thoughts on Hinduism, Buddhism, Muhammadanism and Christianity* (United Kingdom: Dekton Publishing, 2021 [1925]).

26. See, for example, Ross Kane, "The Wisdom of the African Christian Practice of Reverencing the Dead," *The Christian Century,* April 5, 2018, www .christiancentury.org/article/critical-essay/wisdom-african-christian-practice -reverencing-dead.

27. Here I want to extend my deep appreciation to Dr. Moonjang Lee. From a South Korean background, Dr. Lee was by far my most influential professor in seminary, in part due to the unique cultural wisdom he brought. His courses "The Practice of Prayer" and "Spiritual Formation and Mission Praxis" were nothing short of legendary. See also Jeff Ritchie, "I Will Awake the Dawn: An Experience of the Dawn Prayer Meeting in Korea," The Outreach Foundation (blog), October 9, 2016, www.theoutreachfoundation.org /trip-blog/2016/10/8/i-will-awake-the-dawn-an-experience-of-the-dawn -prayer-meeting-in-korea.

28. There are many excellent resources online to help diversify your influences and your bookshelf. See Jody Wiley Fernando's "101 Culturally Diverse Christian Voices," Between Worlds (blog), https://thelinkbetweenworlds.com/2014 /03/24/101-culturally-diverse-christian-voices. Find a list of one hundred books by Christian authors of color at Deidra Riggs, "Books by Christian Authors of Color," www.deidrariggs.com/books-christian-authors-color. You'll find more colorful resource recommendations at https://michelletsanchez .com/colorcourageous.

29. Jemar Tisby, among others, does a spectacular job of tracing the history of the White church's complicity with racism in America. See Tisby, *The Color of Compromise: The Truth About the American Church's Complicity in Racism* (Grand Rapids, MI: Zondervan, 2020).

30. For some excellent resources that explore the connections between racial dynamics and effective evangelism, see Brenda Salter McNeil, *A Credible Witness: Reflections on Power, Evangelism and Race* (Downers Grove, IL: IVP Books, 2008); Sarah Shin, *Beyond Color Blind: Redeeming Our Ethnic Journey* (Downers Grove, IL: IVP Books, 2017); and Rick Richardson, *Reimagining Evangelism: Inviting Friends on a Spiritual Journey* (Downers Grove, IL: IVP Books, 2006).

31. William H. Frey, "The US Will Become 'Minority White' in 2045, Census Projects," Brookings (blog), March 14, 2018, www.brookings.edu/blog/the -avenue/2018/03/14/the-us-will-become-minority-white-in-2045-census -projects.

CHAPTER 8: PRAY (IN THE RAW)

1. Mark Vroegop, *Dark Clouds, Deep Mercy: Discovering the Grace of Lament* (Wheaton, IL: Crossway, 2019), 28.

2. Vroegop, *Dark Clouds, Deep Mercy.*

3. Philip Yancey, *Disappointment with God: Three Questions No One Asks Aloud* (Grand Rapids, MI: Zondervan, 1988), 237.

4. David W. Swanson, *Rediscipling the White Church: From Cheap Diversity to True Solidarity* (Downers Grove, IL: IVP, 2020).

5. Soong-Chan Rah, *Prophetic Lament: A Call for Justice in Troubled Times,* Resonate Series (Downers Grove, IL: IVP Books, 2015), 22.

6. J. E. Eubanks, Jr., "The Confession of Corporate Sins," byFaith (blog), January 13, 2016, https://byfaithonline.com/the-confession-of-corporate-sins.

7. Mark Vroegop, *Weep with Me: How Lament Opens a Door for Racial Reconciliation* (Wheaton, IL: Crossway, 2020), 113.

8. H. B. Charles, Jr., quoted in Vroegop, *Weep with Me,* 79.

CHAPTER 9: PILGRIMAGE (FOR PERSPECTIVE)

1. "Sankofa—ECC | Love Mercy Do Justice," https://covchurch.org/justice /racial-righteousness/sankofa, emphasis added. The Evangelical Covenant Church has preferred the terms *racial righteousness* and *racial reconciliation.* "What Is Racial Righteousness?," Minnehaha Academy, www.minnehaha academy.net/about/racial-righteousness.

2. Leland Ryken, Jim Wilhoit, and Tremper Longman, eds., "Pilgrim, Pilgrimage," in *Dictionary of Biblical Imagery* (Downers Grove, IL: IVP Books, 2000).

3. Ryken, Wilhoit, and Longman, *Dictionary of Biblical Imagery.*

4. Ryken, Wilhoit, and Longman. *Dictionary of Biblical Imagery.*

5. Ryken, Wilhoit, and Longman. *Dictionary of Biblical Imagery.*

6. James Harpur, *The Pilgrim Journey: A History of Pilgrimage in the Western World* (Katonah, NY: BlueBridge, 2016), 6.

7. N. T. Wright, *The Way of the Lord: Christian Pilgrimage Today,* 2014 ed. (Grand Rapids, MI: Eerdmans, 1999), 4.

8. Christian Timothy George, *Sacred Travels: Recovering the Ancient Practice of Pilgrimage* (Downers Grove, IL: IVP Books, 2007), 37.

9. David P. Leong, *Race & Place: How Urban Geography Shapes the Journey to Reconciliation* (Downers Grove, IL: InterVarsity, 2017), 56.

10. It was on this Canaanite woman that Jesus bestowed his highest praise of all, one which, in fact, he never spoke to the Twelve: "You have great faith!" (Matthew 15:28).

11. Leong, *Race & Place,* 41.

12. Tracy Hadden Loh, Christopher Coes, and Becca Buthe, "Separate and Unequal: Persistent Residential Segregation Is Sustaining Racial and Economic Injustice in the U.S.," Brookings (blog), December 16, 2020, www.brookings .edu/essay/trend-1-separate-and-unequal-neighborhoods-are-sustaining -racial-and-economic-injustice-in-the-us.

13. Loh, Coes, and Buthe, "Separate and Unequal."

14. Loh, Coes, and Buthe, "Separate and Unequal."

15. Loh, Coes, and Buthe, "Separate and Unequal."

16. Michael Harrington, *The Other America: Poverty in the United States* (New York: Touchstone, 1997).

17. Douglas S. Massey and Nancy A. Denton, *American Apartheid: Segregation and the Making of the Underclass* (Cambridge, MA: Harvard University, 2003), 1.

18. "Celebrating 10 Years of the Sankofa Journey," Covenant Newswire Archives (blog), January 20, 2009, http://blogs.covchurch.org/newswire/2009/01/20 /6816.

19. The documentary *13th* also tracks this line of bias within the criminal justice system from the past to the present.

20. I'm so grateful that everyone can now experience Hinton's story through his riveting memoir, Anthony Ray Hinton, *The Sun Does Shine: How I Found Life and Freedom on Death Row* (New York: St. Martin's Press, 2018).

21. "Celebrating 10 Years."

22. "Celebrating 10 Years," emphasis added.

23. "Celebrating 10 Years."

24. You can learn more about Debbie Blue's inspiring story at Bob Smietana, "True Blue," *Covenant Companion,* May 6, 2015, https://covchurch.org/2015/05/06/true-blue.

25. Mark Vroegop, *Weep with Me: How Lament Opens a Door for Racial Reconciliation* (Wheaton, IL: Crossway, 2020), 67, emphasis added. See a full itinerary of the Civil Rights Vision Trip in the *Weep with Me* appendix.

26. Harpur, *The Pilgrim Journey.*

27. Vroegop, *Weep with Me.*

28. Jemar Tisby, *How to Fight Racism: Courageous Christianity and the Journey Toward Racial Justice* (Grand Rapids, MI: Zondervan Reflective, 2021), 4.

29. As of this writing, future Washington, D.C., museum projects like the National Women's History Museum (www.womenshistory.org) and the National Museum of the American Latino (https://americanlatinomuseum.org) are under consideration for future development. Both require donors and supporters to advocate for their creation and success.

30. The organization African Ancestry has also conducted similar journeys called "African Ancestry Family Reunions" to Burkina Faso, Cameroon, Nigeria, Senegal, and Sierra Leone. For more on the growing movement of African heritage travel, see Travis Levius, "For Black Americans, a Heritage Trip to West Africa Can Be Life-Changing," *Travel + Leisure,* January 22, 2021, www.travelandleisure.com/trip-ideas/west-africa-heritage-trip.

31. George, *Sacred Travels,* 26.

32. Harpur, *The Pilgrim Journey,* 16.

33. The celebration and/or commemoration of Jewish holidays by Christians, while of course no longer required, is a richly creative way to deepen our Old Testament foundations—foundations that remain vital to our Christian faith. For an excellent family guide on this, see Robin Sampson and Linda Pierce, *A Family Guide to the Biblical Holidays: With Activities for All Ages* (Springfield, TN: Heart of Wisdom, 2001).

34. "Relocation: Living Among the People," Christian Community Development Association, https://ccda.org/about/philosophy/relocation.

35. Michelle Ferrigno Warren, *The Power of Proximity: Moving Beyond Awareness to Action* (Downers Grove, IL: IVP Books, 2017), 22.

36. Dominique DuBois Gilliard, "Rethinking Incarceration to Fight Concentration Camps with Dominique DuBois Gilliard," *Hope & Hard Pills,* podcast, September 28, 2019, https://hope-hard-pills.simplecast.com/episodes/rethinking-incarceration-to-fight-concentration-camps-with-dominique-dubois-gilliard-ure7pT17.

37. Billy Graham, "In His Own Words: Scars of Battle," The Billy Graham Li-

brary Blog (blog), May 13, 2017, https://billygrahamlibrary.org/in-his-own
-words-scars-of-battle.

38. Leong, *Race & Place,* 56–57.

39. Harpur, *The Pilgrim Journey,* 17.

CHAPTER 10: FAST (FOR REAL)

1. David W. Swanson, *Rediscipling the White Church: From Cheap Diversity to True Solidarity* (Downers Grove, IL: IVP, 2020), 51.

2. *Hamilton: An American Musical,* music and lyrics by Lin-Manuel Miranda, 2015.

3. *Biblical Advocacy 101,* Christian Reformed Church, www.crcna.org/sites /default/files/36318_osj_advocacy_brochure_can_web.pdf, emphasis added.

4. Jemar Tisby, *How to Fight Racism: Courageous Christianity and the Journey Toward Racial Justice* (Grand Rapids, MI: Zondervan, 2021), 195.

5. *Biblical Advocacy 101.*

6. Helen Lee, "The Case for Diversity on Your Conference Stage," Helen Lee: Author, Speaker, Missional Mom (blog), November 7, 2015.

7. I am grateful to Tim Keller for this insight: "The first facet of biblical justice is radical generosity. While secular individualism says that your money belongs to you, and socialism says your money belongs to the State, the Bible says that all your money belongs to God, who then entrusts it to you (1 Chronicles 29:14; 1 Corinthians 4:7)." Read more in Timothy Keller, "Justice in the Bible," *Life in the Gospel,* September 18, 2020, https://quarterly.gospelinlife .com/justice-in-the-bible.

8. *Malcolm X—If You Stick a Knife in My Back,* November 5, 2011, YouTube video, 0:28, www.youtube.com/watch?v=XiSiHRNQlQo.

9. Tisby, *How to Fight Racism,* 170.

10. See, for example, Duke L. Kwon and Gregory Thompson, *Reparations: A Christian Call for Repentance and Repair* (Ada, MI: Brazos, 2021).

11. Tisby, *How to Fight Racism,* 187.

12. "Justice Deposits," Community Christian Church, www.communitychristian .org/justicedeposits. See also Eddie Yoon et al., "Could Gen Z Consumer Behavior Make Capitalism More Ethical?," *Harvard Business Review,* December 14, 2020, https://hbr.org/2020/12/could-gen-z-consumer-behavior-make -capitalism-more-ethical.

13. C. S. Lewis, *Beyond Personality: The Christian Idea of God* (London: Centenary Press, 1944).

MICHELLE T. SANCHEZ, MDiv, ThM, serves as executive minister of Make and Deepen Disciples for the Evangelical Covenant Church, a vibrant multiethnic denomination of more than nine hundred congregations throughout North America. Michelle completed seminary degrees at Gordon-Conwell Theological Seminary, spiritual direction training at Boston College, and field studies on the life and times of Jesus at Jerusalem University College. After studying international business at New York University, she worked as an investment banker at Goldman Sachs and ministered to international students with Cru in New York City. Michelle has also served with the Institute for Bible Reading as well as the Lausanne Movement, which exists to connect influencers and ideas for global mission. She is a frequent conference speaker and a columnist with *Outreach* magazine. Michelle is the author of three books with WaterBrook: *Color-Courageous Discipleship, Color-Courageous Discipleship Student Edition,* and the picture book *God's Beloved Community,* all in 2022. Michelle has thoroughly enjoyed experiencing colorful cultures in thirty countries and territories around the world—and counting! She and her husband, Mickey, live with their children in the Chicago area.

For bonus materials, inquiries, and additional resources on color-courageous discipleship and beyond, please visit https://michelletsanchez.com.

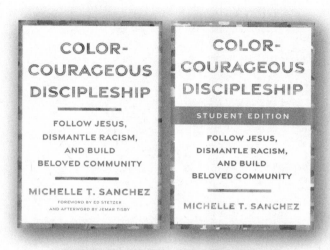